THE
LAFFERTY GIRL

*Rooted in grace
growing in love!*

Rebecca Lafferty

THE
LAFFERTY GIRL

SURVIVING TRAUMA, ABUSE,
and MY FATHER'S CRIMES

a mormon daughter's story

REBECCA LAFFERTY

with KATIE McNEY

**UNION
SQUARE
& CO.**

NEW YORK

UNION SQUARE & CO.

NEW YORK

UNION SQUARE & CO. and the distinctive Union Square & Co. logo are registered trademarks of Hachette Book Group, Inc.

Text © 2025 Rebecca Lafferty and Katie McNey

The author and editor have made every effort to reproduce the substance of the conversations relied on in this book, but some have been edited and condensed for clarity and space. Some names and identifying details have been changed for privacy or at the individuals' request.

ISBN 978-1-4549-6102-4 (hardcover)
ISBN 978-1-4549-6104-8 (paperback)
ISBN 978-1-4549-6103-1 (e-book)

Library of Congress Control Number: 2025009918
Library of Congress Cataloging-in-Publication Data is available upon request.

Union Square & Co. books may be purchased in bulk for business, educational, or promotional use. For more information, please contact your local bookseller or the Hachette Book Group's Special Markets department at special.markets@hbgusa.com.

Printed in the United States of America

2 4 6 8 10 9 7 5 3 1

unionsquareandco.com

Cover design by Pete Garceau
Interior design by Christine Heun
All photos courtesy of author

Frontispiece: Me in front of my student-of-the-week presentation during my first year of public school, 1985.

For my children, who taught me unconditional love.

CONTENTS

AUTHOR'S NOTE

THIS BOOK IS ABOUT MY FATHER, but only insofar as his actions have affected my life. The story on these pages is mine and mine alone.

Sharing my story has been difficult, to say the least. It's taken me fifteen years to finish this book. It was incredibly painful to relive the trauma, heartache, and grief I'd buried deep inside of me, and I had to stop and put the manuscript aside many times over the years. But unearthing and facing this pain has facilitated more healing than I could have ever imagined. That is why I kept writing—so that others who have suffered from similar experiences can know that they are not alone and that healing is possible.

While my father's actions have profoundly affected my entire family, it is my intent in this book to share only my experience. I do not wish to speak for any of my brothers or sisters or to tell anyone's story for them. I feel only the deepest love for everyone in my family, especially my saintly mother, who endured more than any of us and still managed to shower us with love and keep us safe. I am very grateful to the members of both my immediate and extended family who have been willing to answer my questions and share their feelings and recollections. Any errors are mine.

I have also asked my father to share his experience with me. He has been more than willing to provide his perspective and answer my questions, and he has given his consent for me to include them in the book. His answers haven't resolved everything for me—in some cases they've only led to more questions—but being able to open a dialogue with him has been a crucial part of my healing journey.

Most of the names and places in my account have been changed out of respect and protection for those involved, but everything I've written here is true, based on my research and recollection. This is my story and my experience. I've laid my soul bare on these pages, and I ask only that you read with an open heart. I hope that, in doing so, you will find deeper love and compassion for your own journey.

With love and light,
Rebecca

1980

OUTSIDE, EVERYTHING IS GRAY AND BLANK, like the blackboards at church, coated in chalk dust. I'm still not used to our new home. Gone are the swaying palm trees and warm coastal breezes that used to beckon me outside to play in the Southern California sun. Here in this small Utah town, it's too cold to go outside, and the sun always seems to hide behind the clouds. To my four-year-old mind, the frost that spiderwebs across our windowpanes is at once entrancing and frightening.

I seek comfort in the familiar sounds of my family drifting through the house. Mom, tidying up breakfast. Dad, adding coal to the fireplace. Gwen, plunking hymns on the piano.

I'm sitting on the floor of my bedroom, playing with my brother, Johnny, who is three.

Suddenly, for no apparent reason, Johnny begins to cry. I wrap my small arms around my younger brother, trying to comfort him, but he won't stop crying. I have no idea what's wrong.

Loud footsteps shake our house, traveling down the hall to my bedroom. The door flies open, and my father stands in the doorway. I jerk my hands away from Johnny.

"What did you do?" Dad demands.

The anger in his voice triggers an all-too-familiar paralysis in my body. My stomach tightens, and my heart begins to race. My tongue is suddenly frozen to the roof of my mouth, and I find I'm unable to produce a single sound.

Dad repeats his question, his voice rising with each word. "What did you do, Rebecca?"

1

I stare up at him, rooted to the spot. I sense that Dad is mistaking my unresponsiveness for guilt, and this only makes me panic more. I know from past experience that asserting my innocence won't save me. Everything in my small being is desperate to escape the punishment I know is coming.

Then, in the midst of my terror, a thought enters my mind: *He already thinks I did something bad. What if I give him the answer he wants? Would that make him happy?*

I hesitate. I know it's wrong to lie. But my desire to be safe trumps my need to speak the truth.

I take a deep breath and in a small, shaking voice say, "I did it."

My false confession does not save me. Dad lunges forward and hauls me up by my arms. He throws me violently over his lap and yanks my pants down to expose my bare backside. He strikes my tender skin with the palm of his hand, again and again and again. He hits me so hard, I think I'm going to bleed.

Terror and pain course through my body, and I wet myself. This enrages Dad even more. He tells me he's going to punish me for this too, and he hits me harder.

I don't know how long the beating lasts. It seems like it will never end. I'm vaguely aware of Mom rushing into the room and whisking Johnny away. She does not try to stop Dad from hurting me.

Finally, Dad dumps me on the bed and slams the door behind him, leaving me sobbing on the blankets, my wet pants tangled around my ankles.

The pain goes beyond my raw skin. It is sharper than any pain I have ever experienced, a knife wound of shame, humiliation, and abandonment. All I want in that moment is to be reassured and comforted. But there is no comfort to be found. No one comes to check on me.

Possessed by a strong animal instinct to hide, I slide off my bed and crawl toward my closet, where I burrow into the back corner. As I huddle in the darkness, I feel my small heart break. The pain and isolation of this moment, a culmination of all the moments that have come before it, tear at my soul. All I want is for someone to see my suffering and take me away from this place. But it feels like no one in the world is on my side. And even if they were, they wouldn't be able to stand up to my father.

In the depths of my pain, I whisper, "Can anybody hear me?"

To my surprise, I hear a response—a soft but firm, "*Yes.*"

A peace I have never experienced before spreads through my entire body. It is as though someone is holding me and wrapping me in a thick blanket. I lean into the warmth.

"*I have a special job for you, Rebecca,*" the voice tells me. "*You are here to love.*"

The words slip into the splintered crevices of my heart and settle deep.

I don't know how long I stay in the closet. Perhaps an hour passes. Or maybe it's only a few minutes. All I know is that when I open the door, I am imbued with a renewed sense of hope and strength. I know now that I am not alone. I know that I am loved.

I leave my room and find my father. I reach out my arms for a hug and tell him I'm sorry and that I love him.

Dad is surprised, but he accepts my apology.

See? I tell myself. *I can do this. I am here to love.*

I return to my room, smiling. For the first time, I know that someone, somewhere, sees what I am experiencing. They are a witness to my truth. This validation is all I need to continue moving forward.

I have no way of knowing how quickly this resolve of my innocent four-year-old heart will fade. Nor can I predict the depths of darkness I will have to traverse before I feel this love again.

2021

It's a gray February morning in Salt Lake City. Even though I've lived in Utah for decades now, I'm still not used to the way the winter gloom weighs on my soul. In the winter, an inversion happens here in the valley: The Wasatch Mountains form a basin that traps a dense layer of cold air beneath a layer of warm air, and all the pollutants get trapped with it. The result is a thick soup of yellow-gray smog that lingers from December to February.

The dense smog drains my energy, making even the simplest tasks seem like wading through wet concrete. My head is sluggish, but I know I have to keep moving. Because if I stop, the concrete will set, and I'll be trapped forever, just like the air.

I'm mindlessly folding a pile of laundry when my phone rings.

"Hello," says an automated recording. "This is a call from Dan Lafferty, an inmate at the Utah State Prison. To accept this free call, press zero. To refuse this call, hang up or press one."

The words cut straight through the fog, and my heart starts to race. *Why is he calling me?*

I've been writing to him for years now, and I still get butterflies in my stomach whenever I see one of his letters in the mail. But talking on the phone is different, more real. At least with writing there is time to read and process each letter before responding. There's safety in the space between. But on the phone . . . what will I say? What will *he* say?

My finger trembles as I press zero.

"Rebecca?"

Hearing his voice immediately makes me feel like I'm a child again. Out of habit, my body starts to tense, and I have to remind myself that I'm safe. I take a deep breath.

"Hi, Dad."

Dad tells me he only has fifteen minutes to talk. He doesn't waste a moment. He speaks quickly, updating me on life in prison. He's been taking care of an elderly gentleman who has dementia, and he tells me that his new job is to clean the bathrooms. Some of the inmates have complimented him on how clean everything looks, which makes him proud. But that's Dad. Whatever he does, he'll stick with it until he masters it—even if it's cleaning bathrooms in a state penitentiary.

As he talks, my body starts to relax, and my heart softens listening to him. I can't convey how good it feels to share a genuine connection with my father, to be present and hear everything he has to say, to know that he wants *my* approval.

Dad tells me that he's figured out a way to make ice cream using the limited resources they have in prison. He says all the guys raved about how good it was and that they were looking forward to the next batch. His story makes me laugh. I relax even more; the weight around my heart lifts.

Dad says it's nice to hear my voice, and I say the same. Then he tells me he believes things are changing and that soon it will be time for him to fulfill his role as the Prophet Elijah.

And just like that, the spell is broken. That familiar ache returns to my chest—a biting blend of bitterness and disappointment. After all this time, Dad still believes he's a prophet.

"Do you want to hear the script I've prepared to announce Jesus Christ's return?" His voice is so earnest and eager.

I close my eyes against the pain. "Sure, Dad. Tell me."

PART ONE

BEFORE

CHAPTER 1

1976–79

I WAS BORN AT HOME, per my father's orders. There was no one there to assist with the birth.

Dad, who was in chiropractic school at the time, told my mom that finances were tight and they had no money for hospital bills. They were living on a tiny income procured by Mom, who prepared sandwiches every morning to sell to the students at the college. Dad felt confident that studying human anatomy in his courses had given him all the knowledge he needed to deliver me himself. He said that he had prayed about it and felt a confirmation that he was making the right decision. Even though the leaders of my parents' church, the Church of Jesus Christ of Latter-day Saints (known colloquially as the LDS or Mormon Church), expressed their concerns, Dad stayed the course. Once his mind was made up, nothing was ever able to dissuade him, especially if he felt that he was following God's will.

Mom had given birth before—to my two half-sisters Gwen and Marleen—back in her home country of Scotland. But she had delivered my sisters at a birth center with the assistance of midwives. I'm sure she was nervous to be doing an unassisted birth at home. But no doubt she trusted in God, and my dad.

I was born on December 21, the winter solstice. It also happened to be the birthday of my oldest sister, Gwen. Gwen told me she was so excited for my arrival. "You were my birthday present," she recalls.

My birth was not a long one, but there was a complication.

"You came out blue," Dad told me, "with the umbilical cord tied around your neck. I was so nervous I had diarrhea." When he saw my

still, seemingly lifeless body, Dad wondered if following his prompting*
to do a home birth had been a mistake.

Mom calmly instructed him, "Dan, you need to unwrap the umbilical cord from around her neck and suction her mouth out."

A moment later, which felt like eons to Dad, I took my first breath.
"You didn't even cry," he said. "You just looked around as if to say, 'Let's
get this show on the road.'" He said he was so relieved once I started
breathing and took it as a sign that he hadn't misunderstood God's will
after all.

The love I felt for my parents, especially my dad, was immense. Dad
was my whole world when I was a kid; I could feel how much he loved
me. He told me he was thrilled to become a father. It was the most exciting thing to him—and the scariest.

"You were like a new toy to your father," Mom tells me. "He would
rush home at the end of the day and spend time examining every one of
your fingers and toes, commenting on your perfection." There was no
question that I was loved. At least at the beginning.

We were living in Los Angeles at the time. It was the 1970s, and
both Dad and Mom vibed with the counterculture. Dad's focus was on
adopting a holistic lifestyle and living as close as possible to what nature
intended. This meant breastfeeding, using cloth diapers, eating a vegetarian diet, and avoiding conventional medicine at all costs.

Mom was less certain. She told me nursing me was a struggle for
her. She hadn't breastfed my older sisters, and she was unsure about it,
especially without any guidance from nurses or doctors, but Dad was
insistent.

"If it weren't for Betty, who coached me through the undertaking, I
may have given up," Mom told me.

---

* "Prompting" is a Mormon term that means one has received a message from God to take
a specific action.

Betty, a family friend whom Mom met at a church event, proved to be a great support for my Scottish mother, who was still figuring out her way in a foreign country. She also saved my life.

One day, when I was nine months old, Betty was at the apartment visiting Mom. Suddenly, she looked around and asked, "Where is Rebecca?"

My mom froze. "I'm not sure," she said. "I haven't seen her for a minute."

They rushed around the house looking for me but couldn't find me anywhere. Mom said she felt sick to her stomach, imagining the worst.

It was Betty who found me headfirst in a bucket of water, barely able to hold myself up, coughing from the water I'd inhaled and struggling to breathe. Luckily, they pulled me out in time, and I was fine. This was just the beginning of the kind of trouble I would get into.

Sixteen months later, my brother Johnny was born. As the first boy in the family, he quickly became my parents' favorite child. To this day, my parents still say that Johnny is nothing short of a godsend, a special and sweet-spirited soul. I love Johnny and wholeheartedly agree with my parents. He is one of the gentlest and kindest people I know.

I remember when Johnny was a baby, he was very sensitive. Our mother told us that he cried for days after he was born. I could tell he had a harder time adjusting to his new environment. His crying never irritated my mother, though; on the contrary, she found it precious how he would cry over the smallest things.

When I saw Johnny for the first time, I was so excited to meet him. Mom recalls that I was obsessed with trying to hold him and lift him up, which made her nervous. I thought of Johnny as my baby, and as the years rolled by, he became my equal and best friend.

My brother and I shared a close bond. We could always find a way to entertain ourselves and passed the time together in absolute contentment. I loved how we could play with something as simple as a box for hours. Our imagination turned that box into anything we wanted. It could be our home, a car, an airplane. We would put it over our heads and be transported to an entirely new world.

Living as we did in Southern California, Johnny and I spent a lot of time outside. I have fond memories of running around the yard of our Glendale home in our diapers. We spent many days filling up the plastic pool with water from the hose, with no thought for how cold the water was. We loved being out in the sun. We felt so free.

As Johnny and I became accustomed to the outdoors, our curiosity for adventure and exploration grew. Even though we could barely walk, we somehow managed to climb the fence and haul ourselves onto the roof of the house. That became our new adventure. I was the leader, and Johnny followed.

One time, Johnny got stuck and started crying. I remember Mom ran outside and discovered him clinging to the fence by the tips of his fingers. Her eyes found me next, perched on the top of our little apartment roof, where I sat as content as could be. She couldn't believe what she was seeing. She panicked but was able to get Johnny off the fence without a scratch, and then helped me climb down the roof. Now, when she tells me the story, she laughs at our antics. She says I seemed older than my age. She felt like she didn't need to worry about me as much. She thought that, somehow, I would figure things out.

It's a Sunday morning. Our family is gathered around the kitchen table, eating breakfast. I am eighteen months old.

It's almost time to go to church. Dad tells us we all need to say thank-you for the meal before we can be excused from the table. Gwen and Marleen do what's asked of them and leave to finish getting ready. Mom needs to take care of Johnny, so she asks Dad to get me out of my high chair.

"Nope," Dad says. "She's staying in there until she says thank-you."

I'm tired of sitting in my high chair, and I want to get down. I put my arms up, but no one helps me out of the chair.

Dad looks me in the eye. "You need to learn to say thank-you, Rebecca, and you are not getting down until you say it."

I become frustrated that I'm not being set free. I'm sure I'm being clear about what I want. I hold my arms up higher, just in case.

Mom takes Johnny to the bedroom. The moment my mother leaves the room, my father's face changes.

"Say thank-you, Rebecca," Dad snarls.

His expression scares me. I start to cry, but he doesn't let me out. I don't understand what Dad is asking of me. All I know is that my request to get down is being ignored.

Mom and my siblings come back to the dining room, dressed in their church clothes. Dad tells them to go to church without us. Mom looks uncertain, but she does as Dad says.

After they leave, Dad starts to yell at me. My heart and mind grow confused. Why is Dad yelling? What have I done wrong? I don't understand what's happening or what he wants from me.

My tears turn to sobs, but Dad doesn't relent. I cry for a solid forty minutes, until I finally cry myself to sleep.

An hour later, my mom and siblings return from church to find me hunched over in my high chair, my face red and swollen.

"She's still in there?!" Mom cries.

The panic in her voice wakes me up. I can see the alarm etched on my mother's and sisters' faces. I feel a ray of hope at their return.

"Can we please get her out, Dan?" Mom asks.

"Nope," Dad says, crossing his arms. "Not until she says thank-you."

My sister Marleen discreetly takes off one of her black Mary Janes. She tiptoes toward me then holds it up and whispers, "Rebecca, what's this?"

"Shoe," I say.

Marleen whirls around. "She just said it!" she shouts. "I heard her. She said thank-you." Before Dad can question her, Marleen quickly sets me free from the high chair, and my sisters whisk me to safety.

◆ ◆ ◆

Though I had no way of understanding this at the time, this experience—which I can still recall in vivid detail, despite my young age—was the first of many moments that would begin to chip away at my soul. I was starting to realize that the loving, doting father who brought me into this world and examined my every feature with pride and admiration was transforming into a scary, unpredictable monster. Dad loved me. I knew he did. But he also had no issue disconnecting from my cries and pleas when it came to disciplining me. Thank God for my clever and brave sisters, especially Marleen, who was always quick on her feet and determined to save us from Dad when she could.

I asked Dad recently if he remembered the high-chair incident. He told me he doesn't. He does, however, remember getting frustrated with me and my "lies" as a child. He said that he felt a lot of pressure from the church about how to raise us kids, which, he claims, he didn't like. He believed they wanted him to teach us to be obedient and to "kill our spirit in order to please God." He said that he prayed to get answers all the time about how to provide for and direct our family.

Once Dad felt like he had received a directive from God, he *never* backed down. Many times I would hear Mom say, "Your dad is just so damn stubborn. He would cut off his nose to spite his face." There was just no quitting for him when he believed in something. When Dad got that look in his eyes and tone in his voice, I would get extreme anxiety because it was unclear what he expected, and I knew that if I didn't guess correctly, there would be harsh consequences.

Mom later told me that she began to hate my father for his behavior. She was a romantic, but Dad never once told her he loved her. She would have left him, but she was confused by the teachings of the church, which taught her that divorce wasn't the right choice and made her question where, as an immigrant, she would go. So, even though she was unhappy, she tried to make the best of her situation. She gave everything to us children and to Dad, until he took so much she felt like she had nothing left to give and that she didn't even know who she was anymore.

A year after Johnny was born, our family was blessed with another little girl: Rachel, the beautiful princess. My mother saw the stars in her eyes and thought she was perfect. She couldn't stop oohing and aahing over her features and perfect proportions, especially her long fingers and legs. Mom predicted Rachel would be tall and beautiful. That was how I viewed her, too.

Rachel was too young to become the third musketeer to Johnny and me, and since children have a constant need to be included, she became something of a hindrance to our playtime. Eventually, however, she stopped trying to keep up with us. She preferred to stay close to Mom, playing quietly and humming every once in a while to let us know she was content. Sometimes she would say to us, "I'm happy," and then continue playing with her toys.

All of us children were close. The best part of the day was after Dad left in the morning and we were able to play freely. How peaceful those times were, curled up on the couch with a blanket and a bottle of milk, watching *Sesame Street* or *Mr. Rogers*. In the afternoon, we'd wait for Gwen and Marleen to return home from school and then listen to them practice piano, enjoying the music that filled the house.

In those days, my siblings were the best thing about my life, and the time we spent together was always comforting. But as we grew older, these peaceful moments seemed few and far between. Instead, life became more frightening and unpredictable.

I remember one day Dad brought home a box of dates so Mom could make her delicious date and coconut roll dessert. Feeling a toddler's strong urge to investigate, I ran to look in the box.

I was met with an immediate, "No, Rebecca!" and a smack on the hand. "Do not put your hands in that box."

I felt frustrated that my curiosity was constantly being met with a swat instead of being encouraged. So being the inventive and determined spirit I was, I put my toes in the box instead.

My creative choice made my parents laugh. However, the next time I tried to find a way around the rules, I was swiftly reprimanded. I began to feel constantly on edge. I never knew if my actions were going to earn me a laugh or a slap.

Dad was constantly trying to correct my behavior. He told me explicitly that he needed to break my spirit, as if I were an animal who needed to submit to its master. Over and over, I would reach for something and be met with a swat. It wasn't safe for me to explore or to try new things, as a toddler needs to do. In the moments that mattered most, I wanted nothing more than a word of encouragement from him that would have reassured me in my emotional and mental development, growth, and exploration. But I was never given that.

There were times when Dad would seem to show affection, but his love always came at a cost. Sometimes he would come home from work and smother me with kisses until I would smell like his breath. It felt yucky, and I didn't like it. Other times, he would tickle me to the point where I couldn't breathe. I learned that if I could control myself and refrain from showing a response, he would stop. I did everything in my power to show him that his kisses and tickles didn't have any effect on me until he got bored with the game and gave up.

As a result of this hot-and-cold treatment, I became uneasy and anxious. I would cry out in the night, seeking comfort from my mom. This would infuriate Dad. He would get up, come into my room, and tell me to stop crying. When I wouldn't, he would start hitting me, saying he would give me a reason to cry. I was terrified. Where was Mommy? Why was Daddy hurting me?

Imagine being a child, not feeling safe in your own home, and the person terrorizing you is the very person who is supposed to protect you.

There are countless children in the world who are subject to this kind of abuse, and my heart goes out to all of them. I know firsthand the struggle they experience, and the cognitive dissonance that occurs as a result. Studies have shown that children can be severely mistreated by their parents, but the moment these same children are separated from their parents, they will sob and beg to be reunited with their abusive custodians. That was my experience, too. No matter how much Dad hurt me, I only wanted his love.

As I grew older, I observed that Johnny and Rachel didn't seem to be subject to the same treatment. Johnny was always free to show Dad something he'd been working on or playing with, and Rachel would linger nearby until he noticed her and showed her affection. Neither of them suffered from Dad's harsh corrections in the middle of the night. I thought I must be doing something wrong. Whether this was true or not, in my mind I believed that he loved them more than me.

Dad told me I was punished because he couldn't stand my lying and attention-seeking. Over and over, my father would tell me, "Rebecca, you are the oldest, so you need to be a good example for your younger siblings." It hurt me to see how my brother and sister seemed to receive more love and kindness than I did. They were given praise, encouraging words, and attention while I was constantly being corrected. I didn't want to be the oldest. I wanted to be loved, too. (In truth, I wasn't the oldest. Gwen was. But Dad viewed my half-sisters Gwen and Marleen differently from his "real" children.)

Mom was preoccupied with caring for my younger siblings and trying to placate my father. She would become very overwhelmed with my needs and hand me over to my older sisters, who would entertain me for a few minutes before getting sick of me because they were teenagers and couldn't be bothered with babysitting. In my eyes, it seemed that to everyone in my family I was just a nuisance. I was dismissed and ignored, and if I did anything at all to attract attention, I was quickly scolded and disciplined. As a result, I tried to make myself as quiet and as invisible as possible.

One time, I found some entertainment in a balloon that had made its way into our home. I relished in the simplicity of being able to see how high I could get the balloon to soar as I ran in animated circles to try to catch it before it hit the floor. Eventually, the inflated latex hit something sharp and popped. I was startled by the loud sound. Then, realizing that the magic was over and the balloon was gone, I began to sob. My effortless play had come to an abrupt end.

I made the mistake of going to Dad for consolation, explaining what had happened.

My tears were met with: "It would be wise to not cry over material things." I'm sure Dad really believed he was teaching me the correct way to respond to disappointment, but it was just another reminder that my emotions were an inconvenience. Something to be stifled.

What I understand now is that when a child is abused or mistreated, as I was, they are unable to express their feelings because there is no outlet for them. From an early age, my feelings were not validated. If I was angry or upset, I was punished and told to stop making a scene. This taught me that my emotions were the problem. So I stuffed them down deep inside of me and tried not to feel anything at all.

CHAPTER 2

1946–74

AS AN ADULT, I've come to understand that my parents, especially my dad, were following the template for parenting they'd received from their own parents.

My father, Dan Charles Lafferty Sr., was born in 1946 and raised in Spring Lake, Utah, a rural community of only a few hundred people. The census-designated place (not even a town) is so remote, it has no businesses or stoplights, even today.

Dad was the fourth of eight children, born to a proud Irish Canadian father and a hard-working Swedish mother. Watson and Claudine Lafferty were upstanding members of their community, and they expected the same of their children.* But the environment in which Dad was raised was far from easy. Grandpa Lafferty was a force to be reckoned with. He could insult you and then convince you to come into his business the very next day. He firmly believed that his way was the right way, and, trust me, you didn't want to disagree with him.

Grandpa was a chiropractor and homeopathic practitioner in a time when alternative healthcare wasn't popular or even tolerated. But Grandpa

---

* There were two girls and six boys in my dad's family: Cynthia and Catherine (pseudonyms), Ron, Dan (Dad), Mark, Tim, Watson Jr., and Allen. Most of Dad's positive memories are connected to his younger brothers. "Ron was six years older than me," Dad wrote to me during our correspondence for this book, "so there was some distance there, but all the others came close together." He said most of his memories of being a boy revolved around playing on the farm with his brothers: "just playing and having fun down by the barns, mostly with Uncle Mark because of our age proximity. . . . The barns were our world, with Skippy our dog also."

wanted to look good, and he wanted to be seen in the community as a man who had succeeded. He worked hard, and he expected my father and his siblings to also work hard; he believed that children should be useful and earn their keep. Consequently, my dad started working at the age of five, milking cows for a neighbor.* Dad told me that Grandpa was proud of his family and the image they presented to the outside world. He liked to take pictures of them when they came home from church, dressed in their Sunday clothes. Dad told me that Grandpa always felt a strong need to document his life. He kept a journal faithfully and recorded lots of home videos.

Grandpa was very strict. He'd lost his mother as an infant, and his father (my great-grandfather) was incredibly abusive. The abuse was so bad, Grandpa Lafferty ran away from home and joined the navy. He commented later that, had he stayed, he would have killed his father. Unfortunately, we tend to mimic what was modeled to us as children. As a father himself, Grandpa ruled his home with an iron fist, and he wasn't afraid to use force or physical means to correct any member of the family. He showed very little, if any, sympathy or gentleness toward his children or my grandma. He was serious about being the man of the house and enforcing his position of authority. If you stepped out of line, the consequences were dire. When my dad was a boy, Grandpa beat the family dog to death with a baseball bat in front of all the children because the dog was being disobedient—an incident that absolutely traumatized my father and his siblings and solidified that Grandpa governed their home by fear.

Perhaps because he was a chiropractor (or because he was extremely devout), Grandpa had a strong distrust of conventional medicine. One time my dad sustained a severe head injury from a sledding accident; he

---

* My dad explained in one of his letters to me, "This [was] all part of Grandpa's plan. He wanted us to learn to work, and so we were there [on the farm] taking care of the animals and really didn't associate with any neighbors or friends that much until we got a little older."

ran straight into a tree, and his head swelled so much that his face was unrecognizable. I am sure he must have had a concussion, but it was never confirmed because Grandpa didn't let Grandma take him to the doctor. Another time, when my father was a teenager, he and his brother were playing with a bow and arrow. One of the arrows got lodged in my uncle's side, but Grandpa refused to take him to the doctor. He told my uncle it was his punishment for playing on the Sabbath. Instead, my uncle had to suffer a very serious injury at home.*

Grandpa was a convert to the Church of Jesus Christ of Latter-day Saints, and he enforced the rules of the religion as strictly as everything else. All the boys in Dad's family were expected to serve a two-year mission once they turned nineteen, as is customary in the church. There was no discussion. So, even though my father had no real interest in giving up two years of his life in the service of God, in 1972, he traveled to Airdrie, Scotland, as a missionary for the LDS Church.† That was where he met my mother.

My mother, Matilda Burns, was from a small town in Scotland—not quite as remote as Spring Lake, but still very rural. She was the oldest of five children.

---

* Despite this strict environment, my father only had positive things to say about his childhood. He wrote, "I've come to understand that those of us who are children of the God of Love have a tendency to forget negative things but remember happy things. . . . Even though I'm sure there were experiences from my childhood that weren't so good, they just seem to fade away leaving all the happy memories. Except for things that I have done wrong as opposed to the things that may have been done wrong to me."

† I asked Dad how he felt about his church responsibilities as a young man. He said, "I just accepted the line I was being fed that it was true, and I really never questioned anything because I wouldn't have even known what to question. . . . I didn't really enjoy church meetings that much, just like I didn't much enjoy school, but in both church and school, God blessed me with cute girls who helped make it more enjoyable. . . . I would have felt like something was wrong if I didn't keep up with my responsibilities, and the same with going on my mission. I didn't really choose to go. I just went because it was the next thing to do."

Mom's mother was not the most attentive parent. Mom thinks that's probably because my grandmother, who was adopted, was an only child. Nanny wasn't much for cooking or cleaning either. Mom says that the image she remembers best of her mother is her sitting in front of the fireplace reading Catherine Cookson novels. Becoming a mother must have been quite a strain for my grandmother. When Mom was only ten, Nanny left Mom and her younger siblings for a time, to explore her life and take a break from the stresses of caring for five children.

At age sixteen, Mom went to live with her grandmother. She and her gran took a vacation once a year to the seaside. That's where Mom met Jeff Buchanan, a man eight years her senior. Jeff had served three years in the military guarding the Brandenburg Gate in West Germany, something Mom found very attractive. They decided to get married and move to England. Mom packed up her pet budgies and a small suitcase and boarded a train to meet him. She remembers thinking she couldn't believe what she was doing. She felt like a kid still, leaving home and venturing out into the unknown. Shortly afterward, she got pregnant with my sister Gwen and then, eighteen months later, had my sister Marleen.

When Marleen was just six months old, my mom found out that Jeff was cheating on her and that he had stolen money from her. So she left him and moved home. Back in her hometown, raising two toddlers on her own at only twenty years old, my mother felt the need to get closer to God. She discovered the LDS Church and decided to join it. The church gave her something larger than life to hold on to during that uncertain and challenging time and provided a safe social outlet and supportive community for her.

Mom wanted her sister Maisie to learn about the church and share in the sense of hope and belonging it had given her. That's how she met Dad. Every week, he came to the home of a friend of Mom's to teach Mom and Maisie about the Gospel. Missionaries teach prospective members (called "investigators") in the investigators' homes. Mom wasn't trying to keep her church membership a secret by meeting at her friend's house; rather, she did it out of respect for my grandfather, who didn't believe in organized religion.

Dad's missionary companion was a boy named Richard Christiansen, who was quite taken with Mom—another reason they visited her so often. Dad told me, "I kind of just followed whatever Richard wanted to do, not unlike or perhaps good practice for how I gave deference to Ron later on."

Dad said that he also saw something special in my mom. It might have been the fact that she wanted to get closer to God after so much in her life had gone wrong, or it might have been her unbreakable spirit. "She was a recent convert, and I taught the adult Sunday school class that she attended, and I noticed that she gave intelligent answers to questions I would ask," he told me.*

Dad wasn't the best missionary. He was always breaking the rules and looking for ways to make his mission fun and thus bearable. "I remember that I didn't really like tracting [proselytizing from door to door] or having to make reports to account for every minute of every day," he told me. When he was made the leader of his district, he recounted, "I had to be a little dishonest in my reports, because I did some crazy fun stuff with the guys in my district when I took over. We had sleepovers in the carpeted Relief Society room at the church, and I loaded everyone into the car like a circus clown car, and we went to movies from time to time. We would go to other churches, and I even got another member who had a car to camp out at Loch Lomond, a famous lake, that I thought would give them fun memories."

---

* "One time," Dad recalled, "Richard and I got talking about plans for the future as we got near the end of our time together, and he actually asked me . . . what I thought of your mom, implying I could tell that he thought she was special and perhaps I should consider marrying her. I don't remember my exact response but I'm sure it was something like that I would be getting in school and playing the field and learning about that kind of stuff once I left Scotland."

On the last day of his mission, the church members threw Dad a going away party. He told me he embarrassed Mom by asking her for a goodbye kiss, which she granted. Later, he told her he rather enjoyed the kiss and asked for another. "Your mother and I made out for such a long time that my lips were raw," Dad said. "Then I was off to fly across the pond back to America."*

Mom has a different version of the story. She told me that she and Dad would see each other at services; however, there was never anything more between them. After all, Mormon missionaries aren't allowed to have romantic relationships. But Dad had always struggled with following church rules. He was headstrong and did whatever he thought was best.

After Mom and Dad's encounter, Dad returned home to Utah, and my parents went on with their lives, assuming they would never see each other again.

---

* Richard asked my mom to knit him a sweater, but it didn't fit him. Dad wrote, "Coincidentally, the sweater she knitted for Richard was a little small for him but fitted me just right, so I got it and I wore it fairly often and thought of her each time."

CHAPTER 3

1974–75

BACK IN THE UNITED STATES, his missionary service complete, Dad took a welcome break from the church with one of his close friends. They drove around the country, exploring life while living out of his Volkswagen Beetle and smoking a lot of pot. I believe he explored women as well. According to Dad, this was his last hurrah—his rite of passage—before he settled down and focused on church and school.

I can't help but think that Dad only stayed in the church because he didn't want to disappoint his father. I've often wondered how things would have turned out if he had continued with his "rite of passage" and never returned. As it was, once Dad made the decision to go back, he jumped in full force.

Dad told me that the two career paths he had originally considered were becoming an airline pilot or an elementary school teacher ("Kindergarten, no shit"). He said he didn't actually choose to be a chiropractor. "Like many things in my life, God chose it." He told me he had a revelation to become a chiropractor while still on his mission.

> While I was serving in Aberdeen, Scotland . . . I was called out to our tracting area, and I received my first major revelation. The moment is frozen in time. I can still see the little road with the little fish shop we passed to hit King Street, and I can still see the fence along the sidewalk, but for some reason, I can't remember who my companion was. But about ten steps down the sidewalk on King Street, the spirit said, "*You will become a chiropractor.*" It wasn't a voice, but it was unforgettably profound, and from that moment on, I never doubted what my career would be.

Dad told his father he was going to follow in his footsteps and become a chiropractor, but, interestingly, he didn't tell him about the revelation.

Personal revelation is a key doctrine of Mormonism. In fact, the church was established on the principle of revelation: The founder, Joseph Smith, claimed that God and Jesus Christ appeared to him in a vision and told him to restore the fullness of the Gospel on Earth. The Mormon Church preaches that each of its members can receive direct revelations for themselves from God. Dad has always felt confident in his revelations and his belief that God is guiding his life.

The problem was that Dad's revelations often seemed to conflict with what his father wanted or what the leaders of the church taught. Instead, his ideas resonated more with people who were on the fringes of the religion or who had broken away from the mainstream church. It would be some time before Dad acted fully on these ideas, but he always struggled with toeing the line.

Despite his revelation about becoming a chiropractor, Dad felt comfortable taking his time pursuing his education, "following a path that was right for me in the meantime." Eventually, Grandpa got impatient with Dad's slow path. Dad recalls, "One day he told me I should get serious about it and gave me a few hundred dollars and said to go to Iowa and get into school. That is where he went to school and it was the original chiro college. So I did."

Dad enrolled in Palmer College of Chiropractic in Davenport. In one of the letters he wrote home to his parents, he said, "I don't like Palmer, but I'm willing to give it some more time." He also wrote, "I hate school and church; they feel like a prison to me."

After only a semester, Dad decided to drop out. He related, "At the end of the first semester, just before finals, someone got into my locker and stole all of my notes and things. I couldn't prepare for my finals, and I took it as a sign that supported my feeling that it wasn't time. So I left school, and several people told me that if I dropped out I would never go back because they had never seen it happen, but I assured them that I would get back when the time was right." This is how Dad has approached his entire life. His philosophy was that whatever happened was what God intended.

At the time, my dad was dating a girl named Cheryl who was not LDS.* After a while, Dad received another revelation—"an instinctive pulling"—to go to California. When he tried to say goodbye to Cheryl, she "begged" him to take her with him to California as she had a friend there who was getting married. So the two of them went to California together. Dad found work and rented an apartment, and Cheryl lived with her friend's family.

After about a year, Dad decided he wanted to enroll in Los Angeles College of Chiropractic rather than go back to Iowa, but he needed more prerequisites. He decided the easiest way to get them was to go to Utah and take night school classes. Cheryl went with him.

Eventually, Dad's relationship with Cheryl ran its course. Although she was important to him, he had a sense deep down that she wasn't the person he was meant to marry. According to Dad, they parted on friendly terms.

After Cheryl went home to Iowa, Dad became more serious about getting his life in order. The next step in his progression as a faithful Mormon was to marry a righteous Mormon woman. Mormons believe that to reach the highest level of heaven, known as the celestial kingdom, you must be sealed in the temple to another Mormon. I don't think marriage or becoming a family man was something Dad necessarily wanted, but it was very much expected of him. Not only is a temple marriage a prerequisite for going to heaven, but the church also requires celibacy from its single members; having sexual relations outside of marriage is considered a grave sin. Dad was never very worried about sinning,

---

* In a letter to his parents, he said, "I prayed about it, and I want to take it very slow with her, as I am only beginning to feel attracted to her."

sexually or otherwise, but he was not immune to the pressure from his family and community to find an eternal companion. His intent now was to complete his chiropractic degree, find an LDS woman, marry her, and start a family. He felt like he needed to act quickly and that it was part of God's plan for him to get married soon.

Meanwhile, five thousand miles away, Mom went on with her life in Scotland, raising my sisters. One evening, when she was out dancing with a friend, a young man who had been watching her all evening approached her and introduced himself. He was taken by her grace and beauty, not to mention her dance moves. Slowly, they began to get to know each other. His name was Raj.

Raj, who was from India, was studying to become a doctor. His culture fascinated my mom, and they enjoyed many rich conversations about politics, religion, and life. Mom loved how accepting her family was of her relationship with Raj. He would spend a week at their home, sleeping on the couch, before heading back to school. When I listen to my mother tell this story, I can see the regret in her eyes as she says, "I should have married Raj."

In the fall of 1975, Mom made arrangements with a friend to visit the United States and attend the church's semiannual General Conference in Salt Lake City. At this time, Dad was in Utah, working on getting ready to go back to college. He had a job building a dam up in the mountains. He told me, "I bought a little trailer and pulled it up there, and I had my motorcycle, a 250 Yamaha Enduro, that was so fun to ride in the mountains after work. I was making good money, not paying rent, etc. And then one day I accidentally hit my boss in the mouth while trying to hurry and open some cement bags to fix a part of the dam. Long story short, I lost that job." Because Dad was no longer working on the dam, he was able to attend his missionary reunion the following weekend, which he wouldn't have been able to attend otherwise.

The weekend of the General Conference arrived, and Dad went to his mission reunion. As he was leaving the building—literally opening the door to go to the parking lot—he ran into Mom. Crossing paths that way was such a shock for both of them. For Dad, it felt like fate.

Dad asked Mom if she wanted to go get some ice cream. They went for ice cream, and then he took Mom back to the home where she was staying with friends.* For the next three weeks, he continued to court her.† As Dad spent time with Mom, he began to experience those same feelings he'd had when he had taught her during their missionary lessons in Scotland. He started to wonder if this was the girl he was meant to marry.

Dad prayed about it, as he did about everything in his life. He tells me, "Besides Cheryl, there were other girls that I became friends with that I wondered if I should get serious with, but the spirit always directed me that I shouldn't develop relationships of any serious nature with [them]. So you can perhaps imagine my surprise when I fasted and prayed all day at work and received a clear answer that 'Yes, this was the one.'"

After getting his answer, Dad phoned Mom and asked if she would make a little picnic and meet him in a park near where she was staying. (I laughed when I heard that Dad asked Mom to make the picnic instead of making it himself, but it certainly tracks with Dad's view of gender roles and marriage.) Dad writes, "I must admit, I was very nervous when I tried to broach the subject. I stuttered and sputtered a minute, and she could see what a hard time I was having. But then, I just blurted it out. I said, 'I fasted and prayed, and I feel like we are supposed to get married.' And she said, 'I know. That's why I came here. Because God told me to.'"

---

* Dad told me, "She spilled ice cream on her dress, she was so nervous. Bless her heart."

† Dad recalled, "I would either phone her from my trailer park or go visit her if the girls had something planned they wanted me to go with them to."

Once again, my mom's version of events is slightly different. She says that she was rather taken aback by Dad's proposal. Everything felt a bit rushed to her. She was still dating Raj and wasn't ready to end things with him. However, one year earlier, Mom and one of her friends had visited a tea reader who had told my mom that she would marry someone across the ocean with the initials D. L. I suppose it felt like fate for her, too.

Mom later told me, "It all happened too fast. I tried telling your dad that maybe we should slow down a bit and get to know each other." However, it was not in my dad's nature to be deterred. At the time, it was one of the things that my mom found attractive about him.

Imagine meeting a person, and everything about them attracts you in a way that you have never felt before. They don't care that you have scars from your previous relationships. They're willing to do anything to be with you. And so, you don't take into account that they're not perfect or that you've only known each other for a month. You let go of your doubts and decide you're destined to be together.

However, somewhere down the line, the honeymoon phase fades away, and you're left with reality. The traits of the spouse you once loved become an annoyance. Their once adorable refusal to budge on what they want is now an inability to compromise. Their tendency to take the lead, which you once saw as maturity, now becomes an unwillingness to take your views into account. Everything that you loved about them is now the same thing that irks you beyond imagination.

This would eventually become my parents' story. Yet, at the time, they were both so full of hope. I think there is something inside all of us that desires a happily ever after and that wants to believe fate is intervening in our lives. And so, Mom said yes.

Dad immediately got the ball rolling. He had everything planned out. He would finish his last three years of chiropractic college in Glendale, California; then, they would move back to Utah to be close to his family where he could join his father's practice. Dad was very adept at selling

Mom on his vision of an eternal marriage and the life they were going to build together. I can see how it all must have felt romantic and adventurous to her.

Perhaps the greatest influencing factor for my mother was that my oldest sister, Gwen, who was ten, was fully on board. She was excited to give America a try and worked on losing her Scottish accent in order to fit in. Marleen, on the other hand, was very content to stay in Scotland, where she could snuggle up next to her granddad on the couch. Of course, my mother couldn't leave her behind and eventually convinced Marleen, who was only eight, that she needed to come, too. When they reached the States, it took Marleen some time to find comfort in her surroundings; she seemed the most cynical about her new experience. But her presence proved to be an immense comfort to my mom. No one could make her laugh like Marleen.

My parents got engaged in October. It only took my mom and sisters a couple of months to get their visas—another sign in my parents' eyes that their union was divinely appointed. A few days before Christmas, my mom and sisters boarded a thirteen-hour flight, feeling excitement and anticipation for the new lives they were about to begin. They landed in Los Angeles International Airport, jet-lagged and hungry, where they were greeted by my dad and his youngest brother, Allen. The connection between Allen and my sisters was instant and helped make the transition easier for them. They had just inherited an uncle who was charismatic and playful. Everyone laughed when the girls didn't miss a beat asking to go to the beach.

Dad shuffled my mom and sisters to a studio apartment he'd rented and equipped with basic furnishings. A meal was waiting on the table for them as they walked through the door. When they entered, Allen recalled my mom saying, "Wow, this is posh, Dan."

Allen later told me, "Hearing your mother's sincerity took me aback. I couldn't see what she saw. I thought, 'This place is a dump!'"

Dad made all the necessary arrangements for where and when he and Mom were to be married. All of his efforts really touched my mom. A man taking charge felt refreshing to her. I don't think she understood the full extent of what she had signed up for. Dad's entire focus at this time was to get his life in order and live as the LDS Church taught.

My parents were married on the last day of the year in 1975. Their temple ceremony was followed by a reception inside the gymnasium of the local church house. The women of the congregation served cake and fruit punch, and the whole Lafferty clan showed up to attend the event. Dad's family seemed like the ideal happy family, which was what Mom wanted. She especially liked my grandmother, Grandma Lafferty. Mom thought she was very kind and soft-spoken.

However, there was something that didn't seem quite right to Mom. Her heart didn't believe everything she was being taught. She struggled with the strange rituals in the temple—which were quite different from the church's regular Sunday services—and the idea of being subservient to a man. The god she believed in was much bigger than the one the church depicted. Mom prayed and begged God to help her trust in all that she was being told. She wanted to embrace her new life and believe that she had finally found her happy ending and that all her hardships were behind her.

Unfortunately for my poor mother, they were just beginning.

CHAPTER 4

1980

SHORTLY AFTER DAD COMPLETED HIS CHIROPRACTIC SCHOOLING, our days of sunny California living came to an end. We packed up our belongings and moved to Utah so Dad could begin practicing with Grandpa Lafferty.

When we first arrived, we lived in my uncle Tim's home in Payson, a town about an hour's drive south of Salt Lake City. Tim was actually living in California at the time, building studio sets in Hollywood, so he let us stay in his house while we found a place to live.

While we stayed at Uncle Tim's, Dad drove fifteen minutes to the nearby town of Salem every day to work with my grandpa. On his way home, he would pick up raw milk for us from Jerry's Dairy and Burger Barn. On one of his trips, he noticed a little house across the street from Jerry's. He became curious about the house and asked if it was available to rent. The owners of the dairy also owned the house and told him it was. I remember my dad coming home that day, excitement in his voice as he told us he'd just found the perfect home.

And so we moved to Salem. Our new home was in the middle of the town. To the north of us was the dairy. I can still remember the smell. (The raw cow's milk and cheese we bought from them was an important staple for our family.) To the south of us was a large pond shouldering a busy highway—two major concerns for Mom, who was raising three intrepid and energetic small children under the age of four. Beside the pond was a historical monument that marked the site of Pond Town Fort. The plaque read, "In 1851 David Fairbanks and David Crockett located land adjacent to a small stream at the head of Salem Lake and built a dam. In 1856 Eli Ashcraft, Royal Durfey, Silas Hillman, Acquilla Hopper, Jacob Killian, Truman Tryon and their families settled Pond Town and began building the fort for protection . . ." This bestowed an adventurous quality on our new home. We, too, felt like pioneers and explorers. Consequently, we began calling our house "Pond Town Fort."

The thing that excited me most about our new home was the tiny shed that stood directly behind the house; it looked like a miniature version of our home. I wanted it to be a playhouse. However, Dad immediately told me I was not allowed to play in it. The shed was intended for storing large amounts of wheat, honey, water, and other nonperishable food items, to prepare for the end of days. (Later, my mom sold off the items we'd stored in order to pay the rent.)

With the shed off-limits, I soon found other areas to explore. There was a ten-foot plum tree I would often climb for solace, seeking an escape from my outer world. Just north of the shed was a small sandbox where my siblings and I would spend hours playing, making mud pies and tunnels for the boxelder bugs that seemed to abundantly surround our home. We also had a clothesline, and I loved to watch my mom from across the yard, hanging the laundry and bedding out to dry. She always seemed at peace when she did this. Perhaps it reminded her of her home in Scotland, far away. To this day, I still remember the smell of those sun- and air-infused bedsheets, lulling me to sleep at night.

Weeks after our arrival, Dad built a covering off the back porch for storing coal and stacks of chopped wood for the wood-burning stove, which we used to heat our home during the winter months.

As a child, I loved the show *Little House on the Prairie*, and living in Pond Town Fort made me feel like I was like Laura Ingalls Wilder. I deeply related to Laura—who she was as a person, her family life, and the trials she encountered each day. I wanted to be her. I especially loved the relationship she had with her dad. I began to long for that with my own dad. In my mind, Charles Ingalls was what a true father should be.

Our minds are powerful things, and at times I convinced myself that I could see Laura's father in my own. What I didn't yet realize was I would never be Laura and my dad would never be Charles.

Another Sunday afternoon. We're going for a family drive up Payson Canyon to see the fall leaves. I'm almost four.

I'm sitting in the back seat of the car with my sisters, watching the colorful leaves blur by through the window. Suddenly, I have an urgent need to use the bathroom, but I'm afraid to say anything. Dad already seems irritated, and I don't want to set him off.

I hold it until the discomfort becomes unbearable. I intuitively know it isn't safe to speak, but the intense need to relieve my bladder outweighs my instinct to be quiet. I summon my courage.

"I need to go potty," I say, my voice barely above a whisper.

"What?" Dad snaps from the front seat.

"Rebecca needs to use the bathroom," Gwen says.

Dad jerks on the wheel and abruptly pulls over to the side of the road. He reaches back and yanks me forward onto the front seat. Then he roughly pulls my pants down and holds me outside the car door.

"Go," he orders.

I hang there in his arms, my pants down in front of my entire family. My body freezes. I can't relax enough to urinate in front of him and everyone else. I need privacy. I need a toilet.

I can sense Dad's impatience with me. It makes me freeze up more.

I become frustrated with my body. If it would just cooperate, then I could defuse the tense situation.

Dad waits a few more seconds, but my body refuses to cooperate.

"Liar!" Dad snarls. He throws me violently onto the back seat, where I land on top of my sisters.

Being thrown doesn't hurt as much as his words and visible disgust, as if he's discarding something repulsive.

I glance at Gwen. She wears an expression of annoyance that seems to say, "Well, now you did it."

No one else looks at me. Everyone is holding their breath, afraid to set off Dad, who has returned to the road and is driving erratically down the canyon. None of us are wearing seat belts or sitting in car seats. (Dad doesn't believe in them.) Mom clutches Rachel tightly on her lap in the passenger seat, and Johnny is squeezed between my parents in the front.

I curl up on the back seat, drowning in shame and confusion. *What's wrong with me?* I wonder. If only I could stop doing and saying the wrong things. If only I could stop being me.

A few months after this incident, I again angered Dad for something I hadn't done wrong, and again I was hurt and humiliated. This is when I had my experience in the closet, where I felt the love of a divine presence in the wake of Dad's beating.

Lying to my father, telling him I'd done something wrong when I hadn't, was the first time I was conscious of betraying myself to gain approval and safety. When I look back on this experience now, I can acutely recall every detail as if it had happened yesterday. I remember the terror and pain as vividly as the warmth and peace I felt afterward.

I know, of course, that my experience could be interpreted as a trauma response, born of the intense religious programming I had received during my four years of life and a child's need to love and bond with their caretaker. It's been proven that no matter how much your loved ones hurt you emotionally, hurt you physically, or traumatize you, as a child you still crave their attention and love. But I strongly believe this outpouring of love was divine in nature. I've felt it many times throughout my life. It has been a source of strength and hope when everything else around me seemed to have been swallowed by darkness.

However, my newly formed resolve to love slowly faded as, time and time again, I was forced to weather my father's abuse and face what I perceived to be a lack of love from the rest of my family, who were unable to intervene whenever he punished me. It was a devastating and heart-breaking feeling to believe at such a young age that I was unloved and, thus, unlovable. I wondered if things would ever get better. Would I ever again experience that sense of peace and love I had felt in my closet?

What made my situation more difficult was that, from my point of view, my other siblings didn't seem to receive the same treatment from my father. For them, he seemed to have plenty of love and affection. I became extremely jealous of my siblings, especially my older sisters, for the attention they received from my father. I thought it must mean he loved them more than he loved me.

Things were changing with Gwen and Marleen. They started wearing dresses every day, not just on Sundays, and they would wake up in the morning and curl their hair before school. In my eyes, they had become full-grown women, even though they were still teenagers. They no longer practiced the piano. Instead, Dad took them to his office to help him with secretarial work, and I was jealous of the time they got to spend with him.

As an adult, I've come to learn that each of us was scarred in different ways by Dad's behavior. But as a child, I could only see what was visible to me. My siblings' stories are theirs to tell, so I will not attempt to speak for them. I can only speak for myself.

When you see someone else receiving the love that you are deprived of, especially as a young child, it is very hard to digest. As I watched my father set aside time for my siblings, play with them, and make them laugh, I felt betrayed and deeply resentful. Why was he kind to them and not me? What had I done to earn his disapproval?

I became super heightened in my emotions toward and observations of my father. I felt everything very intensely. Just the mere sight of my father playing with my brother or sisters was enough to make me want to cry and act out. However, I knew I couldn't do that because that would only earn me a punishment.

Instead, I tried to imitate my siblings to earn Dad's favor. I noticed that my sisters would smile a lot and laugh at Dad's jokes. As a result, he liked to snuggle with them. I decided Dad must like to receive love.

So I tried to do what I perceived my sisters doing. I would dress up and smile at Dad and try to cuddle with him. Sometimes it worked, and he would let me snuggle up close to him and put my hand around his neck. But at other times, he would snap at me and tell me I was doing something inappropriate. He would push me away and tell me I was like a boy.

I felt deeply confused. Why was my behavior considered cute sometimes and then at other times considered shameful? What was I doing differently? I felt embarrassed by Dad's reaction. I didn't understand. I loved my father and just wanted his love in return. But, once again, I was left with confusing beliefs and an unclear sense of boundaries. The rules about what was appropriate and what wasn't seemed to constantly change. None of it made any sense. How was I ever going to succeed? How could I find the formula that would allow me to get what I needed to feel safe and loved?

Johnny, Rachel, and I are inside, playing with our toys. Suddenly, Dad bursts into the house. We can tell immediately he's in one of his moods.

Dad sees us playing. To our alarm, he moves quickly toward us. In a fit of rage, he gathers up all of our toys then storms into the backyard. We trail behind, frightened and confused.

Dad marches across the yard. Then he systematically catapults every single one of our toys into the pond behind the house.

I stand in the frost-covered grass beside my siblings, my body shaking with silent sobs. I know that if I protest, Dad will just turn his rage on us instead.

Dad finishes throwing the toys in the pond. Then, without offering a word of explanation, he wheels around and marches back into the house.

The next morning, after Dad leaves for work, Johnny, Rachel, and I climb the fence that separates our yard from the pond. We look into the mossy water, searching for any signs of our toys.

The only thing we see is Rachel's spinning top. It has somehow managed to keep its buoyancy and is bobbing on top of the moss.

"Can I get it?" Rachel asks.

Johnny and I shake our heads. It's not safe. Rachel begins to cry, and I give her a hug to let her know that I understand.

I glance at Johnny, but he's not crying. He stands there stoically, staring at the pond.

We return to the house.

I think about that top often in the days that follow. All alone in that big, stagnant pond, barely managing to stay afloat.

When I was four or five, Mom found some little red tennis shoes for me at Deseret Industries. The shoes had laces, so Dad told me he would teach me how to tie them. I remember sitting in front of the big window in the room with the fireplace, the fall leaves beckoning in the yard outside, as Dad showed me how to hold the laces and loop one side then the other and how to pull them tight. I practiced a few times then got it. Dad seemed pleased by my quick progress. I loved how good it felt to actually do something right.

I saw then that to win Dad's approval, I needed to prove my worth through my competence. This was something I could control. When I learned a skill quickly or acted more like an adult and less like a needy child, I would receive Dad's praise. As I grew older, I remained committed to doing everything in my power to prove my worth and earn Dad's love.*

---

* Alice Miller writes in *The Body Never Lies* (2005): "People abused in childhood frequently hope all their lives that someday they will experience the love they have been denied. These expectations reinforce their attachment to their parents."

This intense need to please others and gain approval would stay with me for the rest of my life. I became very good at picking up on cues from others. My emotional body could feel when something was off—if tension was building or if someone was unhappy or angry—and I learned to anticipate and soothe their needs to avoid being hurt and to earn their love. It became a coping mechanism for self-preservation.

In the process, I lost my identity. I didn't know who I was or what I really wanted.* I thought that doing what others wanted and expected of me was how I earned their love. If I failed, then they would take their love away. This created a split inside of me—between the desire to please another person and to do what felt authentic to myself. Over and over again, I was shown that what my authentic self wanted was wrong. So instead, I tried to be what others wanted me to be. I could do it for a while to feel loved and safe, but eventually I felt something snap inside me, like a pressure valve ready to blow.

I became overly focused on how other people seemed to get away with things without being punished, while I was punished for almost every action I took. It seemed to me like other people's emotions mattered but mine didn't. If I tried to explain how I felt to my father, I was told that I was the oldest and should know better. The things Dad said never made me feel better, only more confused, frustrated, and wishing I didn't have feelings at all.

It seemed that Mom was not able to offer me emotional support during this time. I have no memory of her cuddling with me, reassuring

---

* Karol K. Truman writes in *Feelings Buried Alive Never Die* (1991): "A child's identity revolves around family members. In an abused child's pure intent to make things right for everyone around him as he is growing up, he finds himself taking care of others at the expense of his own feelings and needs. Consequently, the child has no identity of his own. This is what is known as codependency." A codependent *needs* the approval of others in order to feel valid. That's why they're always trying to stay and "fix" whatever is wrong with their caretaker. I became deeply codependent as I grew older.

me, or speaking up in my defense. As long as I didn't need anything, I could be close to her. But the second I complained or asked for something, she became frazzled. The message I got was to stay out of her way. Because Mom was busy caring for Rachel, my older sisters were primarily in charge of feeding me and taking care of me. (Mom was also pregnant with my brother Christopher at the time.) However, my sisters were in their own world, and I mostly just stayed away from them. I felt safest hiding and being on my own.

As a result, I became bitter toward some members of my family, especially my older sisters. I would act out in ways that felt justified to me because of the deep hurt I felt. However, things are not always as they appear, and as time passed, I wished less and less to be in my siblings' place.

CHAPTER 5

1982

EVERYONE IN THE HOUSE IS HIDING, waiting for the storm to break.

Dad came home early today and caught Marleen as she was returning from school. She was wearing one of Mom's blouses. And makeup.

Dad grabbed the blouse and ripped it off Marleen. Then he screamed something about harlots and told her to scrub her face clean. I don't know what that word means, but it made Marleen angry. Clutching the torn blouse to her chest, she slapped Dad in the face.

We were all stunned. Dad, most of all. But it didn't take him long to retaliate. His face red with rage, he dragged both Marleen and Gwen out of the house.

Hours go by and they haven't returned yet. I see the anxious way Mom keeps looking at the clock. She's scared.

The familiar sound of tires pulling into the driveway sends us scattering, seeking shelter in our rooms. Mom stands alone in the living room, bracing herself to weather Dad's wrath.

I creep to the edge of the hallway and peer around the corner.

The door opens. Dad steps through the door, my sisters trailing behind.

I clap a hand to my mouth. Their beautiful hair is gone. The curls I've loved and envied my entire life . . . chopped clean off. I barely recognize my sisters without them.

Gwen and Marleen's eyes are red and puffy. They keep their gaze lowered.

"What have you done?" Mom gasps.

"No woman in my house will act like a Jezebel!" Dad shouts.

"Dan," Mom pleads.

"We're taking them out of school. Clearly, the devil has a foothold in the government's curriculum. I should have seen it sooner."

"What do you mean?" Mom stammers.

"They will finish school here at home. There will be no more TV. And no music either! The only books in the house will be the Scriptures. The devil's influence is everywhere, and I will not have him leading this family into temptation."

Gwen and Marleen start crying again.

"Dan, please!" Mom says.

"Shut up, Matilda! This is your fault! You should have taught them modesty."

I try to make sense of what Dad is saying. No more *Sesame Street* or *Mr. Rogers*? Is he going to throw my books in the pond, the way he threw out my toys?

I slip back down the hall to my bedroom and quickly gather up all my picture books. I carry them into my closet and hide with them in the back corner. I can still hear Dad yelling. Louder now. He's working himself into a rage.

"You women need to understand your place!" Dad screams.

I cover my ears and rock back and forth in the darkness. I try to block his voice out. In my mind, I leave my closet and my body behind. I go somewhere far away, where my books and I will be safe.

True to his word, Dad got rid of the television, the radio, and our cassette tapes. We weren't allowed to go to school or have friends or even associate with the neighbors. We were shut off from the outside world and the people in it. The only time we were let out was to attend church on Sunday, but we weren't allowed to linger afterward and socialize. I don't think my dad wanted us talking to anyone and telling them what was happening at home.

Winters seemed so long. I missed being able to go outside and play in the yard. I longed to create some distance between me and the rest of my family in that small house where we all seemed to be on top of each other all the time, slowly suffocating.

Not long after Dad cut off my sisters' hair, Gwen, who was about sixteen, moved out of the house. She went to live with a family who hired her to work in their recording studio. I didn't understand why Gwen was leaving, but I was jealous of her newfound freedom.

Gwen seemed happy with her new life. She would stop by to see us when Dad wasn't home. She was always lit up with smiles as she shared the details of her day in the recording studio and talked about the kind family who had taken her in. Gwen's gift was definitely her smile—and her positive outlook. Even though she was living with a different family, she was loyal to Mom and helped her out in any way she could. Mom was happy for Gwen but seemed sad that she couldn't provide her with the same safety and joy.

Marleen was right behind Gwen. She got a job across the street, flipping burgers at the Burger Barn. It wasn't long before she caught the attention of a local boy named Jordan. Jordan was ten years older than Marleen, and he was making a life for himself working as an electrician.

Jordan later told me he was attracted to Marleen not just because of her outgoing personality and good looks but because of the healthy meals my mom cooked. He said Mom seemed to have it all together, raising us and running the house, and he thought Marleen would do the same for him.

For her part, Marleen saw Jordan as a way out of hell.

After a few weeks of courtship, Jordan came to my father and asked him for Marleen's hand in marriage. Because Marleen was fifteen and still a minor, Mom and Dad had to approve the marriage, which they did.

Within months, Marleen started a family of her own. I believe it was the best thing she could have done at the time. She and Jordan are still happily married to this day.

◆ ◆ ◆

Shortly after my sisters moved out, my dad was excommunicated from the LDS Church. I believe that one or both of my sisters spoke to someone at church about my father's actions and the way his treatment of them had overstepped certain boundaries.

For us at home, Dad's excommunication and my sisters' departure created a major shift in the family dynamic. The future felt more uncertain than ever. The smallest thing would set my father off. We all walked around on eggshells.

Dad believed he'd been given a special calling from God, and he was frustrated that no one seemed to support him—not his wife or his family or the church leaders. He began to believe that perhaps he needed a new community, and that God would guide him to one if he prayed.

I missed not having my older sisters at home, in part because the focus turned to me to step up and help out more. I resented that. I was young and didn't want to be changing diapers. However, it wasn't these new responsibilities that bothered me as much as it was the lack of joy I felt in our home. Things seemed so hopeless and dark. No one ever acknowledged my experiences or the ways that my father's actions affected me in particular, and I was scared about what might happen next.

All of my efforts to love and receive love from my father had created distortions in my perception of myself and reality, not to mention extreme guilt and shame. As a result, I chose to practice not showing my emotions at all. Feelings were a burden, and I started to hate that I felt anything at all. *Why was I made this way?* I wondered. I decided I must be flawed.

My alone times in the closet or the plum tree were now a thing of the past, and my heart began to harden due to the effects of my unexpressed emotions. My only means of solace was singing and staring off into space. I would sit in front of the mirror and gaze into the eyes of the little girl looking back as if to ask, "Are you going to be all right?"

In these moments of stillness, a voice would whisper to my heart, *"Don't give up."*

These messages filled me with just enough strength to keep going. I would feel a renewed sense of hope and a knowing that I would survive. No matter how bad things got, I was going to get through this.

I was becoming more calloused to Dad's punishments. I'd learned I could survive his beatings, and after he threw all our toys into the pond, it felt like there was nothing left for him to hurt me with. I cared less and less about trying to compete for his love, perhaps because Gwen and Marleen, who had been my direct competitors, were gone. Instead, my focus turned toward the outside world—again, likely because my sisters had left home. I, too, wanted to know what else was out there.

Eventually, I felt a burning need to push against the boundaries of my imprisonment and see what was beyond the six-foot fence that confined us in the yard. After a short struggle, I managed to open the gate. My heart raced with excitement and adrenaline as I made my way across the street.

A little girl about my age was playing in her front yard. I shyly said hi, and she told me her name was Cassie Peterson. Soon we started playing.

The elation caused by this unfamiliar taste of freedom—and the joy of playing with a girl my own age—caused me to lose track of the time. I didn't realize it was so late in the day and that my father would soon be returning from work.

Not long after I'd begun playing with Cassie, my dad pulled into the driveway. He jumped out of the car, grabbed me, and started beating me right in front of my new friend. Without a single word, he dragged me back to the house. I wasn't even allowed to say goodbye. I felt humiliated and wondered what she must think.

However, I was not deterred. The next day, I returned to visit Cassie, knowing now to be smarter about my timing and to go back inside well before Dad returned home from work.

Cassie loved showing me all her toys and her trampoline, which is where the two of us spent most of our time. We'd spend hours jumping on the tramp and doing tricks. One time Cassie encouraged me to do a flip. I'd never felt so exhilarated. It was intoxicating.

Cassie was the only person I had to compare my life to. Since she always had a new bike or new clothes and plenty of friends to play with, her life seemed perfect. But looking back now, I can see that she had her own demons and tormentors to contend with. She had an adopted brother, fifteen years older than she was, who called her "Cassie Ass." When I first heard him say it, I laughed and repeated it. She said very seriously, "It's not funny. Don't call me that." I could see how much the name hurt her. I never said it again.

I kept my visits with Cassie a secret from Dad. (Mom knew, but didn't tell him.) My times with Cassie were fun but short-lived. I didn't know it then, but our days at Pond Town Fort were numbered.

Even though I was less focused on earning Dad's approval, I still loved him. However, I was confused about whether or not he was a good parent. On one hand, I had seen a loving father-daughter relationship on *Little House on the Prairie* that did not at all reflect what I had with my father. But at the same time, Dad frequently quoted Scripture to me about biblical parents who behaved quite differently—like Abraham, who was willing to sacrifice his son Isaac simply because God told him to. Dad believed that he was just a puppet and God was the puppeteer. Whatever God commanded, he would do. To him, that was what it meant to be a righteous man and father.

This belief was illustrated quite clearly when my new baby brother, Christopher, only a few days old, caught pneumonia. He had an alarmingly high fever and was struggling to eat. Mom pleaded with my father to take them both to the doctor.

Dad responded, "I'll give him a blessing, and then it's in God's hands."

Mom's heart was filled with great anxiety and panic for the life of her baby. She clung to my brother for two days, nursing him and praying for his health.

Finally, his fever broke. To this day, my mom and Christopher share a close bond. There is nothing stronger than a mother's healing love and a strong will to survive.

After this experience, things started to ramp up. Dad and Mom seemed to be arguing more than ever. Even though our life was no *Little House on the Prairie*, at least it was something familiar. I was in no way prepared for the change that was about to happen to our family.

As a child, I had no concept of what was going on in my parents' lives. I was conscious only of my dad's unpredictable behavior and my unmet needs. I had no way of knowing that my parents had their own needs that weren't being met. I had no way of knowing they were broken, too.

CHAPTER 6

1978–83

WHAT I DIDN'T KNOW AS A CHILD was that Dad was in the middle of an intense faith transition—not *away* from the church and its doctrine, but closer to its more extreme origins.

Joseph Smith founded the Church of Jesus Christ of Latter-day Saints in 1830 in Palmyra, New York, after gaining a following in the wake of publishing the Book of Mormon, which he claimed to have translated from buried gold plates with the help of a seer stone. (Before this, Smith worked as a "glass-looking" treasure hunter and was taken to court for defrauding his clients.) As the church membership grew, Smith adopted increasingly radical ideas, borrowing from other religions and customs that interested him and introducing them as revelations from God.

One of these was polygamy. After being caught having an affair with his teenage foster daughter, Fanny Alger, Smith secretly married her, claiming that God had commanded him to take plural wives and that polygamy was the higher order of marriage. After all, many prophets in the Bible had multiple wives, like Jacob and Abraham, and Smith considered himself to be a prophet as well. In 1841, Smith married Louisa Beaman, his third wife, and over the next two and a half years, he is believed to have married more than thirty women—several as young as fourteen, and ten of whom were already married.

For a time, polygamy was kept hidden from both non-Mormons and members of the church alike. Those who knew about it were sworn to secrecy in special temple rituals Smith adopted from the Freemasons.

Later, however, polygamy was practiced openly; Smith's successor, Brigham Young, had fifty-six wives, and by 1870, about a quarter of all Mormons practiced polygamy. Since plural marriage was illegal in the United States, polygamy became one of the primary reasons that Mormons migrated west to Utah, heading out from Nauvoo, Illinois, in 1846. (Utah was, at the time, a part of Mexico, until the Mexican Cession of 1848; it was incorporated into Utah Territory in 1850, with Young as its first governor.)

Mormons eventually ended the practice of polygamy in 1890 after Congress disincorporated the LDS Church and seized most of its assets for continuing to break the law. The church president at the time, Wilford Woodruff, issued a manifesto ending plural marriage, paving the way for Utah to be admitted as a state in 1896.

My understanding is that Dad, like most modern Mormons, didn't know much about polygamy. However, one Sunday, back when we still lived in California, a church member gave a talk on plural marriage (Mormons have a lay ministry) and asked the congregation to raise their hands if they were descended from an ancestor who practiced polygamy. Mom and Dad were the only ones who didn't raise their hands. For some reason, this caught Dad's attention. He was curious about polygamy and why God had commanded His people to practice it, only to withdraw His commandment later.

After we moved to Utah, Dad became very interested in church history, especially early church doctrines that were later retracted. In his research, he learned about a mine in Salem built by John Hyrum Koyle in the 1890s that was nicknamed the "Dream Mine." Koyle had prophesied that the mine would provide financial support for the Kingdom of God before Christ's Second Coming. Something about the mine and Koyle fascinated Dad and prompted him to do further research. He even went to check out the mine one night without permission from the mine owners. He told me, "That move to Salem and further insights into the Dream Mine was where the journey began that . . . got me into church history that led to finding *The Peace Maker*."*

Coming across *The Peace Maker* was a turning point for Dad. *The Peace Maker* was a small pamphlet written by Udney Hay Jacob in 1842 and printed by Joseph Smith when the Mormons lived in Nauvoo, Illinois. The pamphlet argued for the practice of polygamy as well as the subservience of women. Wives, it claimed, were men's property and should call their husbands lords and masters. This was the true order of the family, ordained by God. The author argued that if this order was restored, it would be the means of driving away Satan's influence from the earth.

Something in *The Peace Maker* struck a chord with my dad—even though Joseph Smith later disavowed the pamphlet, claiming it was printed in his offices without his knowledge. Perhaps it was because Dad saw echoes of its teaching in the temple rituals, where women veiled their faces before God and were symbolically led to heaven by their husbands. (A woman cannot enter the celestial kingdom, the highest level of heaven, unless her husband calls her forward by her "temple name," one assigned to her when she undergoes what is called the endowment ceremony. Husbands are required to know their wives' temple names, but women are forbidden from knowing their husbands' temple names.) Maybe Dad saw reflections of polygamy in the practice of temple sealings, in which men are able to be sealed to more than one woman, but women can only be sealed to one man. If a woman becomes widowed and wants to remarry, she must first request a special dispensation from the First Presidency to have her original sealing canceled, which means she will

---

* Dad recounted, "When we were in Salem . . . I got a book about [the Dream Mine] that I had to ask for special at the library because it wasn't on the shelves, and they pulled it from under the counter. . . . As I shared the story with your mom and she saw the picture of John Koyle, the Dream Mine prophet, she had some kind of spiritual insight or premonition. . . . John Koyle was also excommunicated from the church in Salem. There is a very fascinating story with all of that, that in a way it seems like another chapter took off when I got into it."

not be with her first husband in heaven. Or perhaps a patriarchal system simply felt the most familiar to him, having been raised in the household he was, and he sought a way to take out his frustrations and repressed emotions on his wife and children, the way his father had before him, and his grandfather before that. Perhaps he simply felt it was his due. He had suffered at the hands of his father. Now it was his turn to be the lord of the house. Maybe it stroked his ego and validated his belief that men were in fact the superior gender and closer to God. (In Mormonism, only men can hold the priesthood, the power of God on earth.)

Whatever the reason, Dad took the teachings of *The Peace Maker* to heart and began to enforce these ideas at home, particularly on my mother. He also began to speak explicitly about polygamy. I can only imagine the torment my mom experienced at this time, hearing her husband openly declare he wanted to marry other women.

Inspired by *The Peace Maker*, Dad sought out more early Mormon texts, discovering other principles that had been introduced by Smith and then later abandoned by modern leaders. One of these was a doctrine known as "blood atonement," a principle that was heartily embraced by Brigham Young in particular. The doctrine stated that any heinous acts committed against God's followers ought to be redressed by spilling the blood of the person who had committed the sin. There were many precedents for this in both the Bible and the Book of Mormon. Countless times God commanded the death of evildoers—from the destruction of Sodom and Gomorrah to Nephi slaying Laban (a pivotal event in 1 Nephi, the first book of the Book of Mormon) to drowning the entire world in the flood.

The more Dad studied church history, the more he became convinced that the modern church had fallen away from Joseph Smith's original teachings and was currently in a state of apostasy. Wilford Woodruff and later leaders had acted in error by withdrawing the practice of polygamy and other foundational doctrines to appease the US government.

My father was neither the first nor the last to hold these beliefs. Alongside the Church of Jesus Christ of Latter-day Saints, by far the largest continuation of Smith's church, there are hundreds of denominations and factions, each one claiming to practice the true Gospel as Smith taught it—and each with their own interpretation of his doctrine.

As Dad immersed himself in his studies, his literalism and fundamentalism grew. He began to envision himself on a quest for the absolute truth. Soon he could only see the world through the lens of black and white, good and evil. There was no space for nuance.

Of course, I didn't realize any of this as a child. I didn't know it was his reading of *The Peace Maker* that had worked Dad into such a fit of patriarchal rage that he decided to throw all our toys into the pond (something he claims he doesn't remember doing). All I knew was that my father was growing scarier and more unpredictable by the day.

Joseph Smith also preached that the laws of God took precedence over the laws of men. This really captured Dad's attention. When Dad was in chiropractic school in Glendale, my mom and sisters made vegetarian sandwiches to sell to the students. They would wake up before dawn to prepare the sandwiches, and Dad would take them to the college. Dad got the idea from a man who had previously been selling sandwiches to the students. He was leaving the area and told Dad he could take over the corner he had on this market. The sandwich business was our family's only source of income, but it was quite successful.

However, the business didn't last for long. The board of health shut it down because Dad wasn't following regulations for the sale of food: he didn't have a license and he also wasn't paying taxes on the money he earned. Dad was furious. He thought it was wrong for the government to punish him for being ambitious and trying to support his family. In his mind, the government was forcing him to go on welfare rather than allow him to run an enterprising business. (The irony, of course, is that Dad wasn't doing any of the work himself, apart from collecting the money for the sandwiches.)

Dad recently told me on a phone call that he was very frustrated when the government shut the business down. He claims that someone was jealous of his profits and reported him to the authorities. "The world is just full of assholes," he told me. "Soon we will have our time on earth to reign, and God will separate the wheat from the tares, and the assholes will have to leave." I am sure he considered, and likely still considers, government employees to be among the "assholes" who will burn at Christ's Second Coming.

The Book of Mormon preaches the importance of a "good and just government" that receives its power from the people, and it argues that a government that fails in these duties should be removed. These teachings were a reflection of Joseph Smith's own political views. Smith viewed the founding documents of the United States as sacred texts in their own right (the founding fathers are enshrined in the Book of Mormon and in Mormon culture generally), and Smith himself decided to run for president in 1843 because he was unhappy with the way government leaders were failing to protect the Mormons.

Dad also began to believe that the government was corrupt and that it was preventing him from following God's higher laws. Perhaps inspired by Smith's example, he decided that he needed to get involved in politics. In his mind, everything was connected: religion, politics, business. If he wanted to follow God's laws, he first needed to change man's laws.

In 1981, shortly after Dad started working with Grandpa Lafferty, the LDS Church sent my grandparents to the southern states on a two-year mission. At this point, my uncle Mark, who was a year or two younger than my dad and had also completed his chiropractic degree, joined Dad in running the practice in my grandfather's absence.

Dad and Mark had always enjoyed each other's company. Growing up, they spent a lot of time together doing outdoor activities and taking care of chores. Grandma said the two were practically joined at the hip. When they began working together in Grandpa's office, Dad said that he and Mark got along really well. He joked that it must have been all that time they spent milking cows together. During their work breaks, they enjoyed many conversations about God and religion. They both believed that everything wrong in the world could be made right by restoring God's higher laws.

Even though Dad was the third oldest son, he held a lot of influence over his brothers—not unlike Joseph Smith, who was also the middle son. Soon, his conversations with Mark grew to include his other brothers, and he began holding meetings in Grandpa's office. He talked about treating patients according to the "true way" to live (through Mormonism) and often railed about how the government had exceeded its constitutional mandate, supporting his claims with passages from the Book of Mormon. For example, he believed that the government had no right to require its citizens to have a Social Security number or to pay taxes or even to hold any kind of license. He believed he had the fundamental human right to live his life without any intrusion or authorization from the government.

Dad prayed constantly, seeking guidance for what he felt was God's will. He decided that he needed to send his driver's license back to the state of Utah, return his Social Security card, and revoke his marriage license. Don't get me wrong; doing all of that didn't stop him from driving or expecting Mom to treat him like a husband. He still drove, but he ignored the speed limit, which he viewed as the government overstepping its role, and instead drove "wisely and carefully." He also stopped paying sales tax, which caused all kinds of confrontations with cashiers in local businesses.

In 1982, not long after Dad threw away all of our toys and I began my secret friendship with Cassie, Dad decided it was time to move forward with his political ambitions. He declared himself a candidate for sheriff of Utah County and began campaigning on the promise that he would enforce the laws according to a literal interpretation of the Constitution. He submitted op-eds to local newspapers and did interviews on the radio, expressing his political views.

Like Joseph Smith before him, Dad's campaign stirred up controversy in the community. One of his op-eds was about how the power of the government was being improperly applied and how it was unconstitutional, in particular, to arrest a person when they were driving on the freeway. As you can imagine, the local police force didn't appreciate these views.

One day, when Dad was on his way to a debate with his political opponent, he was pulled over by a state trooper for speeding and not having a vehicle inspection sticker. According to Dad, the trooper had a personal vendetta against him and had laid a trap, hoping to convict him of a felony so he wouldn't be able to run for office.

Dad flatly refused to cooperate with the officer. He locked the doors and declined to get out of the car, claiming the officer couldn't arrest him without a warrant from a judge. Furious, the officer pulled the car window off its track and reached in to grab him. Dad drove off, provoking a car chase with several state troopers in pursuit. When Dad was finally apprehended, he was charged with multiple crimes, including second-degree felony escape, third-degree felony assault, and evading an officer. He was locked up in the county jail.

After spending a few nights in jail, Dad returned home with more intensity and rage than I'd ever witnessed. I can clearly recall my mom sitting on the couch, nursing little Christopher and quietly listening to my father rant as he paced back and forth in our small living room, while the rest of us watched apprehensively from the hallway. The stress was so thick, you could practically taste it.

My poor mother. She always held space for my dad's feelings and extreme views. She supported him as a wife and kept all of us clean and well fed while he was off "fighting the war of good and evil." Dad fully believed that he was meant to fulfill a grand mission in this life. He felt chosen by God. If Joseph Smith could start a movement and restore the truth to the earth, why couldn't he?

Dad's run-in with the law only intensified his radicalism and strengthened his belief that the government was corrupt. He decided to stop paying property taxes on Grandpa's home and business. From his point of view, paying taxes meant he was conceding that the property belonged to the government. He wanted to force a standoff to determine who actually owned the property, working himself into a rage over reasons that only made sense to him.

To no one's surprise, except perhaps my dad's, when this standoff finally happened, he did not emerge victorious. The Utah County assessor notified him that the county was taking possession of my grandparents' home and seizing all of Grandpa's office equipment. Dad informed the assessor that he intended to defend himself against this invasion of his God-given constitutional rights.

Dad's brothers fully supported him in his battle against the state. But when my grandpa, who was still on his mission, learned that his home and business were about to be auctioned off, he was furious. Grandpa accused Dad of hypnotizing his brothers and of trying to hypnotize him and Grandma over the phone. Grandpa cut his mission short and returned home, barely saving his business in time.

Grandpa never forgave my father for nearly losing the home and practice he'd entrusted him with in his absence. Although Dad was saddened by Grandpa's reaction, he was not dissuaded from continuing in his quest. His mission to follow and restore God's higher laws on earth was only just beginning.

CHAPTER 7

1983

NOW THAT DAD WAS FULLY COMMITTED to living by God's higher law, he rejected the idea of working within the constraints of human laws altogether. Consequently, he decided to quit his job—or at least, that's what he claimed. The truth is Grandpa visited Dad when he was in jail and told him he was no longer welcome to practice with him.*

Without an income, we were soon unable to pay rent. Watson Jr., Dad's middle brother, informed Dad about an abandoned property where the owner had allowed him to park his trailer. Dad contacted the owner, who gave us permission to move into the old farmhouse on the property. (Dad's version of events is that we left Pond Town Fort because the landlord's daughter was getting married and wanted to live there.)

The farmhouse was a complete dump and should have been condemned. It was damp and cold and infested with mice. There were holes in the walls, and the carpets were old and rotting. I slept in the basement, in the room where we kept all our food storage. It was disgusting and smelled like mold and rodents. I shared a bed with Johnny and Rachel. We all huddled together to stay warm and safe from the long dark nights.

I dreaded nighttime, especially waking up and having to go to the bathroom. My fear was that on my way to find the toilet in the dark, a

---

* Dad later claimed he was relieved that his father kicked him out of the practice because he didn't particularly like being a chiropractor. "I don't like touching people that I don't like," he told me. "There are people I instinctively like and others that I don't. Perhaps the people I instinctively don't like are assholes. I don't know. But if I only had to treat people I like, I would have liked being a chiropractor, but there were too many people I didn't like."

mouse would run across my foot or I would step in the droppings that literally covered the floor. To prevent this, I made sure I didn't drink too much water before going to bed.

Dad saw the farmhouse as a fresh start, a way to live in alignment with his new "true way" of life. He was determined to live off the grid as much as possible. To this end, he procured two cows that he milked for a time before passing that chore on to my mother, who was now seven months pregnant with my youngest brother, Brian. He also managed to find some chickens that laid little green eggs, which we kids called "Easter eggs." Dad shut off most of the electricity to the house but left the breaker on for a large fridge, where we kept the milk from the cows, and a deep freezer, where we stored homemade butter.

Dad had grand plans for the farmhouse and our off-grid lifestyle. He enlisted Watson in his vision to plant a potato garden. They hooked Watson's truck up to one of the rusty abandoned plows from the 1800s that still stood on the property. I remember riding in the back of the truck as they pulled the plow across the field. My job was to drop the potatoes that Dad had most likely retrieved from a grocery store dumpster into the newly plowed tracks. The planting was a success, but we never saw the harvest.*

I remember one morning Dad came home and announced that he was going to teach me how to make butter. I loved that he was excited to show me something, but once I realized how much work it would require, I quickly lost interest. I couldn't care less about making butter. But no one asked me what I thought or what might be going on with me. There were times when I wanted to yell, "Hello, people! I exist here, too!"

---

* Dad's recollection of this time is a little rosier than mine: "Uncle Watson had us help with his tile business to pay rent, and then we started to buy the cows and the chickens for the farm which I took care of. I just liked having you kids around me there and started to homeschool you. I never planned too far ahead actually. I was just following this strange path that I felt I was on."

It was becoming clear to me that what I wanted didn't matter. I felt like I was viewed as a physical commodity and resource, nothing more. I was to sit on the floor and shake this bucket filled with cream. For what felt like an eternity, I shook that bucket until it turned into butter. I was told that my place was in the kitchen with my mother and that I was not to leave the house. According to Dad, men managed the money, and women toiled in the kitchen. This was the natural order of things. I was to wear dresses and be obedient. Basically, I wasn't allowed to have a voice or an opinion, and if I were to vocalize my feelings, then I would be punished and put in my place. I was told to stop making up stories and not to cry, or I would be given a reason to cry.

Although we were living in abject poverty, Mom still managed to turn the horrible farmhouse into a home. In the kitchen there was a large wood-burning stove that she used to heat gallons of water—that was how she bathed us and cleaned our clothes. She also used the stove to cook all our meals. Every morning, she would feed us homemade bread drizzled with honey and topped with thick cream or a bowl of mush—hot cereal that she had sprouted and then gently cooked on the stove and served with honey, milk, and eggs from our little chickens, which she would let us kids collect. Dinners were whatever vegetables Dad scavenged out of the local grocery dumpster, usually old carrots and potatoes, beets and cabbages. Pure alchemy occurred as Mom managed to transform this garbage into a yummy meal we called "now and later"—so called because we would eat some now and then reheat the rest with olive oil later.

One of my only joys during that period was watching Mom bake bread. I loved watching her grind the wheat in the brown Magic Mill box. She would allow me to pull the chair over and pour the wheat into the machine. I would watch the cup of wheat slowly swirl down the spiral hole before the machine came to a stop. I must have been transfixed because, in those moments, I don't remember having a care or concern for anything or anyone.

Greater magic would happen once Mom opened the drawer. I loved watching how she would scoop out the freshly ground flour and mix it with water, oil, and yeast until it became dough. She had a Bosch mixer that Dad had picked up at the thrift store for her birthday, and she definitely made good use of it. She would plop the dough onto the floured countertop and fold it over and over, sprinkling it with flour many times, before separating the big blob into three or four perfect-sized loaves, shaping them into the well-greased pans, and covering them with a towel to rise. It wasn't long before the warm and delicious fragrance of home-baked goodness transformed the cold, stale house into a paradise.

Mom was truly a miracle worker. She was strong, unfaltering, and committed to making life bearable for our family. As long as I can remember, she was constantly busy: nursing a baby, cooking, cleaning, making our clothes, baking bread, milking cows, listening to my father's rants. And somehow, she would still make time to sit down and read with me. In my mind, there was nothing she couldn't do. But I don't recall Dad ever showing gratitude for her labors. He expected them of her, as he did of all of us.

Mom's main solace during this time was Marleen and Gwen. They lived in the same town and would stop by on occasion to see us. She loved when they came by. The only other source of comfort—and empowerment—she had was finding ways to jab back at my father without him realizing it.

One day, exhausted from running the farm and being pregnant, Mom finally got fed up with the ridiculous chickens, so she let them inside the house and allowed them to shit all over the floor. I remember her standing in the living room, laughing so hard she was doubled in half, as the chickens ran amok around her.

When my dad arrived home and found the house overrun by chickens, he was shocked and asked, "Matilda, why are there chickens in the house?"

Mom replied calmly, "Oh, I don't know, dear. I'm just allowing things to follow the natural order."

To this day, I still wonder how my mother was able to bear my father. All the things he put us through were intensely hard for us kids, but she had to live with the thought that she would grow old with this man and his bizarre behaviors. She cried a lot, but I never saw her break. She seemed to draw strength from a source that allowed her to adapt to any situation. She was truly the beacon of light in the darkest times, an assurance that no matter what, everything would be okay. There's no question I wouldn't have survived without Mom.

Dad decided to name our farmhouse "La Mancha" because he loved the movie *Man of La Mancha*. He clearly saw himself in Don Quixote, a man who wanted to right all wrongs but who was arrested and persecuted for following his dreams. I find it interesting that he related so strongly to Quixote, a character whose name has become synonymous with delusion.

I remember Dad picking up a video of *Man of La Mancha* from the university library and watching it at home. We had a TV for a short time because of Dad's brother Tim. Uncle Tim came to visit from California and saw how we were living. No doubt wanting to ease our torment, Tim told my dad that he needed to get us some children's movies to help our development. Dad went to the library, rented a VCR, and connected an extension cord to the outlet that powered the freezer. I'll be forever grateful to Tim for bringing some small measure of escape into our lives. He returned to California after his visit and never had anything to do with my dad's schemes.

Dad would occasionally bring home movies from the library for us kids to watch. (The fact that he relied on a government institution is an irony not lost on me.) I also remember him bringing home *Jack the Ripper*. Mom expressly told me not to watch it. "It's not appropriate for children," she said.

One day, I was bored after watching *The Sound of Music* and *Mary Poppins* for the twentieth time. I saw *Jack the Ripper* sitting on top of the television. The fact that my mother had forbidden me from watching it made me even more curious. I had watched other adult movies before, like *The Pink Panther* and *Jaws*. Why was this any different?

I snuck the movie into the VHS and watched about twenty minutes before I got the sickest feeling in my stomach. I quickly ejected the movie and strategically placed it back exactly as it had been. I wasn't interested in having any more nightmares. The fear of mice running across my feet in the middle of the night was more than enough for me, thank you very much.

By now, it was clear that my father was completely obsessed with following his new religious beliefs. We children were barely on his radar and only existed in his periphery, as part of his property. The things he did only made sense to him, and he would fly into a rage if we didn't immediately obey even the strangest commands. It felt like he was waiting for some great calling or event to transpire, convinced that the end of the world was upon us.

Later, my mom told me she believed my dad has bipolar disorder and that if he had ever been properly evaluated, he would have been diagnosed. My dad's behavior certainly seemed consistent with bipolar disorder or manic depression, a mental health condition that causes extreme mood swings—an upswing in which the person feels euphoric (mania), followed by a downswing into depression. At times Dad would seem very happy, almost abnormally upbeat and wired. Then, in the next moment, the wrath of God would be upon us. Dad would frequently dissociate. He was always restless, underweight, and constantly making poor decisions, which are also symptoms of the illness. I believe my father experienced a psychotic break, when he fully lost touch with reality, during one of his manic episodes.

Bipolar disorder can be genetic and caused by trauma and stress. I'm almost certain my grandpa Lafferty had the same condition. The illness can be managed with medication and therapy, but neither Grandpa nor Dad would have ever considered turning to conventional medicine for help.

As a child, of course, I didn't understand what was happening. I just knew that things were changing. Life at the farm was becoming even weirder, if that was possible. Dad had strange people come to the house. They didn't make eye contact with us, and I was explicitly instructed not to talk to them. The whole thing was very secretive and unsettling. Dad hung up a heavy blanket to separate the kitchen from the front room so they could have their meetings.

Curious to know what was going on, one time I pulled back the curtain just enough to glimpse someone standing at a pulpit addressing the rest of the group. I didn't know at the time that I was witnessing cult meetings with the School of the Prophets.*

Sometimes Dad talked to me about his newfound beliefs, but he lacked the ability to pause and see if I understood what he was saying or, God forbid, solicit my opinion. He would go on long rants about the evil state of the world and where things were headed. When I asked him about what was going on, I needed a simple answer, not a warped discussion about how everything in the world was wrong, except for what he and his fellow cult members believed. He could always justify his anger and believed he alone had the solutions. Looking back, I can see how the brainwashing was in full force. Even as a child, I knew that something was wrong. I'd known my whole life that Dad was unstable, but this was something new.

One thing I have to give my dad credit for is his imagination and ability to sell others on his dreams. He had—and still has—a way with words and could convince almost anyone to follow him, like his father before him,

---

* The School of the Prophets was founded by a man named Robert Crossfield, who called himself Prophet Onias, and who shared Dad's beliefs that the modern LDS church had strayed from God's sacred doctrines—most notably plural marriage. See page 80.

probably because he truly believed that he was right. Dad managed to fully sway his brothers to his way of thinking (Tim being the only exception). My dad was a smart guy, but IQ is not the same as emotional intelligence. He knew how to survive and live as a minimalist, how to rally other people to his cause, but to any objective onlookers, it would have been clear just how much of a Don Quixote he really was.

There were times I was starving for Dad's attention, so I would willingly listen to his long rants. I was grateful at least that he was talking to me, and I would pretend to understand what he was saying just to be close to him. In these moments, he would call me by his nickname for me, Bert. I liked having a nickname. It made me feel special. I thought the name came from Bert and Ernie on *Sesame Street*, but Dad told me that someone had mistaken my name for Roberta once and that's why he called me Bert. Later, my mom told me the truth, which was that Dad had a flirtatious relationship with a bank teller named Roberta. I have no idea why he decided to call *me* by this woman's name. Perhaps to irritate my mom?

I thought if I was obedient and pleased Dad, he would change his belief about girls staying home and boys going to work with their fathers. I wanted to see the outside world. I wanted something different, *anything*. I was tired of this black-and-white experience. I longed for some color in my life.

But connecting with my father was never an easy task; it felt like preparing myself for the unknown. Would I suffer from frustration and boredom as he droned on about his delusional vision of the world? Would I walk away feeling a little taller from his attention, or would he punish me again?

Johnny, in contrast, was always good at following Dad's orders and never seemed to get in trouble. I wished I could be like him, but it was so hard for me to be obedient and to not question things. Johnny got to go to work with Dad, which he seemed to enjoy. I saw this as further proof of favoritism, although I think my dad just believed he was preparing Johnny for a "man's role" in the world.

Rachel always kept quiet and stayed close to Mom most of the day. She and I slept next to each other, but we rarely spoke. It felt at times as if we lived in completely different worlds.

I asked Rachel recently if she had any memories of life at the farmhouse, and she says she has virtually none. She only remembers the chickens and sleeping in the basement. She thinks that absorbing a lot of our mother's stress may have caused her to lose her memories. When we are under stress or experience trauma, we are often unable to store memories because our brain switches into survival mode, and all of our energy is directed toward staying safe.

Rachel does recall playing in the kitchen. There was a small cupboard that Mom would keep toys in for us, and Rachel would climb inside and play. No doubt she felt safe there, knowing Mom was close by.

By this time, Christopher could walk, and Mom made sure he stayed close by as well. For the most part, he seemed content. Mom would ask me to keep an eye on him when he went outside so she could try and get a break from having us all underfoot. We would roam the yard and chase the chickens until we got bored.

One time, Dad brought home a rusty old bike he'd no doubt found on one of his dumpster dives. I was thrilled and asked him to teach me how to ride it, the way he'd taught me to tie my shoes. But he said no; he was too busy. Then he walked away. This time his rejection actually made me livid. Why bring the bike home at all if he wasn't going to show me how to ride it? I had so many warring emotions in my head and my heart and no idea how to process them. Without an outlet to express my emotions, I did the only thing I could do: I stuffed them down. I'd learned many times by this point that emotions only proved to be an inconvenience, so I ignored them.

I was six years old at the time. Up until now, I had been raised with little structure. I was treated by Dad like I was a pain in the ass and told to entertain myself or else given some ridiculous chore. I didn't know the word for it at the time, but I was resentful. The fact that Dad didn't care about me until he needed something made me angry and bitter.

One of the last memories I can recall in the farmhouse was the time Dad brought home a case of grapefruit. I was thirsty and craved the grapefruit's juice. I remember reaching into the box to grab one of the bright juicy fruits.

Mom quickly said, "No Rebecca, we will be eating dinner soon."

I was confused. Mom had never restricted me this way in the past. Now looking back, I see it must have been because Dad was at home and she was showing him that she was obeying his orders to discipline us kids—orders she followed when he was around but threw out the window when he was gone.

In that moment, however, I just felt angry and frustrated. I was thirsty *now*. Why was Mom changing the rules? So I reached into the box and took a grapefruit anyway. Mom caught me and scolded me, which broke my heart. I felt like she had turned on me, too.

I went outside and sat on the porch, sobbing. Dad saw me from across the yard and came running toward me, asking me if everything was okay. Since Mom was on the verge of giving birth, I'm sure he assumed I was crying about that. But for a split second I imagined I was Laura Ingalls, and my father was coming to scoop me up in his arms and comfort me.

I should have known better. As soon as I told him what had happened, Dad said, "Well, you must have deserved it."

Right then and there, I said to myself, *I don't need your love anymore, Dad.* From then on, I did everything to prove to myself that I didn't need or even desire Dad's love. I didn't care if I ever saw him again. I worked even harder to hide my emotions. I'd learned that sharing them was no use, and when I showed that something didn't bother me, that thing seemed to go away more quickly. I believed I could escape situations if I stayed quiet. In short, I began to close my heart.

I can see this change when I look back at pictures. My body physically took on the appearance of protecting my heart. My shoulders turned in, and I began to hunch over. I truly believed that no one cared if I lived or died. I felt defeated, like I couldn't do anything right.

I was hurting so deeply. I just needed someone to talk to me and listen to me.

But in these moments, I didn't feel like there was anyone I could turn to for solace, not even my mom. Although Mom cared for me, she wasn't emotionally available to hold space for my feelings, not with all of the stress and responsibilities on her plate—four small children and another about to arrive any moment. Most of the time, she was mired in her own thoughts and fears, and I could physically feel her stress. Whenever I did something useful, like help her make bread or watch one of my siblings, I was able to earn her attention and gratitude, and that gave me some peace. But more often than not, I felt lost to an overwhelming sense of powerlessness that pervaded our home.

Occasionally, Mom's stress and fear of Dad made her lash out at me. I remember one time we were getting ready to leave the house, perhaps to go to church, and we were waiting for Dad to pick us up. Mom's anxiety was revved high, and I felt it infiltrate my own nervous system. I tried to brush my hair, but I was so anxious, I ended up tying my hair in knots. When Mom saw the knot, she lost it. She screamed at me, asking me how I could be so useless, and chopped my hair off with her scissors. I stood frozen in place. I was used to this kind of behavior from my dad, not my mom. I felt that I really was useless and unlovable.

I wish I could have felt the love I'd felt in the closet. I didn't realize the presence I'd connected with as a young child was always there, waiting for me to reach out.

My brother Brian was born in the farmhouse on July 23, 1983. There was no way my dad was letting my mom give birth in the hospital, so she had no choice but to deliver him at home. My poor mom was so distrustful of my father at this point; she didn't want him anywhere near her. She went into the bathroom by herself and lay on the cold floor and delivered Brian on her own. (She allowed my father to clean up the afterbirth once she was done.) An hour or two later, she was back on her feet and making dinner for us all. I don't know how she did it.

Mom let me hold Brian and comfort him when he started fussing. He felt like my own baby. I loved him so much.

Around this time, Grandpa got very sick. He was diabetic, but he refused to stop eating ice cream. I think he believed he would get better, but he never did. Eventually, he developed a sore on the bottom of his foot, which only got worse and eventually developed into gangrene. However, because Grandpa had a strong distrust of modern medicine, he refused to have his foot treated or to take any medication. Instead, he asked my dad and his brothers to give him a healing blessing. They did, but nothing changed.

Grandpa started getting sicker. He would take three to four naps a day. Dad could tell he was nearing the end, so he spent a lot of time with him, recording Grandpa's history. They also read the Scriptures together. Toward the end, Grandpa couldn't get out of bed. One day, my grandma went to make tea and returned to find that my grandpa had passed. She called the paramedics, and they took Grandpa to the hospital in an ambulance and tried to revive him. They got his heart started, but he never woke up.

Dad summoned his brothers to the hospital. My uncle Allen came with his wife, Brenda, and their baby daughter, Erica. Dad said he prayed about what to do, but he couldn't get a clear answer about whether they should keep Grandpa on life support or let him go. He felt that in order to receive an answer, only their immediate family should be present. He mentioned this to my grandma. She approached Brenda and said, "If it's all right with you, we would like just the family here for this blessing."

According to my Dad, Brenda replied with a sarcastic, "Yes, Mother. That's fine."

Dad said that he felt a rush of anger and thought, *You bitch, nobody talks to my mother like that.*

Brenda's sister, Sharon, told me that Brenda was very upset by this interaction, but not because she'd been asked to leave the room. She cared deeply about my grandpa and was angry that my dad and his brothers were willing to just let him die instead of giving him the medicine and help he needed. She was also disappointed that Allen hadn't stood up for her and that she wasn't allowed to stay with her father-in-law in his final moments.

After Brenda left the room, the family prayed. Then Dad said they knew that they needed to let Grandpa go. He gets very emotional whenever he recalls this moment. Dad says he remembers that he wished they would have never notified the doctors because of all the money it cost my grandma. He told me he saw a spot in the mountains one day and thought it would have been the perfect place to bury my grandpa.

Dad also told me he was grateful Grandpa passed away before he embarked on his "next phase." He knows that my grandpa wouldn't have been able to understand.

CHAPTER 8

1983

SIX MONTHS AFTER WE MOVED TO THE FARMHOUSE, Dad announced he was going to take a second wife.

Mom, of course, was not happy about this. She had thought about leaving my dad many times over the years. But being as isolated as she was, and with no resources to speak of, she didn't know how to do it. No matter how bad it was for her to live with my father, going her separate way seemed much more difficult. She would be venturing into the unknown as an immigrant (she would not get her citizenship for many years) and single mom raising five young children all under the age of seven. Mom says, looking back, the reason she stayed as long as she did was that she only saw two options: stay and wait for a better path to present itself, or leave and let the state separate us and place us in foster homes, which was never going to happen if she could help it.

Once Mom tried confiding in my grandma Lafferty, asking her what she should do. She hoped that Grandma would show her a way out of the misery she had to endure daily. However, I think my grandma was going through her own trials and was emotionally unavailable. Her only advice was: "Get back in there and keep praying for strength." Needless to say, that was not the support my mom needed at the time.

My dad's insistence on practicing polygamy, however, was the last straw for my mom. She told him if he took another wife, she would leave him. Dad told her she could leave, but she could not take us kids since we were his property.

Seeing no alternative, Mom told Dad she'd prayed about it and was willing to help him find a second wife. To show her support, she started sewing special undergarments for Dad and his new wife that were akin to the garments Joseph Smith introduced to the temple ceremony and that faithful LDS members continue to wear. Secretly, however, she began planning our escape.

My mom's primary solace during this time was Marleen. No matter how bad things got, Marleen had the ability to make my mom laugh. She was the support my mother needed to survive. Marleen had been married for a year now and had her own newborn. Her life was going well. However, her heart ached for Mom. Marleen loved our mother so much that she would frequently stand up to my dad in Mom's defense. There were many times that she got slapped hard for it, but her spirit was strong. She didn't care what my father did to her. She only cared about Mom and us kids. What's incredible to me is that Marleen was only sixteen at the time. But she had more guts than any of us.

Marleen was only eight when she came to this country, but she had always been mature for her age, and she knew how to distinguish between people who were good and people who were bad. She'd figured out Dad a long time ago and had had an easier time getting away from him than anyone else. She knew there were other men out there who would treat Mom much better, and she encouraged my mom in her plans to leave, even though there were many obstacles in her path. I think Mom was too embarrassed to tell her family back in Scotland what had happened to her. She felt like contacting them and asking for help wasn't an option.

I clearly remember Mom sewing the garments and talking to Marleen about how Dad was going to find another wife. They talked mostly in whispers, so as to not let me hear the conversation, but I remember them laughing about how absurd the situation was. Once, Marleen had Mom laughing so hard that she peed her pants. This was just about a regular occurrence whenever Marleen came to visit. Her sarcasm and humor always helped us forget the pain we were going through. She could turn a horrible situation into something we could laugh at.

As a child, of course, this was all a little confusing. I tried to make sense of what was happening by watching Mom's reactions. All I knew was that if Marleen could make Mom laugh, it couldn't be all bad. The fact that I could see her be calm and "happy" brought some peace to my emotionally unstable and fearful world.

Thank God Marleen was able to stay grounded through all of this. She was such a blessing to us. Marleen taught me that happiness is a conscious choice. No matter how bad things get, there is always a silver lining.

Since moving to the farmhouse, Dad and his brothers had continued to meet and obsess over the teachings of *The Peace Maker*. By this point, Dad had persuaded his brothers Mark, Watson, and Allen to his way of thinking. They got rid of their Social Security cards, stopped paying taxes, and tried to impose the same patriarchal principles on their families that my dad had on ours. And they began openly discussing polygamy.

Mom wasn't the only wife to be concerned about these new developments. Her sisters-in-law were extremely alarmed by their husbands' newfound extremism, but they were too frightened to say or do anything—all except for Brenda. Brenda was the youngest wife, married to the youngest brother, but she was the most vocal in her criticism of Dad. She encouraged the other wives not to put up with their husbands' abusive behavior.

Brenda married my uncle Allen, the uncle who met my mom and sisters at the airport all those years ago, in 1982. I remember one time Allen brought Brenda over for a Sunday dinner, when we still lived at Pond Town Fort. She seemed a bit uncomfortable, not that I blame her. I remember thinking how pretty she was and being surprised she was allowed to wear makeup.

After Allen began to adopt Dad's ideas, he refused to let Brenda register her car or take their baby to the doctor when she got sick, and he sabotaged his successful tile business by getting rid of his Social Security card. But Brenda fought back. She told Allen she didn't want him associating with his brothers, and she continued to encourage the other wives to resist and stand up to their husbands.

As talk of polygamy continued, the other wives turned to Dianna, Ron's wife, for guidance. So far, Ron, who was the oldest son, hadn't been roped into Dad's cult. At Dianna's urging, Ron came to the house to talk some sense into Dad and his brothers.

However, instead of convincing Dad to give up this delusion, the opposite happened: Dad managed to convince Ron that he was being called as the next president and prophet of the church and that my dad would be his first counselor and Watson would be the second counselor. (The LDS Church is headed by the First Presidency: the prophet and his two counselors. They are always men, as are the Quorum of the Twelve Apostles and all global, regional, and local leadership positions.)

Somehow, Ron was persuaded by Dad's vision. He followed Dad's example and quit his job; shortly afterward, he had to file for bankruptcy and lost his successful construction company. Simultaneously depressed and emboldened by Dad's teachings, he grew angry and violent toward his family and tried to bend them to his will.

Dianna reached out to friends and family for help, including Brenda. She was advised, by both Brenda and others, to divorce Ron and get as far away from him as possible. So she left and moved to Florida, taking the kids with her and filing for divorce. This was a huge blow to Ron. Even though Brenda wasn't the only person who had encouraged Dianna to leave, Ron held her personally responsible. Brenda had long been a thorn in my family's side for her outspoken behavior and refusal to follow traditional gender roles. This made her an easy target for his rage.

Shortly after this, Ron came to stay with us at the farmhouse. He only had a few things with him, but I remember clearly he had a guitar because my sister Rachel was obsessed with the tuning knobs. Ron would get frustrated when he would go to play the guitar and discovered the strings were flat because she had been turning the knobs. He would yell, "Damn you, Rachel!"

During this time, Dad was working with Watson doing tile work. Watson also got him a job working on Robert Redford's ranch. While he was at the ranch, Dad met a Romanian immigrant named Anne. According to Dad, Anne approached him and said she'd been having dreams about him. (This was not the last time this would happen to my father.) Dad thought it was strange because he could tell that Watson liked Anne, so he tried to keep his distance. However, Anne kept showing him attention. Finally, Dad brought up polygamy. Anne said she was open to the idea, so they "consummated" the relationship. Dad said they never had a marriage ceremony, and it didn't last long.

When things with Anne fell through, Dad decided it was time to find himself a proper second wife. In the fall of 1983, a few months after Brian was born, Dad, Ron, and my mom took a trip to Oregon where they visited a polygamous commune run by John W. Bryant. My poor mother wasn't given a choice about whether to go; however, she hoped she could use this to her advantage to leave my dad. While they were away, I stayed with Gwen, and my other siblings stayed with Marleen.

For three days and two nights, Mom sat in the car, nursing my new baby brother while Dad and Ron toured the commune and experimented with drugs and group-sex activities. You can imagine just how desolate my mother felt in that situation. Even though she was planning to leave my father, this was still a lot of emotional trauma for her to go through. Mom tells me that this was the hardest time of her life. However, her spirit was unbreakable.

Mom's situation was so pitiful that one of the women from the commune approached the car and offered her some food. She invited Mom to come in to avoid the cold outside, but my mom was stubborn and resentful; after all, these were the people who were helping Dad find a second wife. She refused to leave the car and told the woman, "Absolutely not. I don't need anything from you." Mom had no wish to associate with that community, and after all she'd been through, she didn't trust anyone.

Mom was right to be distrustful. The woman, who was actually sent to assess my mother for a potential initiation, returned to my dad and told him my mom would not fit in with the community there. Dad was livid that Mom had been disobedient. Not once did he stop to consider the hell he was putting her through. The only thing he wanted was complete and utter obedience, which I'm sure included satisfying his sexual needs.

When he and Ron returned to the car, Dad beat my mom in front of his brother for her insubordination. Later, when they returned home, he almost strangled her to death in front of us children. He told us that she was being punished and then banished her to the trailer outside the house. Keep in mind that my mom was only a few months postpartum and nursing a newborn.

By this point, my mom was terrified. She was convinced that Dad had lost his mind and if we stayed, I would be married off to some old man who would rape me and impregnate me with his kids, as often happens in polygamist groups.

There had been a recent report of a family in California that had over twelve children who were kept chained to their beds by their parents until one of them escaped and contacted the authorities. My mother was sure that was how we were going to end up. We were only a breath away from living in that situation already. She prayed with every cell in her body, "Please, God. Help me find a way out of here. Help me protect my children."

After Mom's legs had healed from the beating Dad gave her, she decided to put her plan into action. She knew she needed to speak Dad's language to get all of us children to safety and out of that hellhole. She told him that she'd prayed about it and that God told her He wanted her to take us children somewhere so we would be out of his way as he did the Lord's work. She told him God said he was to "go ahead and pave the way." Mom later told me the words just came to her. I believe she was being led by the spirit and shown how to save us.

Dad thought this was a brilliant idea. He handed Mom twenty dollars and said that he would be back in a few hours.

Mom didn't want to risk Dad changing his mind. As soon as he left the house, she yelled, "Rebecca, we're getting out of here!"

I screamed with joy and jumped up and down. I stayed with my siblings while Mom ran across the street to use a payphone to call my sister Gwen. Gwen showed up a few minutes later with a van. We gathered our few belongings and jumped into the van. I believe we were out of there in less than thirty minutes.

As we drove away, I remember wondering if I was really free at last. Had we left Dad for good, or would he find us again? And what would happen when he did?

2006

I've reached a breaking point. I can't take it anymore, and the impulse to flee hits me harder than ever. I let it take over. The moment he leaves for work, I pack the kids into the van. I don't tell anyone where we're going.

I speed down the interstate like a fugitive, ignoring the icy roads. All that matters is getting as far away as possible.

I glance at my children in the back seat. Ten-year-old Erin meets my gaze.

Suddenly, I'm in Erin's place, sitting in the back seat while my mother desperately drives the van that will take us to freedom, gripping the wheel so tightly, I can see the bones through her skin.

Time blurs together, past and present merging into one disorienting moment. I am mother and child both.

I pull the car over. I rest my head on the steering wheel and try to slow my breathing so I don't hyperventilate.

How did I end up here? I wonder. I vowed as a child this would never be my reality. And yet here I am, stuck in the exact same situation as my mother, and her mother before her.

The only thing that feels safe is to run.

CHAPTER 9

1983–84

AFTER LEAVING THE FARMHOUSE, we moved from place to place while Mom found odd jobs and tried to make ends meet. We stayed in Provo for a week, in the rental home of a family friend. After that we moved to Payson.

While we were in Payson, Brenda came to check on my mom. She asked me to help her make a bottle for Erica. I asked if it was okay to use the water from the faucet. I remember the surprised, and concerned, look on her face as she answered, "Yes, it's safe."

She didn't say anything else, and at the time I thought I'd done something wrong. Looking back now, I can see what she must have been thinking. *You poor thing. You've been brainwashed, too.*

I thought Baby Erica was so cute and wanted to play with her, but Brenda held her very close during her entire visit.

Mom got a little bit of help from the church. She was given food from the Bishop's Storehouse (the church's version of a welfare program), but in return she had to clean the church. In order to do that, she had to take all of us kids with her. This, of course, was a disaster and only caused her more stress since we just ran around making noise and not providing any help whatsoever. She would yell at me to look after my brothers, who were out of control and full of energy. But attempting to corral them was always a losing battle.

Eventually, a woman at church told Mom she could apply for government funding. With help from the state, we were able to move back into our old house, Pond Town Fort. None of us were attending school at the time. Mom had some early reader books that she would give me to practice reading.

During this time, Gwen got married. She was eighteen or nineteen. I remember Mom frantically sewing dresses for all of us and thinking everything felt absolutely surreal. We drove up to Twin Falls for the wedding.

Dad never came looking for us. He was more than happy to "go ahead and pave the way" for his new calling as prophet, free of us kids. He told me recently, "I told [your mom] when she was leaving that I felt that I was supposed to follow that journey on my own from that time. I wasn't upset at her or anything. She had made arrangements to be picked up with you kids . . . I left for a while to make it easier . . . When I came back you were all gone." He claims to have felt nothing at our departure. "I felt about the same with each of those three big changes: getting kicked out of the church, kicked out of the office, and when your mom took you kids and left. They each just felt like the next thing that was happening in what I now describe as my predestined journey." As always, Dad believed that whatever happened in his life was God's will.

Prior to our departure, Dad had introduced his brothers to a man who went by Prophet Onias, a fundamentalist from Canada who had founded a cult called the School of the Prophets. Onias, whose real name was Robert Crossfield, shared Dad's belief that the modern LDS Church had strayed from God's sacred doctrines revealed to Joseph Smith, most notably plural marriage. According to Onias, God was also upset that Spencer Kimball, the LDS president at the time, had declared in 1978 that Black men were allowed to hold the priesthood; Onias held the racist belief that people of African descent bore the mark of Cain and were not worthy to wield God's power.

Onias believed he had been charged by God to cleanse the church and prepare it for the Second Coming of Christ. He tasked Dad and his brothers with helping him to prepare pamphlets to send to church leaders. It was these meetings that I had witnessed at the farmhouse.

Not long after Mom fled the farm with us kids, Dad moved the meet-ings to his parents' home. Onias received a revelation that the Lafferty brothers had a special calling from God, and he ordained Ron to be the bishop of the school's Provo chapter.

Ron was struggling. Like Dad, he had been excommunicated from the church. Dianna had left him and taken the kids to Florida. He'd lost his home and the successful contracting business he'd built, along with all of his earthly possessions. He blamed everyone but himself for what had happened. In particular, he blamed Richard Stowe, the man who had excommunicated him from the church and offered Dianna financial assistance; Chloe Low, a family friend who had supported Dianna and helped her leave; and, of course, Brenda.

Brenda refused to allow Allen to join the School of the Prophets and frequently got into arguments with Dad and Ron over matters of church doctrine. She was well versed in the Scriptures and wasn't afraid to stand up to them. Both Dad and Ron grew annoyed with Brenda's efforts to thwart the Lord's work.

With both of their families gone, Dad and Ron threw themselves into the School of the Prophets. Preparing the church for the Lord's Second Coming became their sole purpose in life. At the end of February, Ron claimed he'd received a revelation from God. It was directed at Dianna and chastised her for her rebelliousness. The tone and wording of this revelation were very similar to the revelation Joseph Smith received for his wife Emma in Section 132 of *The Doctrine and Covenants*, in which he told Emma that she would be destroyed if she didn't accept the doctrine of plural marriage.*

Later, in March, Ron received a revelation about Richard Stowe, Chloe Low, Brenda, and Baby Erica. In the revelation, he wrote (speaking

---

* *The Doctrine and Covenants* is a book of LDS scripture, containing revelations Joseph Smith claimed to receive as he was growing and organizing the church.

for God), "It is my will that they be removed in rapid succession." Dad and Ron pondered this revelation for some time. They truly believed it came from God and not Ron's own bitter resentment.

A few weeks later, Ron received another revelation, in which he was told that he was the "Mouth of God" and Dad was the "Arm of God." They both interpreted this to mean that if a removal were to happen, Dad would be the one to actually do it. In Ron's revelation, God compared Dad to Nephi, a Book of Mormon prophet who killed Laban at the Lord's command (see page 52). At this point, Dad was so deep in his delusion that he was willing to do anything that he thought God was commanding him to do, even take someone's life. After all, such commandments are quite common in the Bible and the Book of Mormon, and even in church history.*

Onias, however, after hearing about this revelation, did not support it. He kicked Dad and his brothers out of the School of the Prophets. This paved the way for Dad to decide that he was also a prophet. He adopted the title the "Hand of God" and began to amass a following of his own.

Dad and Ron shared the revelation with Allen. Allen didn't accept it, either. He asked why God would want to punish his daughter, an innocent child. Ron told him, "Because she would grow up to be a bitch like her mother."

I don't know whether Allen warned Brenda about the revelation or not. If she had known, she could have fled and returned to her family in Idaho. Did he think he could protect her? Maybe he thought his brothers wouldn't actually act on the revelation.

After their separation from the School of the Prophets, Dad and Ron decided God wanted them to build a city of refuge. They latched onto

---

* Such as the Mountain Meadows Massacre of 1857, where Mormon militiamen massacred a group of pioneers from Arkansas near Cedar City, Utah Territory. Approximately 120 to 140 men, women, and children were estimated to have been killed.

the Dream Mine (see page 50)—the mine in Salem built by John Hyrum Koyle in the 1890s that my Dad had visited—as the means to finance the city, probably because Koyle had prophesied that the mine would provide financial support for the Kingdom of God before Christ's Second Coming. Dad and his brothers intended to build the city near the mine's entrance. They planned to mine the gold that they knew must be there and demanded that the owners of the mine turn it over to them, lest they "feel the hand of the Lord." Not surprisingly, the mine directors were not impressed by these threats and refused to give them the mine.

Undeterred, Dad and Ron decided to travel across the Western US and into Canada to visit different polygamist groups and seek support for building their city of refuge. They left in May and were gone for most of the summer. As they traveled, they continued to contemplate the removal revelation Ron had received.

During his travels, Dad's delusion that he was a prophet grew stronger. As he and Ron visited different groups, they met other like-minded people and experimented with orgies and drugs. He became particularly enamored of cannabis and was convinced that marijuana had been used by ancient prophets to commune with God.

On a visit to a commune in Big Water, near Lake Powell in southern Utah, Dad reconnected with a woman named Laurene Grant, whom he'd originally met in Oregon. According to Dad, Laurene approached him and said she wanted to marry him. The marriage lasted for about a week until, the honeymoon phase abruptly over, Dad decided to return home.

Dad hitchhiked back to Salem and found us in our little home at Pond Town Fort. (He had been in communication with Grandma, who told him where we were.) I think Dad came by because he knew it was almost time to fulfill the prophecy and wanted to see us one more time. My mom and us kids were the only normal thing in his life. Maybe he missed us. Or maybe he was just following Ron's orders.

I remember seeing Dad peek through the window and becoming immediately alarmed. What did this mean? Were things going to change again? I had adjusted to life with Dad gone and was finally beginning to feel somewhat safe. His return threatened all of that.

It happened to be Brian's first birthday, but Dad's timing was just a coincidence. He didn't really know Brian. He'd been too busy growing his cult and taking other wives to get to know his youngest child.

Luckily, Dad didn't try to take any of us children away from Mom. He barely interacted with us at all. Mom acted very cautiously. She fed him and made sure he was placated. After spending two days with us, he said he was going to Grandma's home in Provo to meet Ron for the Pioneer Day celebrations. He kissed Mom and us kids goodbye and left. I remember Mom said she had a bad feeling about what Dad was up to.

At the time, I remember I wasn't sad that Dad was leaving. I didn't want any more changes in my life, and Dad brought nothing but change.

I'm woken in the middle of the night by someone pounding on the door. It's strange how many emotions a knock can convey. I know immediately that something is wrong.

I sneak out of my room to see what's happening, my eyes still blurry with sleep. Mom opens the door. A police officer is standing on our front step. I can't hear what he says.

"What?" Mom says. I hear the panic in her voice. "All right, give me a minute to get the kids dressed."

I run back to my room, where Mom finds me a moment later. "Rebecca, get up and grab some clothes quickly. We have to leave. Now!"

My heart pounds as I grab the few articles of clothing I own, pulling on some pants beneath my nightgown.

Mom and all five of us kids pile into the police car. I can tell we aren't in trouble because the cop speaks gently to Mom and she's riding up front without any handcuffs on. We kids huddle together as we drive for about twenty minutes.

Finally, we stop at the house of Laura Richardson. Laura was one of my father's chiropractic patients. She was the only other person, besides Gwen and Marleen, who came to visit us when we lived in the farmhouse.

Laura always seemed a little on the fringe to me. Every time she left our house, she would say, "God bless you." I thought she was swearing, but the way she said it sounded so sincere. I don't know how my mom got her phone number, but I guess somehow they stayed in touch.

At Laura's house, Mom puts us kids to bed. I wait until my siblings are asleep. Then I sneak out again. I tiptoe to the end of the hall and listen to Mom talk to Laura in the living room.

"They have no idea where he is," Mom says. I'm alarmed to hear her crying. "How could he do this? What if he comes for me and the kids?"

"We won't let that happen," Laura says. "The police will make sure you're protected."

Protected from what? I wonder. *What's going on?*

"You should get some sleep," Laura says.

I steal back down the hallway before they see me. I climb into bed and stare at the unfamiliar shadows cast on the wall by the street lamp outside my window. They stretch across my ceiling like slow, hulking monsters.

Eventually, I figured out the person we were hiding from was Dad, but I had no idea why. Had he decided to take us kids away from Mom after all?

We stayed with Laura for about a week. Mom didn't let us turn on the TV or radio, and no one told me what was going on. I had no clue what was happening. Why were we here? When were we going home?

Anytime I asked Mom a question, I was met with a blank stare. I would frequently walk into a room and see that she had been crying. But before I could ask her what was wrong, Laura would jump in and say, "Your mom is fine." Then she'd have one of her kids usher me away.

It bothered me that I was being kept away from my mom. In the past, whenever Mom and I were alone, she would talk to me and tell me what was going on, even when Dad was at his most bizarre. Now it was like I couldn't gain access to the Real Mom. When she was around other adults, she acted like she was a different person, a copy of her former self. It frustrated me that she was being (what I viewed as) fake.

Looking back, I'm grateful that Mom had other adults there to hold space for her and reassure her, and I understand why she kept me in the dark. How in the world was she supposed to tell her children the truth, when she was struggling to process it herself? Of course, as a child, not knowing why our lives had been upended yet again was deeply unsettling. I would hear Mom up late, talking on the phone, probably to one of my sisters, in a hushed voice. They would talk for hours and hours. It was hard for me to be at peace when I knew something was terribly wrong.

I heard Laura tell her kids not to talk to me about anything that would make them uncomfortable. This struck me as odd—and hurtful. Why was she worried about *them* feeling uncomfortable? I was the one staying at a stranger's house, without a clue as to what was going on. How on earth would I make them uncomfortable anyway? I wasn't doing anything. Her words seemed to imply that I was a bad person. I already believed there was something wrong with me, so I started to wonder if maybe this entire situation was somehow my fault.

It was the longest week of my life. I spent so much time in Laura's basement, watching movies. I think I watched every Disney movie that was ever made.

Occasionally, I would go outside to the backyard, but I couldn't play. I felt a heaviness everywhere I went. It pinned me down and kept me in a state of constant unease. *Why is Mom avoiding me?* I wondered. *When is this going to end?*

After a week, we relocated to another house, a rental owned by the friend of a friend. Even though it was August, the house was cold, dark, and dirty. It smelled weird and gave me a deeply unsettled feeling. I later learned that the owner was a predator who had abused his daughters. But we didn't have much of a choice about where to go. He was letting us stay there until it was safe to come out of hiding.

Mom did her best to make the place cozy. I remember she had to light the pilot light because it was out, which explained why the house was so cold. Mom seemed so smart and strong to me. She was always able to figure things out. In the days to come, we had a bed to sleep in and we were fed, and that brought me a measure of comfort.

Mom still didn't let us turn on the television. I'm sure she was afraid we would see the news. She did her best to protect us, but it was distressing when she wouldn't give me a straight answer about what was going on. In the absence of an explanation, everything felt precarious.

The days were warm and long, but the summer sun brought me no joy. Even though I was free to go outside and explore my new surroundings, I stayed close to home. Sometimes I would walk around aimlessly, but mostly I stared off into space. I had finally entered the wider world I'd so desperately longed to join, but everything felt foreign and wrong to me. On the farm, there had been rules. I knew my role in the family. I knew my limitations and restrictions. I hated them, but at least they offered a sense of structure and certainty. Now, there were no limitations, but there was also no certainty. I felt like I was floating in space, untethered.

My seven-year-old mind had so many questions. What was expected of me in this new sphere? How could I know the right way to act? How could I know who to trust? My brain filtered everyone I met into two categories: safe and unsafe. Mom and my sisters were safe. Dad was unsafe. And maybe so was everyone else.

We stayed in that house for another week or so before returning to Pond Town Fort. That's when I learned that Dad had been arrested.

PART TWO

AFTER

CHAPTER 10

1984

THE PRISON FRIGHTENS ME, with its guard towers and thick walls, strung with tight coils of barbed wire. We stop in front of a large metal gate and wait for it to open. Then we shuffle forward and wait for a second gate to open. The tall metal fence looms over us. A guard asks to see Mom's driver's license again. There's a gun on his belt.

Inside the prison, we pass people wearing orange suits. They look deranged and unhappy. Everything is dark. I'm familiar with the dark, but this is a kind of darkness that seems like it could swallow me up. Only scary things happen here, I'm sure of it. For the first time, I realize Dad must have done something really bad.

I look at my mom's face for reassurance, but she's wearing that blank stare she seems to always wear these days, and she's biting her lip, which is a sign that she's nervous. My heartbeat picks up. If Mom's nervous, I'm nervous, too.

How long are we going to be here? I wonder. *Can we please just go?*

A guard leads Mom and the five of us kids to a large visitation room. The first thing I notice is how cold it is, how empty and sad. Everything is gray and smells like metal. We have the room to ourselves, apart from the guard, who stands by the door. He's carrying a gun and handcuffs, and the way he frowns at us makes me anxious.

We wait for a while before Dad finally enters the room. He's wearing an orange jumpsuit like the other inmates and handcuffs on his wrists and ankles, which prevent him from walking in a straight line. He has a sad look in his eyes, and I can feel his heaviness—and nervousness—as he looks at the six of us standing there. He has a big mustache, long hair, and a beard. I notice he's wearing flip-flops with socks, which strikes me as being extremely uncomfortable.

As soon as Mom sees Dad, her posture changes. She stands up straight and goes to embrace him. Dad gives Mom a kiss on the lips. I frown, confused. Part of me is reassured. If Mom and Dad are getting along, then maybe things can't be all that bad. But another part of me is repelled. I know how much Mom hates Dad. Why is she letting him kiss her? Why is she being so nice to him? The way Mom switches between her different personalities unsettles me.

But as I look at Dad, the pain and anger I feel toward him starts to fade. It hurts my heart to see him chained up like a helpless animal. He is still my dad, and all I want is for everything to be okay. I don't know what he's done; I just want our family to be together.

The guard removes Dad's chains. Dad puts on a big smile and holds out his hands to us. I run toward him, and as I hug him, I find myself saying, "I'm sorry, Daddy. I'm sorry."

Tears well in my eyes. I have no idea why I'm crying, or why I'm the one apologizing. I'm just so overwhelmed by the strangeness and uncertainty of the situation—happy to see my dad, but heartbroken to know that he's imprisoned in this miserable place. I'm deeply confused about what's happening to my family and what will happen next.

All of my siblings, except for Brian, who clings to Mom, give Dad hugs and kisses, too. Dad seems genuinely pleased to see us and tells us how much he's missed us. We kids huddle on the floor around Dad. Rachel stays really quiet and just observes everything while she fiddles with her fingers. Christopher, who is three, plays with Dad's long hair, while Johnny and I climb all over him. I keep grabbing Dad's face so I can look at him.

There's a door in the room that leads out into the yard. After wrestling with us for a few minutes, Dad tells us to go outside and play so he can talk to Mom for a bit. Johnny and Christopher go outside, but Brian, Rachel, and I stay where we are. I'm too scared to leave Mom's side. While my brothers run around, Mom scoots closer to Dad, and they speak in quiet whispers.

I don't know what my parents say to each other. I'm overwhelmed, so I retreat into myself and just sit and watch. Seeing my parents sitting so close together makes me feel a little safer, though I'm still confused.

The time goes by very quickly, and soon the guard yells a five-minute warning. He walks over to Dad and begins putting the chains back on his ankles.

Saying goodbye to Dad is terribly sad. I don't know when I'll see him again. He's been in jail before, so I assume he'll be getting out at some point, but this is not like the last place. It's clear to me for the first time that he won't be coming home with us now, and maybe not anytime soon.

We walk back through all the gates and security checkpoints, past all the barbed wire. It takes much less time to get out than it took to get in.

I sit quietly in the car during the hour-long drive back to Salem, drowning in a wave of anxiety. I have no mooring, nothing to ground me.

A single thought keeps replaying in my mind: *What will happen to us now?*

The months that followed Dad's arrest were clouded by confusion. I had no earthly clue why Dad was in prison or when he was going to get out. I kept trying to ask my mom and sisters for information, but no one would talk to me about what had happened. Mom and the other adults seemed to speak in a secret language. Whenever I would enter the room, they would go quiet, and my sister Marleen would usher me into another room or tell me to check on one of my siblings. I felt infinitely frustrated. I wanted to understand what was going on, but anytime I asked an adult what was happening, I was told to be quiet and to stop asking so many questions.

I was given a baby doll to play with, probably to keep me occupied so I would stop pestering my mom. As I thought about what to name her, the name Erica popped into my mind, perhaps because Erica was the last female baby I'd interacted with. Or perhaps because I was sensing her spirit nearby.

One time I was playing with my doll, and I called her Erica. My mom, who was in the room, gasped and grabbed my arm.

"Do not use that name!" she hissed.

"Why not?" I asked, startled.

"Because that's the name of your dead cousin," she said.

I stared at her in confusion. What was she talking about? But she wouldn't answer any more of my questions, and I was left feeling like I had done something wrong, though I couldn't understand what.

Everything at home felt tense and dark, and our interactions with neighbors and acquaintances became strained. It seemed like people wanted to get close enough to witness our tragic situation—offering a kind word in passing—but not close enough to offer any real help or support. No one from church ever brought us a meal or offered to clean the house or let us play with their kids, the way they would for other families dealing with hard times.* No one ever asked me how I was doing or if I needed to talk to someone. In retrospect, it's wild to me that none of us were taken to speak with a psychiatrist. But therapy wasn't as widely accepted then as it is now.

Visits with Dad's family were just as difficult. It felt as if there were a huge elephant in the room, but no one wanted to talk about it. I noticed

---

* The Mormon community is well known for its incredible efficiency in providing meals and other forms of support (babysitting, cleaning, mowing lawns, shoveling snow, etc.) whenever a family or individual, Mormon and non-Mormon alike, is dealing with life events such as a birth, death, illness, moving, or unemployment. The women's organization, called the Relief Society, was literally founded for this purpose: "To work in unity to help those in need." On the rare occasion someone did bring us a meal, it was always accompanied by the suggestion that we come back to church.

I was never allowed to play with my cousins. Again, I started to wonder if *I'd* done something bad. Dad was the one in prison, but everyone was avoiding *me*.

I didn't know how to feel about Dad. Clearly, he'd done something wrong. But the lines between right and wrong were murky for me. Dad had done wrong things to my family and me my whole life, but he was also my dad, and he loved me. He always told us he was following God's will. So that made those things right . . . didn't it?

There had been times when I'd been able to see the wrongs for what they were. Before we fled the farmhouse, Dad had very clearly been the bad guy in my personal narrative. It was because of him that I wasn't allowed to leave the yard or do anything interesting. It was because of him that I was perpetually being punished. The negative things that Mom and Marleen said about him further cemented that idea in my mind.

When we finally left the farm, I had been excited by the prospect of change and adventure. I'd fed off Mom's energy and the adrenaline rush of quickly grabbing our things and leaving. But after we moved out, life didn't seem to get any better. Mom was on her own now, struggling to make ends meet and to provide for five small children, and I still didn't have the attention I craved—not that that was Mom's fault in any way. Life wasn't fun or happy. If anything, things felt more strained and stressful, especially in recent months.

The result was that, after more than a year apart from Dad, he didn't seem like quite the villain to me anymore. In fact, seeing him chained up in prison made him seem more like a victim. Life was still miserable, but he wasn't there to blame for it. I began to miss our interactions, however small or unpleasant they'd been, and the validation I'd derived from them. In my seven-year-old view of the world, I felt that if we could all be together again, maybe things would be better.

Mom took us to visit Dad a few more times. So did my grandma Lafferty. Grandma came to our house frequently and was always a comforting presence. My poor grandmother didn't understand how such horrible things could have happened to her family, but she put her trust in God's plan, and her faith never wavered.

I remember one time I stayed the night at Grandma's house in Provo, and the next day we drove to the prison. On the way there, I started to feel really sick. My head hurt, so I lay down in the back seat of the car while she drove. After we finally got through security, I was happy to see Dad. My other siblings weren't there fighting for his attention, and he could see that I was unwell, so he pulled me up onto his lap and began to stroke my head. I went into a trance. The combination of his affection and the stroking motion on my hair was so comforting that, before I knew it, an hour had passed, and I woke up feeling so much better. It felt like a miracle. My dad always had that special healing touch.

It reminded me of the last time he held me like that. It was when we were living at Uncle Tim's house, when we'd first moved to Utah. I was four. I was confident I could fly, so I jumped up onto the banister and promptly fell forward face-first, smashing my two front teeth. Dad held me and my mouth for what felt like hours until the bleeding stopped. In the end, my teeth were fine. My lip was a bit puffy and bruised, but there was no serious damage. Another miracle.

Who was my father? I wondered. This man who seemed at times to be an angel and other times a devil? Why would he sometimes heal me and sometimes hurt me? Sometimes love and sometimes hate?

One time, Grandma took me with her to see Uncle Ron. I hadn't realized he was in prison too until, during one of my stays at her house, she asked if I felt okay going to see him. Even though I was unsure, I said yes.

It wasn't the same visiting Uncle Ron as it was visiting Dad. I felt uncomfortable being there. I noticed he wore a blue jumpsuit, while Dad wore orange. Now I know that it was because he was in the psychiatric hospital rather than in prison. When we arrived, Ron smiled at me and told me my mom was a wonderful woman, which seemed to me like an odd thing to say. I sat quietly while he talked to Grandma. Afterward, Grandma seemed very heavy and tired. She checked in with me to see if I was okay. I told her I was.

After that visit, I never saw Ron again.

I continued to visit my grandma on weekends when I just wanted some one-on-one attention. It was very healing and peaceful for me to be in her company. I felt truly loved being in her presence. She would walk me to the library and let me pick out books that we would read when we got home, and we would sit on her porch swing and stay up late watching *The Golden Girls*. The only thing I didn't like was that she made me go to church with her, but the three hours of torture was worth it if it meant I could spend time alone with her.

Dad called us regularly from prison. But I soon noticed that every time I spoke with him, all he did was talk about himself—his interests and hobbies in prison, his plans once he got out (he always believed he would be getting out). He never asked me about what was going on in my life or even how my day was.

It was the same in his conversations with Mom. I'm not sure why she accepted his calls. I suppose she still felt some kind of obligation or sense of loyalty to him. But then Dad started asking her to do favors for him. He wanted her to pick up his friends who were being released from jail and connect them with other people he knew. He even asked her to smuggle drugs into prison for him. These requests made her extremely uncomfortable, and after a while, she stopped taking his calls.

One day, after Mom had refused one of Dad's calls, I asked her, "When is Dad getting out?"

All of my questions must have worn her down, because she sighed and said, "Never."

I frowned. My mind couldn't grasp the concept of never. "Why not?" I asked.

"Because," Mom said, "Dad and Uncle Ron killed Aunt Brenda and Baby Erica."

I stared at my mom, not comprehending her answer at all. This combination of words made no sense. I'd seen Aunt Brenda and Baby Erica just a year ago, at the park for a family picnic. How could they be gone?

I remembered very clearly how Brenda had held Erica on her lap as they sat on a swing, all the love and attention she'd given her baby, the way I'd tried to soak it in. I remembered, too, a moment when Brenda had stared off into the distance, a sad look in her eyes.

I tried again to process Mom's answer, but it was as if a black hole opened in my mind and swallowed up her words. My brain felt fuzzy and confused. I opened my mouth to seek clarification.

Mom quickly cut me off, "Don't ask any more questions, Rebecca."

And that was that. I wasn't allowed to talk about it again. Anytime I tried to ask a question, I was immediately shut down. So eventually I stopped asking.

However, the black hole in my mind remained. It was literally impossible for me to process the concept of my dad killing anyone, let alone my pretty aunt Brenda and my sweet baby cousin. I couldn't believe it. And so I didn't. I let the black hole grow bigger, swallowing everything until I forgot those horrible words altogether.

In their place, I planted a new belief: that Dad had been imprisoned by mistake. I didn't know any details about Brenda and Erica's passing and we didn't attend their funeral (I didn't even know about it), so it was easy for me to compartmentalize things in this way. None of it felt real, so it wasn't.

I can see now how my mom must have been carrying so much shame. We all were. My dad had dumped his shame on us, staining us with his sins and leaving us to deal with the consequences of his actions. We couldn't go anywhere or do anything without his shadow hovering over us. Mom didn't want us talking about anything connected to what Dad had done, but that just made it easier for me to pretend that it had never happened.

Instead, I started to fixate on the things in my life that did feel real. I became obsessed with the idea that Dad was never getting out of prison. *If he was going to be in jail forever,* I wondered, *who was going to baptize me when I turned eight? Go with me on my first daddy-daughter date? Walk me down the aisle at my wedding?*

To my young mind, it didn't matter that Dad hadn't been spending quality time with me before his imprisonment. Before, there had always been the possibility of *maybe.* Maybe things would change. Maybe he would finally give me the love and attention I craved. But now even the chance for maybe was gone.

CHAPTER 11

1985

WE KEPT A LOW PROFILE FOR THE NEXT YEAR. When summer ended, Mom sent Johnny and me to a neighbor's home to be homeschooled with a small group of other children rather than to public school, and she took us to church less and less. I think she just wanted to hide from the world. She even changed our last name from Lafferty to her maiden name, Burns.

As we moved into fall, Mom's mother and her husband William traveled from Scotland to stay with us for six months in our little Salem home. How we found room for everyone, I have no idea. But we made it work.

I know Mom was embarrassed for her mother to see what had become of her life in the six years since she'd left Scotland. She felt like she'd made a huge mistake by marrying my dad and moving to America. I can only imagine the shame she must have felt when she told my grandmother that Dad was in prison, and why. But things had escalated beyond her control, and it was time for her to admit that she needed help.

Nanny didn't view my mom or our family as victims. Her mindset was, "Best just to get on with it." She rolled up her sleeves and got to work helping my mom manage all of us.

I enjoyed Nanny and William's visit. They brought tea and coffee into the house, which was a surprise to me. I was even more surprised to see Mom drink it, since I'd been taught at church that such things were of the devil. But seeing Mom laugh and chat with Nanny over a hot cup of tea made me consider that maybe the drinks weren't so bad after all. Those were some of the only times I ever saw Mom relax.

Nanny drank black tea with milk and sugar in it. One time she offered to let me try it. I gathered my courage and took a sip. To my astonishment, it tasted delicious. After that, I surrendered my prejudice against tea and coffee. I decided the church leaders must have never tried it or they would have changed their position.

It was a great comfort to our family to have Nanny and William there. One time they went with us to visit Gwen in Twin Falls where she lived with her husband, James. The long car ride always made me sleepy. I remember I was sitting next to Nanny in the back seat, and as I fell asleep, my head would drift to the side. I would jolt awake and straighten my head again. I did this a few times until Nanny gently took my head and laid it on her shoulder. Her kindness made me feel safe.

But Nanny was also always on my case, telling me I needed to help Mom more. She would give me chores and then stand there and critique my execution, saying I need to put a little more elbow grease into it. I found it was ultimately in my best interest to stay out of her way as much as possible.

Motivated by my desire to get out of the house, I decided it was finally time to learn how to ride a bike. I found an old abandoned ten-speed. It had a bar that ran across the top; I wasn't tall enough to reach the seat so I had to duck my shoulder beneath the bar and pedal in a crouch, but I soon learned how to balance myself. After a few tries, I got the hang of it. One time, Gwen's husband, James, saw me riding and said, "Wow! You're really determined."

Mom eventually found me a used bike that was my size. It was painted baby blue. I loved that bike and rode it everywhere. Being able to ride a bike was my ticket to freedom. I'd spend the entire day cruising around town, my hair fluttering behind me in the wind.

On one of my bike rides, I met a girl who lived up the street. Her name was Lindsey, and we soon became good friends. Lindsey really hit it off with Granddad William, and they remained pen pals after he went back to Scotland, which I thought was sweet.

I spent a lot of time at Lindsey's house, and her mom would often invite me to join them for dinner. I loved eating dinner with Lindsey and her mom and dad. It felt so calm and reassuring, compared to the chaos at my house. I was jealous that Lindsey had both of her parents in her life and wondered if she knew how lucky she was.

Sometimes I would sleep over at Lindsey's house, too. I remember during one sleepover we discovered her dad's *Playboy* magazines. As I looked at the photos in the magazines, I felt a strange but not unwelcome tingling sensation in my body. I thought the women were beautiful, and I wondered if I would look like that when I grew up. I also wondered why they were standing the way they were, in exaggerated poses, making curious faces.

Lindsey and I were friends for almost a year. And then, one day, she told me her mom didn't want us hanging out anymore. Maybe her mom had learned who my dad was and that scared her. Or maybe she felt like I was a bad influence on Lindsey. (*Was it the* Playboy *magazines?* I wondered.) I never learned the reason, and I was devastated to lose my only friend.

Most friendships I formed ended in the same way: Once my friends' parents learned who I was, they banned their children from associating with me. I didn't understand why. I guessed it was probably because of my dad, but why would that disqualify me from having friends? Were they afraid that I would do something wrong, too? No one ever gave me a straight answer, so I began to believe, once again, that it was because I was a bad person.

Things weren't any better at church. We rarely went, but occasionally we were invited back and Mom felt guilted into taking us. I hated it. It felt like the people there judged me and didn't care about me or my family. Their love seemed conditional and shallow, nothing at all like what Jesus had taught. I wanted Jesus to comfort me, not these hypocrites.

Cassie Peterson, the girl across the street, would sometimes ask me to go to church with her. I thought maybe she wanted to be my friend again, but I should have known better. I'm certain that her church leaders put her up to it, because the moment we got to church, she wasn't interested in sitting with me or even talking to me. It was like I became invisible.

I remember one time in Sunday school I was asked to read from the Scriptures. I'd had very little schooling at that point—I was still only reading easy readers—so I struggled immensely trying to read the biblical passage out loud. All of the kids laughed, and Cassie joined in. I felt like a freak.

Another time I received an invitation to attend a church activity for girls my age. It was a daddy-daughter dinner. I thought it must be some kind of cruel joke. But Granddad William offered to go with me, and we made the best of it. We made quite the pair: a timid seven-year-old girl and a little old Scottish man who smelled like cologne and cigarettes. (William smoked like a chimney.) It was a sweet experience, and I was so grateful to William, but at the same time I felt painfully out of place as the only girl there without her dad.

We struggled through the rest of that first year. Nanny and William went back to Scotland, leaving us to push forward on our own. Mom was, understandably, very bitter about her situation. I can only imagine how she must have felt. Relieved, to some extent, knowing she would never be back under my father's thumb and that he could never touch her or us kids again. Overwhelmed by trying to provide and care for five small children on her own. Frustrated that she'd found herself in this position.

Mom kept people at a distance and didn't let anyone in. She was polite, but she didn't exactly have time to sit and chat with friends— and she didn't have the energy to deal with people's gossip. The only person she confided in and who seemed to be able to lighten her mood was Marleen. Marleen had the gift of getting Mom to laugh about anything, even her crazy past. The only downside for me about Marleen's visits was that she had kids of her own, so this meant I was in charge

of managing my nieces and nephews as well as my brothers, sometimes for hours. This wasn't much fun for me or Rachel, who was also
charged with babysitting (she was around five years old at the time).

Even though Rachel was a few years younger than me, we were close
to the same height and sometimes passed as twins, especially when we
wore the same clothes. Mom sewed most of our clothes, and she would
save time by making the same outfits for Rachel and me.

When she wasn't making us clothes or cooking or taking care of the
house, the rest of Mom's time was spent sewing doll dresses for a local
boutique and doing other odd jobs, like firing pottery, painting shirts
with little flowers, and making over-the-top vests that looked to me like
mini carpets. I always wondered who was actually buying these things.
Marleen and I would help her, and sometimes my other siblings would,
too, if she was crunched for time. It was a good way to get out of going
to our school lessons.

Mom's preoccupation meant that my siblings and I had a lot of time
to ourselves. Most days, we roamed around outside, looking for things to
explore and getting into trouble. My brothers, in particular, were completely directionless. There was no structure in our house. It was very
much a fend-for-yourself environment.

Johnny's friends would come over every night, and they would spend
hours skateboarding around the neighborhood then come back to the
house and eat cereal and milk. Mom would get angry and yell at them
to stop eating all our food. We could barely afford to feed ourselves, let
alone the rest of the neighborhood.

Johnny, age seven, was the role model for my two younger brothers,
Christopher and Brian. If he did something, they would, too. The neighborhood knew them as the Burns boys. They would get into all sorts of
mischief. It started with catching guppy fish. Then it grew to swimming
in the pond. Then, eventually, they were jumping off the top of the arch
bridge. One time, Johnny got ahold of some matches and set the small

field behind my sister's apartment complex on fire. The fire department had to come to put out the flames. It was quite the spectacle.

Trying to rein in my younger brothers always felt like such an ordeal. I hated being around the constant chaos and seeing my mom in tears from so much stress and frustration. She'd often break down and say, "What am I, the village idiot?" That's when I knew Mom had had enough and needed me to step in and help.

I never acted out like my brothers did. I'd learned at an early age to behave or get beaten, but Dad wasn't around anymore to dole out punishments, which suited Mom just fine. In fact, she told me later that one of the reasons she stopped taking us to see him was that he kept trying to discipline us during our visits. She said it was just too much for her to deal with.

Life was certainly never boring with my brothers around. But despite all the trouble they got into, I loved them and their sense of adventure and how they could always find a way to entertain themselves. I never blamed them for their antics. After all, they didn't have anyone to guide them. They lacked a father figure, and Mom was too overwhelmed trying to provide for all of us to set any kind of boundaries.

Johnny and I had always been close, but there came a time when he seemed to lose interest in me as a friend. He no longer followed me around, and he didn't want me to hang out with him and his friends. I felt pushed away, and it hurt.

One summer afternoon, Mom went out to run a quick errand. She left me in charge of watching my siblings, per usual. I hated the pressure it put on me. I didn't really know how to watch over them or keep them safe, and it made me anxious to have this responsibility. I felt like I had to keep them in line, and I often found myself yelling at them, the way Dad had yelled at me.

Johnny and I got into an argument. I can't remember what we were fighting about, but I'm sure it had something to do with me trying to tell him how to behave in front of his friend. The dynamic between us had changed. No longer were we the best friends who would play together in a simple cardboard box for hours. Now, I was trying to step into a position of dominance and make him yield to my authority. Our yelling turned into shoving. It was as if we had both forgotten our true selves. We were acting out a violent drama, stepping into roles that had been modeled for us by the adults in our lives.

Suddenly, I had the sensation of being outside my body, observing my behavior. In that moment, I saw the way I was treating my brother, whom I loved and respected. A deep sadness came over my heart. I didn't want to force anyone to do anything. I only wanted to love my siblings and have peace in our home.

Something similar happened to Johnny. Simultaneously, we stopped fighting and just looked at each other. Then we hugged as I began to cry.

I realize now that I was being spiritually adjusted. A force outside of myself—a tangible spirit of love, kindness, and compassion, what some people might call Christ Consciousness—had intervened to transform my heart and actions. This divine presence knew how much Johnny and I needed each other.

Johnny and I have recalled this incident many times. We both consider it a pivotal moment in our spiritual progression. I have nothing but the deepest love and respect for my brother. I'm so grateful I had him, and this spirit of love, by my side in those dark days.

The summer after Dad's incarceration, Mom asked Gwen if Rachel and I could stay with her for a little while. Gwen, who was starting a family of her own, agreed. This allowed Mom to keep a better eye on Brian and Christopher. Johnny stayed at home; he had started helping out more with chores and earning money by mowing the neighbors' lawns.

I jumped at the chance to leave our little town, where I constantly felt weighed down by an invisible force. I was ready for a change of scenery— something, *anything*, different.

Most of the six-hour drive was spent in silence, which was fine with me. I felt more at peace that way. When we arrived in Twin Falls, a feeling of hope filled my chest. It was as if I'd been holding my breath, and now I was given permission to exhale. Here, away from Salem, it felt like it might be possible to start fresh.

As I tapped into this burst of warmth in my heart, I decided I wanted to share it. In particular, I wanted to express my appreciation for Gwen for taking me out of that dark place I had been in for so long. So, about a week into my stay, I found a pen and piece of paper and wrote her a little note. I had the idea to put it in the mailbox, which I knew she checked every day. I imagined her finding it and being pleasantly surprised by my small gesture.

I had a very limited vocabulary, but I did my best to find the words that described the admiration I felt for my oldest sister. I wrote:

Dear Gwen,

I am so happy to be here. I envy you, Gwen. I am so happy that you are my sister. Thank you so much for letting me stay with you.

Love your sister,
Rebecca

I placed the note in the mailbox, where Gwen found it shortly afterward. As she came into the house, I eagerly awaited her reaction.

I vividly remember the look on Gwen's face as she marched into the room and held the note up high. "You *envy* me?" she snapped. "Why would you envy me? Don't you know what your dad did to me?"

I stood rooted to the floor in shock. This was the opposite of what I had envisioned. It felt like something sharp had pierced my heart, and the joy drained out of me as Gwen gave voice to her anger and pain. I'm not sure what hurt more: her rejection of my love or the way she emphasized the fact that he was *my* dad, as if she were implying I was an extension of him and thus somehow to blame for her suffering. Her words continued to play out like a puzzle that I couldn't quite piece together. But it was clear that the message my heart had so badly wanted to share with her had been lost in her own pain.

The following days were very confusing for me. I felt a wide range of emotions that I didn't know how to define. I'd gone from feeling some hope for a new beginning to despair that my sister hated me for reasons I couldn't control. Gwen had called him Dad, too. I recalled how I used to be jealous and angry that she got all of his attention, the attention I so desperately craved. And now she was throwing him back in my face.

It had taken so much courage for me to open my heart to Gwen like that, so to have her respond in this way cut me deeply. She couldn't even acknowledge how difficult living with Dad had been for me, too.

I lay about the house for days, confused about what all this really meant. There were so many messages I tried to decipher in my sister's words, but none of them made sense. I found myself wanting to go home. At least there, the darkness was familiar and predictable.

Gwen eventually made her peace with me, inviting me to lie out in the sun with her in her little backyard. This became our time together. I forgave her for hurting my feelings, but she never said sorry and we never talked about what had happened again.

Gwen took Rachel and me with her to church. I protested, but Gwen didn't give me a choice. Her house, her rules. She was extremely concerned that I hadn't been baptized yet. Mormons are baptized as soon as they turn eight, which they believe is the age of accountability—when you know right from wrong. It's an important ritual in a child's life and marks their official entry into the church. Usually, a child's father is the one who performs the baptism. Of course, in my situation, that wasn't going to be possible. So Gwen's husband, James, offered to do it instead.

Gwen talked to my mom about it, and after we returned to Utah, James baptized me.

By this time I really trusted James, and the fact that he baptized me made me feel close to him. I looked up to him as a father figure. He was a caring and strong man. He would talk to me about his childhood and how he would tie flies to sell to fishermen in the Idaho summers. He was always prompting me, in a very gentle way, to think about what I was going to do when I grew up, how I would work and contribute to society. He never forced me to do anything. He was going to school at night to complete his bachelor's degree in psychology and seemed to have an astute understanding of my personality and what my struggles were. I loved him for that and always enjoyed his company.

Gwen and James liked it when Rachel and I stayed with them. However, whenever my brothers visited, it was a struggle. My brothers sorely needed guidance. They had no structure or discipline in their lives, and their visits always resulted in chaos.

After my first stay with Gwen, I began to wonder if Dad had done something bad to me that I didn't remember. My mom assured me that he hadn't. But that seemed to play tricks with my mind as well. Why had he acted a certain way toward my older sisters and not me?

Despite these concerns, I still yearned for a connection with him. After Mom stopped taking Dad's calls, I began to write letters to him instead. He wrote me back—he always called me Bert in his letters—and sent me lots of drawings. Sometimes they were cartoons (he went through a phase where he drew a lot of *Simpsons* characters), but most of the time they were beautiful sketches, drawn with pen. Dad is a talented artist. He also has very good penmanship and a knack for poetry. He would make homemade cards and fill them with poems and artwork: drawings of bears and snow leopards and seagulls flying over the beach. I remember one sketch of a jaguar that looked so lifelike it could have jumped off the page.

Dad's favorite sketch that he did was of a polar bear looking up at the moon in the sky. On the drawing he wrote a quote: "The moon will shine from noon until nine." According to Dad, this quote was a revelation he had received from God. It was a sign for when he would be asked to play his next role as the Prophet Elijah and announce the return of Christ. When he told me this, I remember knowing in my heart that he was never getting out and feeling sad that he was going to be so disappointed when that day never came. I felt obligated to assure and pacify him, to agree with him. But inside I knew that he would never be released.

Dad sent me other crafts, too. There was a time when he made a lot of braided crosses, which was interesting to me, as Mormons don't use the symbol of the cross in their worship—not that Dad had ever been a conventional Mormon. Even though these gifts touched me, I still noticed that Dad never asked me any questions about my life. However, in every letter, every time, he said he loved me. It was enough to keep me writing.

I began to miss my dad a lot. Enough time had passed that all I remembered were the good things. I missed seeing him and giving him a hug. I would fall asleep at night wishing so hard that I could give him one more hug until I started having recurring dreams that I was doing exactly that.

I still didn't have many friends, so I passed my time by riding my bike around town and exploring by myself. Salem is a curious place. It's an old pioneer town, originally occupied by the Ute Indians and later claimed by Mormon settlers, and the energy I would pick up as I biked around was so interesting. The old buildings told a story of a not-too-distant past, and the land itself seemed to speak to me. It felt like such a sad energy. I pondered this sadness. Was it mine? Or did it come from somewhere else? I started to wonder about the people who had lived here before me and what their lives had been like. I would be inclined to stop and pick up a rock or crouch down and use a stick to make designs in the dirt. During these times, it felt like I was entering another realm and connecting with the people who had walked on this land before me. It was very soothing.

It was because of my solitary bike rides around town that I was able to write to Dad without Mom's knowledge. We didn't have a mailbox at home; instead, we had a P.O. Box in Salem's small post office. Every week, Mom gave me the key and asked me to check the mail. That meant I was able to receive Dad's letters without her knowledge. In the summer, I would pick the grapes that grew behind the post office, find a comfortable spot to sit, and read Dad's letter as I ate the delicious, juicy fruit. I never had any candy growing up, so the grapes tasted like ambrosia.

I was the only one who maintained contact with Dad. (By the time I was nine, Mom had stopped taking us to visit him and was refusing all his calls, but my grandma Lafferty continued to take me on occasion.) Johnny didn't seem to have any bad feelings toward Dad. He never said anything negative about him, though he also didn't understand what had happened. Rachel, however, had no desire to see him or talk about him. She didn't like when I would share about my visits or tell her that he sent his love. She wanted nothing to do with him. Brian and Christopher had no memory of him either, and no interest in knowing more. It felt like even within my immediate family I stood alone.

In my isolation, I would spend hours walking around the pond, studying the trees and wondering what was hidden in the long grass. I would always find some old shoe or a shirt someone had taken off to jump into the pond to cool off then left behind. *What was that person's story?* I wondered. There were so many fascinating things to touch and smell, especially in the little marshy area behind my house that my brother and his friends called the Tootie Fruity Jungle. (This area was also a refuge for my brothers. It became their hideout and dumping ground for the wrappers of penny candies they would get daily from the local gas station.) It was such a fun place to explore. I loved the smell of the fresh trees and different grasses and mosses that grew there. The whole area was covered in undergrowth except for the well-worn trail that seemed to go on for miles. I would take my bike down there and find a rock to sit on and just listen to the sound of the trees gently swaying in the wind.

Life seemed so simple in these moments, when I was able to forget about everything and just sit in stillness. A wonderful aura of peace would wash over me. It felt like something was fortifying me.

Summers were the best—the only time I was able to forget about my troubles and actually feel alive. My siblings and I would play outside for hours until the sun went down. Then we knew that it was time to get home, where Mom would have something cooking on the stove or bread baking in the oven.

There was a canal road that ran north into the neighboring town of Payson, where they had a public swimming pool. During the summer, I swear we lived there. Mom would usually drop us off when it opened around 10:00 a.m., and we'd swim all day long until around 4:00 p.m. when it closed. Sometimes we would walk home. We would be absolutely starving by the time we got back. I remember I would eat half a loaf of bread, three potatoes, and a third of a watermelon all by myself. I'd never felt so happy or free.

Then Mom sent us to school.

CHAPTER 12

1985–89

I ENTERED THE PUBLIC SCHOOL SYSTEM as a third-grader. I had never attended a real school before, and my education up to this point had been sorely neglected. Consequently, I was incredibly nervous.

My teacher, Mrs. Peterson, was Cassie's mom. You would think, given her proximity to my family, that she would have been sympathetic and understanding of my situation. But that couldn't have been further from the truth.

On the first day, Mrs. Peterson asked us to listen to and then repeat back arithmetic equations. Most likely it was multiplication tables the students had memorized the previous year, but I had absolutely no idea what she was saying. While reading was something I enjoyed and was decently good at, math was a different story. I had never done any math in my life. It sounded like Mrs. Peterson was speaking a foreign language.

I looked at the other students. They were all repeating the strange words in tandem. How did they know what all of this meant? I tried to copy them, but I soon learned that faking wasn't going to get me through. I might as well have been trying to speak Chinese.

Then Mrs. Peterson called on me and asked me to answer a problem. I stood there like a deer in the headlights. In a quiet voice, I told her I didn't understand.

"Well, I guess we'll have to teach you the slow way," she said, sounding exasperated. She pulled me to the back of the class and sat me at a table away from everyone else. Then she took out a piece of paper and started drawing lines.

When she was finished, she looked at me expectantly. I realized she was waiting for a response. I stared at the paper, feeling my face flush with embarrassment. She hadn't explained what the drawing meant, and I had no earthly clue how to decipher what to me looked like a bunch of sticks.

Mrs. Peterson gave a sigh of frustration, and I felt my cheeks turn a deeper shade of red. The entire class was staring at me in judgmental silence. I felt mortified and wondered why she was being so cruel. Did she not know that I'd never done a math problem in my life? Why was she so angry with me for not understanding? Wasn't it her job to teach me? Did she think I was holding back the rest of the class, as if we were a sports team and I was making us lose?

Things never improved. I progressed through the school year constantly overwhelmed and confused. I never seemed to understand what was being taught. I felt lost while all the kids around me appeared to be thriving.

Looking back, I desperately needed tutoring. However, knowing my personality, it's likely I wouldn't have trusted what I was being taught anyway. I had already created a story in my mind that adults had their own agenda, and I was always being tricked or blamed for some wrongdoing. I truly believed that nobody cared about me or what I felt.

In addition to enrolling us in school, Mom took us back to church. Perhaps it was because of Gwen's influence and my recent baptism. Or maybe she finally felt that enough time had elapsed and that our new last names would give us some distance from Dad's reputation. But it was a false hope. In a small town like Salem, everyone already knew what had happened, and our interactions with other church members always felt strange and cold.

Things were no better with our extended family. I remember one time Grandma had all of us over at her home. I was sitting on the porch swing with my cousin, Rachelle, Mark's daughter, with whom I had been homeschooled. I opened up to her about how challenging school was for me, assuming it must be the same for her. I asked her if her family had changed their last name, too. She looked at me strangely and then told me she had to go inside. I assume she said something to her parents, because that was the last time we were invited to a family function. I suppose Aunt Heather and Uncle Mark were offended by what I'd said, though I didn't know why. I later learned that Aunt Heather had made it clear to my grandma that she would not attend family gatherings if my mom and us kids were there.

That was the first time I felt a real separation between my family and the rest of the Lafferty clan. It was confusing for me to see that the people I loved and cared about—and who I thought loved and cared about me—could reject me in this way. I didn't understand why Grandma was siding with Aunt Heather over us. Everyone refused to talk openly about what had happened, which made me unsure about what I was doing wrong and deepened my belief that there was in fact something wrong with me *as a person.*

As a result of the neglect I felt at school, at church, and even within my own family, I walked around with a huge chip on my shoulder and a constant scowl on my face. Marleen said it looked as if I were angry at the world. Really, though, beneath all that anger was hurt and grief. I withdrew and spent most of my days curled up on my bed, hugging my doll. I was almost certainly depressed, even though I had no idea at the time what that meant.

Whenever Marleen saw me, she thought it was funny to sing a church Primary song (Primary is the LDS Sunday school organization for children) about turning a frown upside down. She would make an exaggerated frown and then rotate her head so that the frown looked like a smile. I'm sure her gesture was sincere, but it felt like she was mocking me. She didn't understand that I *couldn't* find a reason to smile. In my mind, there was nothing to be happy about. All I could see and feel was misery.

Thank God for the times we had a television. Watching *Mr. Rogers* and *Sesame Street* and Saturday morning cartoons allowed me to escape into a different reality, at least for a little while. I would flip through the channels on TV until something caught my eye. One day I stopped on a sitcom called *Silver Spoons*. I was sucked in and started watching it regularly. I was particularly enchanted by the actress who played the role of Kate, Erin Gray. I loved her beautiful brown hair, her dimples, and even her name. I wished I could be like her. Confident and pretty and liked by my peers.

It's September 1986. I stare at the invitation in my hands, reading it over and over, as if it might vanish in a puff of smoke at any moment. I've been invited to a party at Melinda's house. And not just any party. A sleepover.

I've never been to a party in my life.

In the days leading up to the party, I can hardly contain my excitement. I still can't believe I've been invited. It seems like maybe the other girls are finally accepting me. Maybe I can be like Erin Gray after all.

What excites me most of all is that we're going to have McDonald's for breakfast in the morning. I've never had McDonald's, and I just know I've been missing out on something amazing.

The day of the party arrives, and Mom drops me off. My stomach is contorting into such painful knots that I think I might throw up.

Melinda opens the door, and I follow her into the house as Mom drives away. Suddenly, I am terrified. I've spent the night away from my family before, but never with a bunch of strangers.

I take a seat in the living room, clutching my overnight bag to my chest. There are six of us. The other girls are chattering away, but I can't seem to understand a thing they're saying. It sounds like they're speaking a foreign language. Mysterious words like *mascara* and *Walkman* and *Wham!* float around my ears. They giggle about boys I've never heard of and talk about nail polish and brand names I don't recognize.

All of the girls look so pretty. I realize how differently we're dressed. They're wearing jeans and T-shirts they bought at the store. I feel out of place in my handmade shorts and matching blouse.

After we eat pizza, we change for bed and gather in the dimly lit living room with our sleeping bags. I stare at the other girls' pristine white nightgowns, with their puffy sleeves and ribbons, then look at my own drab nightshirt. I burrow into my sleeping bag, praying no one notices it in the low light.

"Let's play Truth or Dare!" Melinda says.

I've never heard of Truth or Dare, but since everyone else seems to know what it is, I don't say anything.

We go around the circle, and each girl answers a question. Most of the questions are about which boys they like at school or if they've kissed anyone. I squirm in my sleeping bag, praying no one will ask me that kind of question.

Suddenly, it's my turn.

"Truth or dare?" Melinda asks me.

"Truth," I say.

Melinda opens her mouth to ask me a question, but before she can say anything, I blurt out the only secret I have, "My dad is in prison because the police think he killed my aunt and baby cousin."

The room falls silent. Five pairs of eyes stare back at me, wide with shock.

I wait for someone to say something. But no one says a word.

Finally, Melinda clears her throat and turns to the girl beside me. "Truth or dare?" she asks.

I slink down into my sleeping bag, wishing the ground would open up and swallow me whole.

The next morning, everyone pretends I'm not there. I can't even enjoy my Egg McMuffin, which tastes like sawdust in my mouth. I can't wait to escape.

Finally, my mom picks me up. I rush to the van.

"How was the party?" Mom asks.

"Fine." I slam the door and turn to stare out the window. I know now that my fantasy of being like Erin Gray is just that. A fantasy.

None of the girls from the sleepover speak to me after that, and I'm never invited to another party again.

Fourth and fifth grades were no better than third. I continued to lag hopelessly behind in school, and the other kids continued to avoid me like the plague.

There was one exception. Her name was Riley.

Riley's brother was Marleen's husband, Jordan. I first met Riley back when Marleen and Jordan got married and were living in a little camper parked on Jordan's parents' property. I was only six at the time, but I remember driving with Mom and Dad to check on Marleen. She had cut her knee on a metal can and needed medical attention.

While we were there, Jordan said to me, "I have a sister your age. Want to meet her?" Riley came outside, and we instantly connected. Being around another person my age was so exciting for me. We were instructed not to wander too far off, but in our short thirty minutes together, we managed to run around the entire property.

I didn't see Riley again until my fourth-grade year when we happened to be in the same class at school. We immediately rekindled our friendship. Soon, we were passing each other notes during class and walking home together and playing after school. Sometimes I would go to her house and help her feed her dogs and do her other chores. We would hang out for a couple of hours until her parents got back from work, and then I would go home. Before long, we were best friends.

Riley was the kindest person to me. She knew my story, but she didn't ask prying questions. She also came from a tumultuous home life—her father was abusive, though I didn't know this at the time—and together we got into all sorts of trouble. We'd skip school, sneak onto other people's property to go swimming in the canal, even shoplift fireworks. In fact, we got into so much trouble, her mom would regularly ground her from seeing me.

Riley was a total tomboy and incredibly strong. When I didn't have my bike, I would ride on Riley's handlebars, and she would pedal for both of us, even uphill. She was so much fun and helped me forget about some of the difficulties in my life.

My siblings found comfort in their friendships as well. Rachel had a close friend named Joan with whom she spent most of her time. She told me that when she saw how Joan's family lived and treated each other, it made her feel safe and helped her realize that there were kind, healthily functioning families in the world that genuinely loved each other. Joan's family loved Rachel and welcomed her into their home. Rachel told me recently it was because of their influence that she eventually decided to go to college—the first one in our family—and become a nurse.

Despite the comfort I found in my friendship with Riley, my preteen years passed in a blur of pain and isolation. School and church continued to be a challenge. I hated how people looked at me, like I had some kind of disease, or else pretended I wasn't there at all. Their behavior continued to reinforce my belief that I was worthless and unlovable. I wanted to hide and never be found.

The treatment I received from my peers was even worse at church than it was at school, especially once I turned twelve and moved from Primary to the Young Women's program. The other girls and even my leaders routinely excluded me. I would sit in the back of the classroom, feeling invisible.

The other girls seemed to have new dresses every Sunday, while I wore the same dress—the only one I owned—every week. I might as well have been wearing a sign around my neck that said, "I'm poor." For a church that preached that greed and vanity were a sin, people there sure seemed to care about their appearance. I don't think they heard the part where Jesus said to give all your money to the poor.

I hated the lessons. Whenever someone read from the Bible or the Book of Mormon, it made me feel like I was reliving my childhood, with Dad quoting Scripture at me that I didn't understand. The meaning of the words continued to remain opaque.

The meaning that did come through, however, was that my presence was patently unwelcome. It was communicated to me in every way possible that people didn't want me there. I wasn't wearing the right clothes. I didn't understand the Scriptures. I didn't have a worthy priesthood holder for a father.

One day I woke up and decided that if the Mormon Church didn't want me, I didn't want it either. People who preached love and Christlike behavior but didn't show it were not the kind of people I wanted to be around. I was tired of dealing with their hypocrisy and cruelty. I got enough of it at school. I didn't need it here, too. So I walked out the doors and never went back.

At my core, I think I believed that I didn't belong because I wasn't good enough. If I wasn't being welcomed into God's church, that could only mean one thing: that I was wicked and impure. Instead of fighting it, I decided I might as well embrace it. I began to gravitate toward the outsiders, the rejects, the rebels, hoping someone somewhere else would accept me.

I informed Grandma Lafferty about my decision and asked her to please not take me with her to church anymore. I'll never forget the grief and disappointment in her eyes. She looked defeated, but she respected my decision and never took me to church after that. I felt a sense of power that I'd taken a role in shaping my own life, but it was accompanied by a deep sadness. Why was it that all the choices that felt good to me seemed to disappoint others?

◆ ◆ ◆

One day in my sixth-grade year, I was riding the bus home from school. My forehead was pressed against the window as I tried to find solace in the verdant fields rolling past outside. Behind them, the maroon slope of Lone Pine Ridge rose toward the bright blue sky, its peak capped with snow.

Suddenly, a girl I'd never spoken to before turned around in her seat and looked me dead in the eyes.

"Your dad is a baby killer," she announced, loud enough for everyone on the bus to hear.

I stared back at her in shock. "He is not."

"Yes, he is," the girl declared gleefully. "He tortures babies and rips off their fingernails!"

In that moment, I felt something snap inside of me. My entire life, I'd been stuffing my pain, anger, and frustration down. My father's cruelty. The shame I felt from his actions. The rejection I experienced from my community, peers, and even my own family. It had all been bottled up in my chest, like a bomb waiting to explode. All the bomb needed was someone to light the fuse.

Unfortunately for this girl, she was the unlucky soul to strike the match. Something inside me took over. I stood up, marched over to her seat, and slapped her in the face.

"Shut up!" I shouted.

The girl stared at me in complete shock for several moments. Then she and her sister started yelling at me. "You're just like your dad!"

I can't remember what happened next. It felt like I'd entered a tunnel. Everything around me went black and fuzzy, and I stumbled my way off the bus.

I don't know why I felt the need to defend my father. I suppose because, even if he was no Charles Ingalls, he was still the only father I had.

Over the next couple of weeks, every time I encountered that girl and her sister, they would taunt me and say cruel things. Then, one weekend,

I saw them playing on the playground near my house. "There's that baby killer's daughter again," the girl jeered.

This time, when I walked up to her, I didn't just slap her. I pulled my hand back and let my fist connect with her face with full force. The punch knocked her off the swing and onto the ground.

I'm not proud of what I did, but at the time I truly felt like the girl deserved it. How could she say something so hurtful to me, when I'd never done a single thing to her? Couldn't she understand how much pain I was in?

When I returned home, Mom could see that I was upset. She asked me what was wrong.

I told her what had happened with the girl. "Why would she say that?" I asked. "Uncle Ron was the one who did it."

"No, Rebecca," Mom said, drawing a deep breath. "It was your father who killed Brenda and Erica."

I stared at Mom in horror. I refused to believe what I was hearing. I had convinced myself that Uncle Ron had been the one to commit the murders and that Dad had been wrongly convicted as an accomplice. Maybe Mom was mistaken. There had to be some other explanation. I wanted it all to be a big misunderstanding. A nightmare I could wake up from.

After Mom left my room, I couldn't move. I felt frozen in place, unable to process this revelation. Why had no one made this clear to me before? Suddenly, all of the whispers and rumors that had followed me for the past five years took on new meaning. I felt a surge of anger at Mom and all the adults in my life for keeping me in the dark. Worst of all, I felt foolish and embarrassed that I hadn't allowed myself to recognize the truth.

My anger soon shifted to Dad. How could he have done something so abhorrent? So inhuman? How was this even possible? I thought of all the conversations we'd had on the phone, the trips I'd taken to visit him in prison, the letters he'd written me. How could he tell me he loved me when he'd done something so monstrous? It changed everything I knew about him.

I tried to imagine Dad killing Baby Erica . . . and I couldn't. My brain simply refused to acknowledge this reality.

Instead, my thoughts turned inward. What did this mean about *me*? If my own father could do such a thing, was I equally capable of such violence? Was I also a monster? No wonder people didn't want their kids playing with me. The confusion and pain that flooded my mind was almost unbearable.

The only outlet I had was my diary, which I had started keeping the year before. I reached for a pen and wrote,

Dear Diary,

I don't understand. How could Dad do this? I'm scared to ask him if he really did it. I know he will tell me, but I don't want to hear it. I don't want this pain anymore. It's too much. I just want to be normal.

I look outside, and all I see are people getting on with their day. Going to work, watering their yards. The neighbors are outside playing with their dog, and I'm lying here in pieces.

Desperate to escape my building emotions, I put a cassette tape in my boom box and turned the volume all the way up. The lyrics from Cinderella's "Don't Know What You Got (Till It's Gone)" filled my room. For the first time, it finally, truly sank in that I was never going to have a normal father-daughter relationship. As long as I hadn't accepted the truth about why Dad was in prison, I'd been able to pretend. But now the illusion had completely crumbled.

Perhaps the strangest feeling of all was how desperately I still wanted my father's love and validation. There seemed to be a never-ending void inside of me, and I knew that the one thing that could fill it would never be mine.

The next time I wrote to Dad, I didn't say anything about what I'd learned. Part of me wanted to know the truth, but at the same time, I was terrified to hear it from his own lips. Once he confirmed what he'd done, it would be impossible to deny. It was better to just never discuss it. Pretend it hadn't happened.

I had no one to talk to about any of these things, and nobody would have listened anyway—probably because they didn't know how to. It was too heavy for all of us. Consequently, I felt utterly, unbearably alone.

2003

There's a package in the mailbox. The return address is the Utah State Prison.

With trembling fingers, I tear the package open. Inside is a book and a letter from my dad. I open the letter first.

Dear Bert,

Here's the book Jon Krakauer wrote about me. I believe it's a sign from God that the time is getting close. I hope you'll read it.

Love,

Dad

I read the letter three times before the words sink in. I stare blankly at the book, which is titled *Under the Banner of Heaven: A Story of Violent Faith*. On the cover is an image of a craggy, red-striped mountain—Canaan Mountain, which towers over Colorado City, Arizona, where Warren Jeffs's fundamentalist followers live. For a moment, all I can see is that mountain.

It looks like a hacksaw.

I'm vaguely aware that I'm holding my breath as I flip over the cover. On the title page I'm surprised to find an inscription from the author.

For Dan—

With gratitude for all your help.

Cheers,

Jon Krakauer

My brain struggles to make sense of what this all means. *Krakauer signed a copy of the book for Dad.*

He interviewed Dad.

Dad sent me his signed copy.

Dad's proud *of this.*

The last thought hits me like a sucker punch.

I can feel myself starting to dissociate as I turn the page. I slowly read the first line of the prologue. "Almost everyone in Utah County has heard of the Lafferty boys."

I grip the book tightly as my eyes skim over the words. In cold, objective facts, Krakauer lays out the events of the murder. Until this moment, I've never heard any of the details of that day. I read about how Allen returned home from work to find Brenda "sprawled on the floor in a lake of blood."

I slam the book shut and throw it across the room.

CHAPTER 13

1987–90

MOM EVENTUALLY ATTEMPTED TO DATE AGAIN. She desperately needed a social life away from us kids, and I'm sure she was hoping to meet a nice guy who would support her and maybe help relieve some of the burden she carried. I would get scared when she would go on dates because I didn't know what it meant for our family. Were things going to change again?

What I know now is that it is very rare for a woman to meet a man who is willing to take care of someone else's kids, especially men in their thirties and forties. By that point, they are already pretty set in their ways. In fact, most of the men Mom met seemed to want *her* to take care of *them*. Consequently, most of her relationships didn't last long, although there were a few exceptions.

When I was ten, Mom dated a man named Sam. He was an ex-Navy SEAL, and they met at an LDS Singles dance. He was from San Diego and seemed to really like Mom. For Mom's part, she was so private that whenever I asked her questions about him, I couldn't tell if she really liked him or not. He seemed nice enough to me.

One time, Mom went to visit Sam in San Diego. Johnny, Rachel, and I stayed at Grandma's house while Christopher and Brian went to Marleen's. I would have preferred to stay at a friend's house where I could do something fun, away from my siblings. Grandma's house felt boring to me now. I think I was also scared and anxious about being left behind. So as soon as Mom drove away, I began to throw a fit.

Grandma couldn't handle my tantrum. She took out a wooden spoon and hit the counter saying, "You want to cry? I'll give you something to cry about." It was exactly what Dad used to say.

Grandma hit me on the hand with the spoon. I began to scream louder, so she pulled me over to the kitchen sink and shoved my head under the faucet.

After she pulled my head out from under the water, I immediately blurted out, "Grandma, I love you"—the way I used to do after I'd been punished by dad.

This snapped her out of it. She blinked at me, as if confused by what she'd done. Then she hugged me and said, "Let's get you cleaned up."

Rachel and Johnny were in the other room. They stayed quiet and curled up on the big recliner, watching. After I dried off and returned to the room, they looked at me but said nothing. They were probably in shock, but I misread their silence to mean that they thought I deserved it, that they were against me. I felt like I was on the outside and they were on the inside.

I decided I must have been in the wrong, as always. I plastered on a happy face for the rest of the weekend. I had no idea how to process all the emotions I was facing. All I could do was try to suppress them.

At Christmas that year, Sam paid for all of us to ride the train to his home in San Diego. It was so exciting to ride a train that far. Of course, it was stressful for Mom because she had to try to keep my younger brothers under control. They had so much energy and were always bickering and hitting each other. Whenever they behaved this way, I was embarrassed to be around them and wished I were somewhere else. I could sense the stares and hear the whispers from strangers on the train about how my mom should be doing something to correct their behavior.

As the ride continued and my brothers' antics failed to subside, I could feel the resentment building among the other passengers. I found myself wanting to tell people to stop staring and mind their own business. I pictured myself standing up and shouting, "Unless you want to help, just shut the hell up! You have no idea what is going on for us or for my mom, you judgmental snobs." Although I was at times embarrassed of my family, I was also very protective of them. I would have done anything to keep them safe or from being hurt if I could.

After a fifteen-hour train ride, we finally arrived in California. As soon as I saw the palm trees and felt the warmth of the sun, it immediately felt like I'd come home. It was such a nostalgic moment. I felt a peace in my heart that I hadn't felt in a long time.

Our Christmas was nice. Mom and Sam made it so cozy and warm. We all had gifts, too—something we'd never had before. My brothers got cool new toys, and my sister and I both received baby dolls and a cradle to put them in. Sam had built and stained the cradle himself, and my mom had made the bedding. All of that thought and effort made the holiday so special. I really liked Sam. I asked Mom if she was going to marry him. She said she would have to wait and see.

These special moments and acts of kindness started to give me hope again. They seemed to pull me out of the darkness, at least for a time.

The next summer, Sam came to stay for a weekend. He started to build us a treehouse, and we were so excited. Everything was going so well. And then, that Saturday morning, while Sam was setting up a basketball hoop for the boys in the living room, something happened. Perhaps it was the stress of being in our tiny little home or dealing with my brothers' exuberant energy as they ran around his feet. Maybe one of them had shouted or made a loud noise. I don't know. Whatever it was, it triggered Sam. All of a sudden, Sam picked up Christopher, who was standing closest to him, and threw him across the room.

After that, it was over. Mom told Sam to leave, and we never saw him again. It was my granddad William who ended up finishing our treehouse.

When I was thirteen, Mom did get married again—to a man from England named Matthew. Rachel reminded me recently that my mom pulled us kids aside to tell us she was getting married and that she needed us to do our best to help out and come together as a unit. I really wanted Mom to be happy, and I wanted to be there for her. I desperately wanted things to work out for all of us, and I saw this as a new beginning, a chance to have the family I longed for. So I replied, with all the sincerity and intent I could muster, "Okay, Mom. I will try to be perfect." I suppose my response really stood out to my sister, since she still remembered it all these years later. She told me she could feel the heaviness of my commitment.

Unfortunately, Mom's new marriage didn't last long. Matthew was a kind person, and I truly believe he tried his best, especially at the beginning. He was the first person to offer me money for anything (I needed some cash for a school activity), but my heart was so closed at the time, I remember being extremely uncomfortable about it. Over time, however, things deteriorated. Matthew ended up being severely depressed. He worked the graveyard shift, so he would sleep during the day. One time, we kids were being too loud, and he burst out of the bedroom and yelled at us to shut up. He was completely nude. We had never seen a naked man before, so it made us all feel deeply uncomfortable.

A power struggle began to develop between Matthew and us kids. He would try to discipline us for our rowdy behavior. The boys were always up to no good, but I was getting into my fair share of trouble now, too. During this time, Riley and I were skipping school a lot and stealing fireworks, and I was failing to help out with the chores or come home when Mom requested. One day, Matthew tried to ground me from seeing Riley, and I yelled at him that he wasn't my father. That was the final straw for him. He chased me through the house and pinned me down and demanded that I respect him and never yell at him like that again. He sent me to my room, and I wasn't allowed to come out for an entire day.

Now, as an adult, I have a lot of empathy for Matthew. It wasn't an easy thing, trying to step into the role of father to five unruly children. But his temper didn't improve, and after two years, he moved out and got his own place. Mom continued to visit him for three more years until he eventually moved back to England. I don't think they ever officially got divorced.

I later learned that Mom got pregnant when she was with Matthew. She knew without a doubt that she could not handle raising another child, especially with Matthew as the father. She finally felt empowered enough to choose for herself—something she certainly hadn't been able to do with my father—so she had an abortion. I'm so happy Mom was able to make that decision for herself and exert some measure of control over her life. Having another baby would have almost certainly taken her to her breaking point.

After Matthew left, we were back to being on our own. As a kid watching my mom struggle to raise us by herself, her third marriage over, I swore to myself that I would never end up in her position. I would never allow a man to mistreat me or abandon me. I would never become a single mom, raising my kids alone.

CHAPTER 14

1989–92

THE FIRST DAY OF JUNIOR HIGH WAS A NIGHTMARE. I was terrified that I would forget my locker combination, and the entire day I felt like people were laughing at my clothes. I was wearing hand-me-down pants that were much too big for me, and I had to keep pulling them up. After school, I was nervous I was going to miss my bus, so I ran to the end of the line, looking frantically for the right number. As I ran, my pants fell down, and a group of older girls started laughing at me. I felt so humiliated and never wanted to go back, but of course I didn't have a choice.

Every morning, I woke up sick to my stomach. And by the end of each day, I was starving because I hadn't eaten anything due to my nerves. Home was the only place that felt safe. I wished I never had to leave my room.

Mom and I started arguing a lot. She expected me to help out around the house with dinner and cleaning up, but I just wanted to escape the hellscape of my day and forget about the homework that I never completed because I wasn't present enough to understand what I was learning and didn't feel like I could ask for the help I needed. I felt entirely alone in the world, even within my own family. Everyone always seemed to need something, and all I wanted was to go to sleep and never wake up.

I felt angry all the time, but no one around me seemed to grasp the extent of the pain in my heart. I wanted desperately to express it, to be understood, to finally be at peace, but I had no idea how to do that in a productive way.

Riley did her best to help, but she didn't really understand what I was going through. Whenever she came over, we would just listen to music and talk shit about the kids at school. I regret buying my yearbooks because I ended up scribbling the meanest things on the pictures of people who had bullied me or hurt me in some way.

By the end of seventh grade, my friendship with Riley had faded. My changing hormones and teenage moodiness made me want to spend all my time alone in my room. I began prioritizing my solitude over hanging out with her, so she found other friends, and over time, we drifted apart.

Music became my new best friend. That and journaling were the only outlets I could find for my emotions; it was the only time I felt free to express my inner world.

When I wasn't blasting music or writing out my thoughts, I would immerse myself in movies and television shows. Mom let me put a television in my room, and I would watch *Beverly Hills, 90210* every week. As with most shows I watched, I became obsessed with the characters and their lives. I lived through Brenda and longed to be just like her. Of course, that meant I needed to find my own Dylan. I thought Dylan, played by Luke Perry, was the most gorgeous guy alive. I desperately wanted someone to love me the way he loved Brenda. I was mesmerized by the chemistry between them and hooked on their drama. I never missed an episode.

This is when I began to internalize the idea that physical chemistry equaled love. If two people felt a strong sexual attraction to each other, I reasoned, then nothing else mattered.

I had next to no education about sex. Sex ed in Utah was (and continues to be) minimal at best, with a strong focus on abstinence. My mom, who has always been very private, also told me nothing about sex or caring for my body, so I was deeply unprepared for puberty.

I was a late bloomer. There was a boy at school named Nick (who knew my real last name was Lafferty) who would tease me relentlessly. He told me I was a carpenter's dream because I was flat as a board, which was true. I was incredibly skinny, with no curves whatsoever. The other girls got their periods well before I did—another way I felt awkward and left out.

Finally, one afternoon when I was fourteen or fifteen, I went to the bathroom and discovered blood on the toilet paper. Thank God I was at home. I remember thinking, *Ohh, this is it.* I told my mom. She bought me pads and told me how to clean my underwear, and that was it. I was on my own after that.

I continued to write to Dad, but his letters never helped me feel better. I still didn't want to acknowledge the truth about why he was in prison, and I didn't want him to acknowledge it either, because it would only make it real. I preferred to invent my own story. Consequently, our correspondence remained at a superficial level. As always, he would focus on his life. Whenever I did share something, it felt like I was pretending. I wasn't able to tap into what I wanted to express to get what I needed from him. I just knew I wanted to please him and to be there for him. So I would write that I loved him and that I missed him, and he would reply with the same old story about how this was all part of God's plan, which did nothing to soothe my pain.

One summer, when I went to stay at Gwen's house, I gave Dad her address so he could write to me while I was in Idaho. A letter arrived, and I sat down in the living room to read it. When Gwen saw that the letter was from Utah State Prison, she freaked out and asked what my dad wanted. I told her that Dad and I wrote to each other and he was just updating me on his life.

Gwen told me he wasn't allowed to send any more letters to her house. She said they brought a dark energy with them, and she didn't want that in her home. She also wasn't comfortable with Dad knowing her address. I respected her wishes, even though I felt like she was being a little extreme, and I told Dad not to send any more letters to me while I was at Gwen's.

◆ ◆ ◆

The beginning of high school was even worse than junior high. My friendship with Riley had officially ended, and I felt wholly alone.

All that changed when I met Curtis.

Curtis was one year older than me—I was sixteen, and he was seventeen—and he was extremely attractive. His look was hard rock meets outdoorsman: His hair came below his ears, but it was soft and clean. Curtis was very quiet and had a way of thinking deeply that felt mysterious and alluring to me. He drove a small black Mazda truck and would invite me to go for drives up the canyon. He taught me how to drive a manual. We loved spending time together, whether it was driving or hanging out in his room listening to music. He worked at the local grocery store, in the produce section, which was where my mom's husband Matthew worked, so they interacted sometimes.

Curtis was LDS, but his family was very kind to me. He had one sibling, a brother my age. His parents got along, and his whole family was very close. They looked out for each other and did lots of activities together, and I was always invited to join them. Curtis's parents even thought we would get married and let me know that they approved of me. I loved receiving their approval, but the talk of marriage scared me a little. We were still just kids.

I did, however, want to lose my virginity to Curtis. I felt ready. I told my mom I wanted to get on the pill and asked her to book me an appointment at the clinic. She stood there, speechless, but then finally agreed that it was a good idea. I didn't know why she was so shocked. I thought I was doing the responsible thing.

One weekend during my junior year, Curtis invited me to go for a campout at his family's cabin, just the two of us. I thought this was such a romantic gesture. We packed up our things and headed up the canyon. Once we arrived, we unloaded all our stuff and explored the property for a bit. Curtis showed me a badger's den and explained how aggressive badgers could be, which made me stick very close to him as we walked around. I remember I wanted to physically attach myself to him, like he would protect me.

Back in the cabin, we made tinfoil dinners to cook on the fire and shared our beliefs about life and our love of music. As we talked, we snuggled and then began to make out. I thought this was the perfect time for us to take it to the next level and assumed that our making out would naturally lead to sex. I'd been looking forward to this for months, and I was certain it was going to be a spectacular experience.

I was hoping Curtis would take the lead, just like Dylan did with Brenda on *90210*. I assumed all boys were like Dylan—confident and experienced. But Curtis's hands stayed safely on my back. I wondered if he needed some encouragement. So after several minutes, I slid my hand inside his pants.

He froze.

I looked up at him and asked, "Do you want to go further?"

He just looked at me with wide eyes and said, "Well, if you want to."

We continued making out, but his body language gave me the impression that I was pressuring him to do something he wasn't comfortable with, which made *me* uncomfortable. It felt like he was rejecting me, so I pulled back and shut down.

We didn't talk after that—not that I would have had any idea how to express what I was going through. In my mind, since Curtis wasn't jumping at the chance to have sex with me, it meant he didn't love me. In reality, I'm sure the prospect of sex probably terrified him, especially as a Mormon. We went from having a wonderful evening, feeling so close to each other, to sitting in awkward silence, both of us too confused and upset to utter a word. This pivotal moment that had been building for me for months had crumbled into disappointment and shame.

The only solution was for him to take me home. Once there, I retreated to the safety of my room. I threw myself on my bed and cried and cried. I decided I was never going to talk to Curtis again. I was too ashamed and embarrassed. His rejection hurt too much.

Curtis tried calling me a few times, but I never answered the phone. We would pass each other in the hall at school, but he never approached me to talk. To me, this was further confirmation that he didn't want me enough. I just wanted him to say, "Rebecca, I want to be with you. Please talk to me." But I'm sure he was just as confused as I was. I still loved him, but I lacked the courage to reach out. The wounded girl in me preferred to grieve the loss of Curtis rather than step into the unknown of communicating my emotions and thoughts. I'm sure with a simple conversation, we could have resolved the issue and found a way to move forward, but I was too afraid. Rejection felt familiar to me, so that was the experience I chose.

It pains me now to think of how my behavior must have hurt Curtis. But I felt broken emotionally, with no idea how to remedy it. In my mind, Curtis was too normal for me. Too good. He could do so much better— find a nice, virtuous Mormon girl—and I was standing in his way. I hadn't gone to church in years, but all my old feelings of being impure and wicked returned. Clearly, *something* was wrong with me. For the first time, it occurred to me that Dylan and Brenda weren't raised Mormon, but instead of recognizing that people outside of Utah and the church lived within a different paradigm and that it wasn't fair to expect Curtis to act like someone raised in Beverly Hills, I felt that I was being sinful and worldly. I was one of those wicked women in the Scriptures that my dad would rail about, a harlot whose only purpose was to lead men astray.

Eventually, Curtis stopped calling me. I found out later that he was called to serve an LDS mission in Germany.

Despite our unfortunate ending, my relationship with Curtis was a very uplifting time for me. It was the first time I had an understanding of what a partnership could look like, and the first time I began to develop romantic and sexual feelings.

Looking back, I can see that with Curtis I was exploring how to get my needs met; however, I didn't really understand what those needs were or how to communicate them. I didn't know how to express my emotions or what I was experiencing inside my body. No one had ever modeled this for me before. And since neither of us had received any guidance about how to approach relationships and physical intimacy, things were never going to end well.

However, I will always be grateful to Curtis and his family for the love they showed me. They gave me a glimpse of what was possible.

CHAPTER 15

1993

A FEW WEEKS AFTER MY BREAKUP WITH CURTIS, Mom announced that we were going to go to Scotland for six weeks to visit her family. I was over the moon. This was exactly what I needed. I loved the thought of getting on an airplane and flying far away from Utah and all the heartache I'd experienced there. I knew things had to be better in a different country. Mom was so lit up, anticipating seeing her siblings again, and I enjoyed seeing her happy.

Preparing for the trip was a bit stressful, but Marleen helped us figure out all the paperwork for our passports, and she drove us to the airport on the morning of our departure. Our flight to Scotland felt like embarking on a real adventure. I didn't even mind how long it was.

We flew into Edinburgh and then took a smaller plane from there to Glasgow. When we arrived, we were greeted by my mom's sister, Aunt Fiona, and her husband, Uncle Angus, as well as my older cousins Sonya and Alison. My mom's brother, Clyde, and his wife, Iona, were also there. It felt so exciting to meet them. They were very welcoming and loved and accepted all of us right away. I remember it was rainy when we landed, and we were all tired and jet-lagged, but I was just so happy to be there.

Scotland was absolutely magical. I couldn't believe it was a real place and that people got to live in a country with cobblestone streets and medieval castles. Everything was so much older and smaller than in America—the homes, the streets, the cars, the fridges—but it felt so much more efficient. Everything worked together like a beautiful puzzle box. I remember being impressed by the way the Scots drove their cars on the narrow streets. When another car approached, they'd pull over to make room and flash their headlights to tell the car to pass. Everyone was so respectful. I also loved how people were always outside, walking and using the bus system. One time we took the bus to Glasgow, and I thought it was the most fun thing I'd ever done.

The weather shocked me. I couldn't believe how quickly the clouds would gather, drenching us in rain. And then, just as suddenly, the skies would clear again, and the sun would be beaming down on us once more. It would all change in an instant. I was used to Utah's slow-moving storms and gray winters, the gloom that would never lift.

The rain made everything so green, the land practically glowed. I drank in the sight of the verdant woodlands and rolling green hills, dotted with sheep. It filled my soul in a way nothing else ever had.

And the food! Oh, the food. I'd never tasted produce or seafood so fresh. My aunt would go to the supermarket every other day (her fridge was too small to stock up with a week's worth of groceries the way we did at home), so everything was always at peak ripeness. I remember she made me a toastie with tomato on it. Never in my life had I tasted a tomato so juicy and delicious. I literally couldn't believe what I was eating. And trying fish and chips for the first time had me in raptures. The battered cod practically melted in my mouth. Even the potatoes tasted better there.

My cousin Sonya, who was twenty, was excited to have a cousin visiting from America. I remember being shocked that she smoked, ate sweets, and drank soda. She even had her own soda machine in her room! That seemed unreal to me.

Sonya asked me if I liked to go clubbing, but I wasn't sure what clubbing was. Sonya seemed thrilled by my ignorance. I think my naivete fueled her. She wanted to show me what I had been missing. Aunt Fiona gave me money to buy some new clothes, and Sonya and I took the bus into town to check out the shops. For the first time in my life, I felt like I belonged somewhere. I loved every minute of it.

I also met Aunt Maisie, my mom's sister who took the missionary lessons from my father, back when she and Mom were in their twenties. Aunt Maisie had a tanning bed in her home, which I thought was unbelievable. She let me use it, and I think I lay there for over an hour. When I got out, my skin was nice and golden.

Everything felt like a dream. But there were a few moments of tension between me and my family. Because Sonya and I had hit it off so well, I stayed with Aunt Fiona, while Mom and the rest of my siblings stayed with Uncle Clyde and Aunt Iona. I liked being able to spend time with Sonya, but I soon noticed that my mom and siblings were doing things without me. They would go on ferry rides and bicycle tours, and I wasn't invited. I began to feel like my mom had pawned me off onto Aunt Fiona so she wouldn't have to deal with me.

I was also annoyed by Mom's behavior. Since we'd arrived in Scotland, she'd been acting like a different person. I didn't understand why she was suddenly treating me so differently. It felt alienating and reminded me of when Dad had first been arrested and I'd felt like my real mom had been replaced by a copy.

I understand now that my mom has always been deeply embarrassed by everything she went through with my dad. I think she was worried her family had lost respect for her. She knew if her sisters had been there, they would have said, "What the hell were you thinking?" Being back home probably made it clear to her just how much she had given her true self away. The saddest part was that she had done it in hopes of finding something better, when in reality it had made her life worse.

In retrospect, it's no wonder my mom wasn't paying as much attention to me. She probably assumed I was having a great time with my cousins and was giving herself permission to enjoy being back in her home country surrounded by the people and things she loved. She was probably feeling like herself again. As a teenager, however, all I saw was my mom acting in ways that felt foreign and strange to me.

Things came to a head one day when Mom and Rachel went to the body shop and purchased some body oils. They generously brought me back a rose-scented oil. However, in my teenage angst, all I could feel was annoyance because I hadn't been invited to go with them to the shop. I thought rose was an old lady scent, and I would have liked to pick out my own oil. Rachel got mango, which appealed to me much more. I was annoyed that they'd given me something I didn't like and jealous of the time Rachel got to spend with Mom. It felt like Rachel was her favorite daughter, and I was the problem child she didn't want to deal with.

I don't know if it was teenage hormones or the stress of being in a new situation that made my turbulent emotions break through the surface, but I got so angry I snapped at my mom, and then I shoved her.

The whole family immediately jumped down my throat. I knew what I'd done was wrong, but it felt like everyone was against me. I stormed off to Sonya's room.

After we'd both had some time to cool off, Mom went out and bought a really nice white wine for me as an apology gift. It was such a kind thing for her to do. She knew I'd already tried alcohol and she thought I might as well drink the good stuff. But while she was bringing it to me, she lost her balance and fell. The bottle broke, and the glass cut her face. She had to get stitches.

I felt terrible. Mom had injured herself bringing that wine to me, when I was the one who had lashed out. After that, I vowed to be a better daughter.

By the time the weekend rolled around, however, I'd forgotten my vow. I was more than ready to go out dancing and forget about the week's drama. Sonya and I had chosen a club, and I'd put together my outfit. I couldn't wait to experience my first taste of nightlife.

We started the night by going to our cousin Anna's house. Anna was eight years older than I was and far more experienced. As soon as we arrived, Anna asked if I wanted a drink. I said sure, not knowing that the orange juice was heavily mixed with vodka. She then asked if I wanted to take some E. I had no idea what "E" was, but she assured me that it would make the night magical. Anna produced a small, flat pill. She broke it and gave me a piece, which I swallowed with the orange drink. Then we called a taxi and rode into Glasgow to stand in line at a popular nightclub. By this point, I was already tipsy and feeling the effects of the ecstasy. Everything was so colorful, like I was in a dream.

Inside the club, the music pumped, making my whole body come alive. That's when the drug really kicked in. I let go of everything except moving to the beat, feeling it pulse inside of me, taking me outside of myself and at the same time deeper within. I'd never heard techno before, and the heavy beats were taking me to a dimension I didn't know existed. The energy was indescribable. I couldn't stop smiling. I'd never felt so much joy or excitement in my entire life. I never wanted it to end.

The music kept getting better and better, and soon we were dripping with sweat. I remember we were getting looks from guys, which felt amazing. For the first time in my life, I felt seen. No one here knew who I was, or who my dad was. I was just a girl, dancing and feeling free and alive. It was like being in a movie. The lights flashed, the music filled my whole body, and I felt myself dancing and moving in ways I never imagined possible. The 1990s club scene in the UK was second to none, and I—the weird, outcast girl from a tiny, insular town in rural America—was getting to experience it. It was absolutely unreal to me.

Before we knew it, it was five o'clock in the morning, and the sun was starting to come up. We were starving, so we stopped at a street cart and grabbed a kabob. It was my first time eating off a street cart, and it tasted heavenly. We caught a cab back, chatting the whole ride home about how much fun it had been and when we could do it again. When we got back to Sonya's, I immediately crashed and slept like a baby the entire day.

On our next outing, we went to a karaoke bar. Sonya thought this was something that I would also enjoy, and she was right. I couldn't believe the attention I got for being American. It felt like I was a movie star.

The guy who managed the bar was named Ian. He flirted with me like no one ever had before. He called me "doll" in his charming Scottish brogue and made lots of eye contact with me, which I wasn't used to getting from guys. Ian had spiked hair in the style that was just starting to take the decade by storm. His shirt was open, exposing his chest, which I thought was very hot, and he had a cleft chin, which looked good on him. He had massive arms and a strong masculine energy. *This is a real man*, I thought.

When it came time for us to sing, Ian introduced the song. "These girls are gonna sing 'Like a Virgin,'" he said, "and none of them are."

We laughed along with everyone else. After Madonna, we sang Irene Cara's "Flashdance . . . What a Feeling."

One of the popular songs at the time was "No Limit" by the Eurodance group 2 Unlimited. Everyone in the bar screamed the title lyrics in the refrain at the top of their lungs.

Singing and dancing along with everyone else made it seem like there really was no limit. After all, I was here on the other side of the world. Anything was possible.

I couldn't stop thinking about Ian. Sonya and I went back to the bar a few more times, and the flirting and sexual tension continued to build. Finally, emboldened by the energy of the club and the vodka cranberry I had just downed, I asked Ian to take me home. I was still hurting from Curtis's rejection, and I wanted to see what someone older and more experienced—a real man—was like. After all, I reasoned, if Ian wanted to have sex with me, it meant he must love me.

It was a disaster. My excitement quickly deflated when we reached Ian's house and I discovered that not only did he live with his mom, but he also had a kid. Our time together was nothing like in the movies. I had a vague idea about what sex was like, but I thought it would be romantic and passionate, the way it was in *90210* or *Dirty Dancing*. This was anything but. There was no foreplay of any kind. Ian didn't kiss me or hold me or tell me he adored me or even try to get to know me, like Curtis had. Instead, he told me to be quiet so I wouldn't wake up his mom or son. Then he laid me down on the carpet in the living room, took off my pants, and immediately proceeded to have intercourse with me. It was very painful. I bled a lot and felt ashamed and lost. I just wanted to go home.

I had no idea where I was, but I knew my aunt's address. So after Ian finished, he took me back to my aunt's house. My mom was there waiting for me. She had been sitting up all night, worried sick. I never told Sonya I was leaving with Ian or when I would be back, so she'd been looking for me everywhere and was terrified I'd been kidnapped. I suddenly realized how irresponsible I'd been. I'd just wanted to do something spontaneous and liberating, to break all the rules, to feel loved. I hadn't thought about how it would affect my family or the stress I'd put them through as they imagined the worst.

My mom and aunt thought I'd been raped, but I assured them that everything was consensual—although looking back, I can see now that it clearly wasn't. I lied and told them I was fine. However, Ian hadn't used protection, so they took me to the pharmacy to get the morning-after pill. It made me sick. I puked and puked all day. After that, I was told that I wasn't allowed to go out again.

At the time, I was incapable of fully processing what had happened with Ian. In my naivete, I didn't view it as rape or assault, and even if I had, I don't think I would have known how to handle that. Mostly, I was angry and frustrated that the taste of freedom I'd experienced was being taken away from me. It felt like I was being forced back into my cage. I promised I wouldn't leave my cousin's sight if they would just let me go out again, but Sonya didn't want to have anything to do with me.

I was crushed. Stuck in my aunt's house, I looked for something closer to home to entertain myself with.

I found it in the boy next door.

The boy, named Rory, looked like trouble, but at that point, that was exactly what I wanted. I felt like if the adults in my life were going to treat me like I was a rebel and a rule-breaker, then that was what I was going to become. I was tired of being cooped up, of having no fun. My experience clubbing with Sonya and Anna and of going home with Ian, as horrible as it had been, had sparked my curiosity and desire to cross into more forbidden territory. After all, certain parts of it—our flirty, sexual exchanges at the bar—had been exhilarating. I needed to feel that thrill again. More than that, I longed to find someone who would actually love me the way I so desperately wanted.

Rory was cute and much closer to my age. During our first conversation, he offered to roll me a spliff. It was my first time smoking weed, and it was fantastic. I loved how it made me all giggly and out of my head. We visited and kissed and laughed for hours. I sneaked back to my aunt's house before Mom knew I was up to something. This continued for the remaining five weeks of our trip.

By the end of the five weeks, I had convinced myself that I was in love. I decided I wanted to stay in Scotland and that my family could return to the States without me. I figured I could get a job and live with my aunt. I had it all planned out. Nothing about going back to America appealed to me. In Scotland, I had finally found acceptance, excitement, and even love. I never wanted to leave.

As you can imagine, this plan did not go over well with Mom. I told her I was in love with Rory and that I wanted to stay. She laughed at how ridiculous it sounded. She didn't understand how, at the time, I felt as if I had finally found something worth living for. My feelings for Rory, and his for me, felt real. It felt like I was finally experiencing real connection, and, in my mind, true love.

I regret all the stress I put my mom through. But I didn't do it out of spite. More than anything, I wanted to escape the depression and darkness that waited for me back in Salem. When Mom forced me to go back, I was livid. I didn't talk to her for the entire flight home. My need to rebel and break free from the prison I felt at home increased exponentially.

Looking back now, it's clear to me how my codependency, formed from childhood trauma, was propelling me to find healing and validation in romantic partners. I attached myself to people so quickly and deeply, to the point of surrendering my own needs and even losing my identity. This pattern was only just beginning to emerge, but it was one I would be doomed to repeat for quite some time.

2016

My phone buzzes, and I look at the screen.

"Hi, Mom," I answer.

"Maisie is gone," she says, stifling a sob. Mom asks if I'll fly with her to Scotland for the funeral.

"Of course," I tell her.

We fly to Scotland and attend Maisie's funeral. It's a beautiful service, but there's an undercurrent of anger. My mom's family blames Maisie's partner for her death.*

During and after the service, I observe Mom's interactions with her siblings. I can see how my mom still changes when she's around her family. It's fascinating to me how they all revert back to the dynamic they had as kids. My mom is the oldest, and I see how she easily takes charge, while her sisters listen to what she has to say.

I reflect on the passage of time, how much we change and mature and yet, in some ways, stay the same. *Do I do the same thing with my siblings?* I wonder.

On the last night of our stay, my cousins—Uncle Clyde's kids—invite me out for dinner at a local restaurant, where we enjoy a nice dinner.

---

* Maisie's health hadn't been great, and she would frequently become dizzy and black out. One evening, she lost her balance coming down the stairs. That's how she died. I was told she lay there for a whole day before the authorities were contacted. Her partner, who was dealing with mental issues, was not able to cope with Maisie's needs.

Afterward, my cousins propose going to a pub. I'm hesitant because my mom and I have an early flight the next morning, but my cousins insist.

As soon as we arrive at the pub, which has a dance floor, it becomes evident that my cousins have no intention of going home anytime soon. The drinking has only just started, and I can see that they intend to have a full night. I start to become anxious. I know I need to go home or Mom will be worried, but I can't exactly bail on my cousins.

After a couple of hours, I ask my cousins to take me home, since my mom and I have an early flight the next day. I knew Mom will be wondering where I am, and I'd also like to get some sleep before our long flight. But they laugh it off and say I should enjoy my last night. I don't want to be rude, so I stay at the pub with them, even though I am a bit worried.

When we finally return home, it's about one o'clock in the morning. To my surprise, my mom and aunts are still up.

"What were you thinking?" my aunt yells at me. "Worrying your mum like that?"

I try to explain, but before I can get a word out, my other aunt jumps in. "How could you do that to your mother? She needs to catch an early flight."

I can't believe it. I'm sorry for worrying my mom, but I'm shocked by my aunts' reaction. My mom knew who I was out with. I knew how to get back home. There was no reason for her to worry. I'm thirty-nine years old, a grown woman, but suddenly it's like I'm seventeen again.

I apologize and tell my mom that if I had known she was waiting up for me, I would have taken a taxi back. For some reason, my answer seems to infuriate her even more. Despite my continued apologies, she doesn't speak to me for the entire flight home. I shake my head, thinking about our first trip to Scotland. Now it's my mom who's icing me out. Mom always shares what she's thinking when we're alone, but when we're with her sisters, she becomes a different person.

I have no idea why she is reacting so strongly. Clearly, something has triggered her. Perhaps it's rooted in the abandonment she experienced as a child, brought to the surface by being back with her family, and she's angry with me for going out and drinking with my cousins when Maisie has just died. Or perhaps she's just mourning the loss of a dear sister and processing the realization that she'll never see her again. But I don't know, because my mom refuses to let me in.

I feel as if I've failed a test, maybe even been tricked. Did my cousins intentionally keep me out late? Why would they do something like that? Does my Scottish family still view me as that teenage girl who went home with Ian? Are we all just reliving the past, frozen in the same roles?

How much have I really changed? I wonder. How much have any of us changed?

CHAPTER 16

1993–95

AFTER WE RETURNED FROM SCOTLAND, I went back to high school and went through the motions of going to class, but mentally I wasn't there. I was fully zoned out, dreaming about the larger world I had glimpsed in Europe. Everyone around me felt so small. The high school drama bored and disgusted me. It all felt stupid and inconsequential. I was still angry at my family for how I'd been treated, and I found myself lashing out more frequently.

Mom grew tired of my moping and sent me to live with Gwen in Idaho for a semester. One weekend, Marleen came to visit with her boys, ages six and eight. Whenever my older sisters got together, they would dump their kids on me and go out shopping, without telling me when they would be back. They'd go spend money they didn't have on clothes and then find ways to lie to their husbands about where the clothes had come from. I didn't care what they did, but I was pissed off that they didn't even ask me if I would babysit for them. They just acted like I was expected to, as if I was the hired help (except I was never paid).

One afternoon, while I was watching their kids, a neighbor girl and one of her hot guy friends invited me to go swimming. At this point, I was tired of doing the responsible thing and more than sick of babysitting for my sisters, something I'd been doing for over half my life. An opportunity for some fun had come my way, and I wasn't going to turn it down. So I took off and left the boys by themselves for an hour.

When my sisters returned home and found the boys alone, they were livid. Gwen sent me straight back to Utah, telling me to inform Mom that she was done raising me. I had a good laugh about that.

149

"Enjoy having to pay a babysitter from now on!" I clapped back.

Back in Salem, I returned to the high school I hated. Even though I kept a low profile, I still continued to attract the attention of bullies. Some of the senior girls would have a stare-off with me in the hallway as they walked by. One afternoon at lunch, without any instigation on my part, two of these girls strolled up to me, grabbed me by each arm, and pulled me outside. While one of the girls held me, the other one started yelling in my face, asking me what my problem was. I felt so much fear and adrenaline pump through my body, I started shaking. Suddenly, the girl smacked me on the side of the head.

My flight-or-fight response surged. I broke free of the other girl's grasp and pounced on the girl who hit me. I pinned her to the ground and laid into her for what felt like ten minutes, pummeling her with punches. When we finally broke apart, there was a huge circle of students around us, shouting and cheering. Their cheers disgusted me. I didn't feel like I'd won a victory—more like I was living among animals and that I was slowly becoming one of them.

My shoe had come off during the scuffle, so I picked it up and walked back inside. Cassie Peterson ran up to me, asking if I was okay.

I gave her a look as if to say, "Oh, please. Don't act like you care." Then I walked away without answering.

The bully girl never bothered me again. No one did. But it didn't matter. I was done with this small, stupid town. I had seen how big the world was, and I couldn't go backward. I was done subjecting myself to the oppressive environment at school, done following other people's rules, so I decided to finish high school by home study. This was one of the most empowering decisions I ever made for myself. I only wish I had done it sooner.

After I finished my home study and graduated from high school, I passed my time idly. The letdown after returning home from Scotland continued to make my life seem small and depressing. I kept searching for something that could help me reach that same high, but there just wasn't much for me to do. Most days, I would walk to the local swimming pool or drive to Orem and hang out at the bowling alley where they had pool tables. In order to afford the gas money, I would help my mom out with her sewing jobs.

Not long after graduating, I met a girl at the bowling alley named Ashley. Ashley was a year older than me, and I thought she was so pretty and fun. She brought exactly the kind of adventure into my life that I'd been searching for.

I began to imitate Ashley. I started to curl my hair the way she did. And I started going with her to the tanning salon. I loved lying there in the warm blue lights; it made me so happy. I would fall asleep in the bed, and when the timer went off, I would resist climbing out. I had no knowledge of skin cancer at the time, nor would I have cared. As I started dressing less like a tomboy and more like Ashley, I began to feel pretty, too.

I was thrilled to discover that Ashley also loved to go clubbing. We found a dance club in Provo that allowed anyone eighteen or older to enter. They didn't serve alcohol, so Ashley and I would mix our own drinks in the car and get a buzz going before entering the club.

One Friday in January, I called Ashley and asked if she was up for going dancing. She of course said yes, and we jumped in the car and drove up to Provo. We waited in line for what felt like an hour. Finally, we got inside the club. As soon as I heard the music, I felt the tension slide from my body. I let go and allowed myself to slip into a trance. We danced all night, closing the place down. But after the club kicked us out, we weren't ready to go home. We walked back to our car, still coming off the high from all the dancing and drinking.

Parked next to our car were three brand new crotch rockets. Their owners were young guys, just a few years older than us. They were smoking and talking next to the bikes.

I looked at the boys, then back at Ashley. Ashley caught my drift and smiled in agreement. We walked up to the boys and asked if we could bum a cigarette. I had already tried smoking once or twice while in Scotland, so it seemed like a natural thing to try again.

One of the boys stepped forward. "Sure thing," he said, offering us each a cigarette and lighting them for us. "I'm Jake," he said. "I saw you ladies in there. You're good dancers."

The five of us made small talk while puffing on our Marlboro Reds. Then Jake looked me in the eyes and asked if I wanted to go for a ride on his bike.

The next thing I knew, I was sitting behind a complete stranger as we tore down the city streets on his motorcycle. I found myself wondering what the hell I was doing. I was wearing shorts in the middle of January, for Christ's sake. But I didn't feel the cold at all. I just felt warm and exhilarated, even relaxed. For the first time in a long time, I felt my mind going blank.

Jake drove faster and faster. And then he yelled at me to hold on. Before I understood what was happening, he popped a wheelie.

I shrieked and held on to him tighter. *What the hell?!* I thought. But I loved it. It felt like being weightless. I didn't know how this guy could be so damn sure of himself, but I couldn't get enough.

After Jake took me back to Ashley's car, I found myself giving him my number and saying, "Call me."

Jake called the next day. We instantly connected. We shared the same rebellious attitude and anger at the world. Jake was new to the area; his family had just moved from Sacramento, and he was having a hard time transitioning from boy to man. He had a nice bike and a truck, but he felt angry and confused about life and the responsibilities that came with being a twenty-three-year-old. He had a heaviness about him. However, he was always kind and gentle with me.

Jake's parents were amazing. His dad was a commercial airline pilot, and his mom was an incredibly loving and generous woman. Both of them accepted me instantly. I felt so welcome in their home. His mom let me know that she approved of my being with her son and that she enjoyed having me around. The two of us talked for hours. I loved listening to her share stories of all the places they had lived and visited due to Jake's dad being a pilot.

Over time, I opened up to them about my family's past. They never showed an ounce of judgment toward me or made me feel uncomfortable about who my dad was. Jake's mom listened while I talked to her about my life. It was therapeutic and felt like being with a good friend. His family showed me nothing but love and compassion and even asked to meet my mom. In fact, they wanted to meet my whole family. This made me feel so safe and loved.

My mom loved Jake, too, and he loved spending time at our home. My mom's ability to talk with him and never lecture or judge him was a big deal for him—something he said he had never experienced with girls' parents in the past. He was becoming a member of my family, just like I was becoming a member of his. I loved how things seemed to be moving forward. I began to open my heart to Jake more and more.

Jake was very respectful and always treated me like a lady. He would pick me up, and we would go back to his house to watch movies. He loved to cook for me, which was something I had never experienced before. We would spend lots of time cuddling on the couch, and I would end up falling asleep. I felt so comfortable with him.

We hung out for three months before we became intimate. We drove up the canyon to a lookout spot to park, talk, and smoke. One thing led to another, and we made love in his truck. The chemistry between us was great, and Jake knew exactly what he was doing. He had no trouble taking the lead, just like Dylan from *90210*. It was the first time that sex didn't hurt and was actually enjoyable for me. We even climaxed together, and I thought, *Okay, wow, this is what it's supposed to be like!* It was like tasting a delicious dessert that you couldn't stop eating. I wanted more.

Jake and I started doing odd jobs together, like moving and laying sod, which was hard work. He always commented on how strong I was and how he thought I was a unique girl. He also said that I was a great driver and trusted me with his truck. Working with Jake allowed me to finally start saving money.

Later that year, Gwen—who had forgiven me for failing in my babysitting duties—and I started to talk about going back to Scotland. I'd talked up the nightlife so much to her, she was curious to try it herself. By this time, Gwen was thinking of leaving her marriage. She'd begun drinking coffee and wanted to leave the church, too. I loved all the ways she was changing and growing.

At this point, Jake and I had been dating for about five months. He was supportive of my going to Scotland, so Gwen and I made all the preparations. I was so excited to go back.

One week before our trip, I suddenly got very ill. I was throwing up a lot, and it felt like I had caught the flu. I figured it would be a quick thing and I would recover and be back to myself in no time. But five days later, I was still sick to my stomach, with no appetite.

I was sitting at my mom's kitchen table, talking to Gwen about our plans, when Mom walked in. She took one look at me and said, "Rebecca, you're pregnant."

I stared at her in shock. *No*, I thought. *Impossible.* I was on birth control, so I couldn't be pregnant.

Gwen took me to the store to pick up a pregnancy test. The second we got home, I took the test, then waited in anxious anticipation. A couple of minutes later, the pink positive sign appeared in the little window.

I refused to believe it. I took the second test out of the package and tested again. Still positive.

In a daze, I walked out of the bathroom and showed the tests to my mom and sister.

Gwen looked at me with empathy. "We can still go to Scotland," she said, "and make the most of it."

I sat down and tried to process what was happening. Once the initial shock wore off, I began to feel excited. I loved Jake so much. Surely having a child with him would only bring us closer together. Our little family would provide me with all the love I'd been missing in my life. We could be so happy.

Jake was planning to stop by the house to drop off some soup. When he arrived, I took him by the hand and walked with him into the backyard. We lay down on the trampoline and looked up at the sky. After lying there for a while, I broke the news to him.

He lay there, stunned. Then he said the thing I'd dreaded hearing the most. "I'm not ready to be a father," he stammered. "I'm still trying to figure out my own life. I can't bring another one into the world. I'm only twenty-three, and you're eighteen. We're too young!"

I was devastated. I thought for sure Jake would be excited and say, "Let's get married!" Instead, he asked if I would be willing to put the baby up for adoption.

I couldn't believe he would propose such a thing. Furious, I rose to my feet and said, "I'm going on this trip, and then I'm having this baby, whether you want to be a part of our life or not."

I went inside and refused to speak to him further. Later, after he left, Mom came into my room to talk to me.

"I'll support you in any decision you make," she said.

I felt a huge sense of relief, knowing I wouldn't be alone. "I want to have this baby," I said fiercely.

"Okay then," Mom said. "I'll help you."

I couldn't believe how strongly I'd become attached to the idea of keeping a child I hadn't even known existed until that morning. Perhaps it was because I was still craving true, unconditional love—the kind of love I knew I would receive from a baby—and I knew in return I could give her all the love I'd lacked as a child. Regardless of the reason, and even though I had long sworn never to be a single mother like Mom, everything inside me knew I wanted to have this baby. I knew it would be a little girl, too. I could just feel it.

Gwen and I finished preparing for our trip. I didn't speak to Jake again before we left.

Unfortunately, the trip was miserable. I threw up the entire time, and I couldn't be around the smell of cigarette smoke, which was everywhere, without puking. There was no clubbing for Gwen and me. Instead, she babysat me the whole time and did her best to support all my cravings for fish and chips and my unquenchable need for vinegar. I could have dumped the entire bottle over the fries, and it still wouldn't have been enough. I was so grateful for Gwen's help, but I felt awful for letting my sister down after talking up this trip for months.

When we returned home, I finally spoke to Jake again. But every time we talked, we ended up arguing. Jake was struggling financially; his bike and truck were going to be repossessed by the bank, and even though he was working, he wasn't earning enough to make the payments. I also didn't know that his family was putting pressure on him to step up and marry me. As a result, he was incredibly stressed.

For my part, I was moody and emotional. I needed to get away to clear my head, so I went to stay with Gwen for a few weeks. While I was there, Jake called and said he didn't believe that the baby was his. I was crushed that he could accuse me of cheating on him, but I didn't have the energy to try to convince him that I hadn't been with anyone else.

I went to all the prenatal checks on my own. Every time I sat in the waiting room and saw the other women there with their partners, I felt so sad that I didn't have Jake by my side. But going through the pregnancy alone helped me become acquainted with my own inner strength.

After my second ultrasound, it was confirmed: I was having a little girl.

I was determined to go through the pregnancy with minimal expenses. So I never bought any maternity clothes, which wasn't a problem since the only thing that really grew was my belly. It was easy enough to put an elastic band around the top button of my shorts to give my stomach a little more room. It was amazing when I began to feel and see movements inside my belly, signs of the little miracle growing inside of me. One night I was lying in the bath and saw my whole stomach move from one side to the next. It freaked me out and made the whole experience so surreal but special at the same time. I took this time to journal and keep notes of my progress throughout the remaining months.

When I was six months pregnant, the reality of my situation began to sink in. I remember one day I was with my mom, coming home from a job I had helped her with. We pulled into the McDonald's drive-thru for a fish sandwich. Thinking about how hard we'd had to work to make the money to afford a simple sandwich suddenly made me realize just how much it was going to cost to raise a child. I hadn't even bought a crib yet. I felt so unprepared. All of my confidence that everything would work out was suddenly overwhelmed by fear of the unknown, and I started to cry.

Mom asked me what was wrong, and I told her all my fears and worries.

She just smiled and said, "Oh, Rebecca, let's go get you a crib and bedding, some baby clothes, too, whatever you need to feel prepared." She always had a way of calming me in those moments. Even though I was taking on this adult responsibility, I was still such a little girl.

I got a job at a boutique up the road, painting and decorating custom shirts, the way Mom had done after we left Dad. It was a small job, but it kept me busy and allowed me to earn some money. I did this until the summer ended. I remember driving to the shop in the mornings, listening to Fleetwood Mac, getting lost in nostalgia as I felt myself teetering on the transition from girlhood to womanhood.

CHAPTER 17

1996

ON THE EVENING OF JANUARY 19, 1996—one year after I'd taken that fateful ride on the motorcycle with Jake—my mom and I were driving home when I felt a sharp pain in my lower back and stomach, a kind of pain I'd never felt before. I told my mom that I was having bad cramps. Then I understood what it meant: I was in labor.

We rushed home, grabbed my things, and went to the hospital. I was both nervous and excited. But after the doctor checked me, he told me that I was only dilated to two centimeters; I needed to be dilated to four before they could really do anything for me. This was not the news I wanted to hear. They sent me home and advised me to walk around until the pain got worse and more consistent.

Three hours later, I returned. I was convinced I had dilated to a four, but they checked me again and said I hadn't changed much. I asked them to please not send me home. I needed to be around people who could reassure me about what was happening. They said that they could induce my labor, and I agreed, not knowing what the procedure entailed.

They placed an IV in my hand and gave me Pitocin. This made the pain I was experiencing ten times worse. I just kept breathing through the tightness and the cramping for as long as I could until they offered to give me an epidural. I couldn't believe the relief I felt afterward. I fell asleep for about an hour and then woke up to the pain again. They gave me more pain medication, but it wasn't working. My left leg went numb, but that was it.

I explained to the nurse what was going on, but she said that there was nothing they could do at this point, so they just coached me through the pain. Mom was by my side, talking in my ear, telling me that I was doing great. But the pain was unreal. I thought I was going to die.

The nurse asked me if I wanted a mirror to watch my baby come out when she started to crown. It horrified me to think of my vulva being ripped and stretched open. I quickly said no before going into another contraction.

I almost passed out. But then I thought of my mom and how she had done this seven times without medication—five of them at home, by herself. Clearly, she'd survived. This gave me the strength to endure the final minutes.

"Last push," the nurse yelled.

I pushed with everything I had.

"She's out!"

Just like that, the pain stopped. They took my baby away to weigh and clean her before giving her back to me. The moment they handed her to me, I felt the most incredible peace fill my body. She was a perfect little bundle of seven pounds, seven ounces, all wrapped up and ready to suckle. Her face was a bit red and bruised from the rough transition into this world, but she was perfect, nonetheless.

Choosing a baby name was easy. When I first saw *Silver Spoons* and became enamored of Erin Gray, I'd decided then and there that when I had a daughter of my own, I would name her Erin.

So when the nurses asked me what her name was, I immediately said, "Erin."

My baby girl was perfect. Just like Erin Gray.

I was absolutely exhausted but so happy to meet her. I felt as if the angels were present in the room with me. The spiritual experience I had holding her was so beautiful, I cried.

However, after we returned home, the reality of motherhood set in. I had no idea how exhausting it would be to care for a new baby. The first few nights were especially rough, and my mom had to wake me up so I could feed Erin. I didn't know there was a proper way to have her latch, so my nipples cracked and bled. I wondered if I was really ready to be a mother.

But the love and support I received from my family was overwhelming. I wasn't used to so much positive attention. My brother Christopher rode his bike eight miles from our home in Salem to come see me in the hospital in Payson and welcome Erin into the world. I was so touched by that.

Riley also stopped by the hospital to give me flowers and congratulate me. Her gesture meant so much to me, and I was excited to rekindle our friendship. Riley had been keeping herself busy, working with her brother as an electrician. She's the strongest girl I know; she could always hold her own against the boys.

Riley never did marry or have children of her own. She had a couple of relationships with women, but they didn't work out, and now she lives with her sister. We're still in touch to this day. Occasionally, we call each other and laugh as we reminisce about our crazy times together getting in trouble and how her little sister would often tag along, threatening to tattle on us if we didn't include her in our shenanigans. I'm very grateful for Riley, and she remains an important person in my life.

I thought I should let Jake know that he had a little girl, so I called him.

"Hi, Jake," I said over the phone. "I wanted to let you know that you're a father. I named her Erin."

Jake was silent for a moment. Finally, he said. "Oh, wow." Another pause. "Why did you choose Erin? What if she gets made fun of for having that name?"

I frowned, beyond confused. "What the hell are you talking about? Erin is a beautiful name." I was so angry and frustrated. *That* was his reaction?

I didn't understand why Jake would say something like that or why he would feel that way. But he couldn't explain it to me, either. We really had a hard time communicating and understanding each other.

"Well," he said, "I guess I should come by and see her. Let me check my work schedule. I've been working graveyards and trying to get my sleep in has been tricky for me. But I'll let you know what day."

I rolled my eyes. "Okay, talk to you soon," I said, then hung up the phone. *Bye, jerk!* I thought angrily.

I called Jake's mom next and told her the news. Unlike her son, she was elated and came immediately to meet her new granddaughter.

The next day, Jake showed up at my door with flowers—no doubt at his mother's prodding.

Jake continued to visit and eventually suggested we get married. It was bittersweet. Finally, I was getting what I wanted. But I felt empty inside. Jake had missed my entire pregnancy and Erin's birth. Only now that she was here did he want to be involved. To make matters worse, I was pretty sure it wasn't what he wanted at all. I was certain his parents were pressuring him.

Despite my doubts, getting married still felt like the best option for me. I was terrified about raising Erin on my own. So I said yes.

We had a small gathering at Jake's parents' home in Orem when Erin was three months old. Everything about the wedding was very elegant, and I was touched by the way both of our families came together to make it happen. Jake's mom decorated the yard and made our cake. My mom helped me pick out my dress. And someone from Jake's family who was a photographer took our pictures. It was a beautiful affair.*

I look back now and realize how loved and cared for I was. I didn't see it at the time because I was still letting my fear and trauma run the show. I didn't think I was worthy of all the love and attention I was receiving.

As the time for the wedding approached, it suddenly got very windy, and I had a moment of doubt. I wondered if the universe or some kind of

---

* At the time, my younger brothers were getting into a lot of trouble. They seemed to always be testing boundaries with the law—rolling boulders down hills into residential areas, starting fires in fields, trespassing on people's property. It was a constant source of stress for my mom, and trying to coordinate anything that involved getting us all together to act like a typical family was a struggle. One of my brothers was unable to make it to my wedding, and this upset Mom, which in turn upset me. But the wedding was still special in its own way.

higher power was trying to get my attention. *Is this a sign?* I thought. But it seemed too late to turn back.

After the wedding, Jake and I moved in with his parents. We lived with them for five months. At first things were good. Eventually, however, I started to feel suffocated and lost. My family moved to California because Johnny had an opportunity to work with my uncle Tim, building movie sets. It was good money, enough to help support my mom and siblings. They could have a new start in a new state, far away from anyone who knew about our past.

I missed my mom terribly. Jake got a job working swing shifts, so I rarely saw him, either. I'd gotten married so I wouldn't have to raise my daughter alone, and yet that's exactly what was happening.

A few months after the wedding, when Erin was eight months old, I started feeling sick again. I called my mom and told her I was struggling. She had the same hunch as before, that I might be pregnant. I took a pregnancy test, and she was right. The thought of having another child was overwhelming and terrifying. Mom told me I had a choice. This time I knew I wasn't ready to have a baby. Mom flew me out to see her, and we went to a clinic together, where I had an abortion. I'm so grateful my mom was able to support me in this decision. I never told Jake.

After that, it felt like I was going through the motions, moving through life without really living. My days felt monotonous and tiring. I was severely depressed. I had no direction. I didn't know what I was working toward, nor did I have any kind of schedule. I felt alone and isolated. I'm so grateful that Erin was such a good baby. She was so pleasant and never fussed much. I was able to keep her clean, safe, and fed. But everything else in my life felt like a blur, and I saw no end in sight. I missed the days, not so long ago, when I could do whatever I wanted. Now I felt scared and locked in to a life that was not what I thought it would be.

One day, Ashley reached out. We reconnected over the phone, and she came to visit me to see Erin. She was single, and her stories about dating and other adventures made her life seem so exciting in comparison to mine. She also looked extremely skinny. As a new mom, I was still feeling self-conscious about my weight, so I asked her what she was doing to stay thin. She told me she'd met a guy who made a powder called meth that gave you lots of energy and made you lose weight. That sounded like exactly what I needed. (I'd never heard of meth before, so I had no idea how destructive it was.) I told her I wanted some. I arranged for Jake's mom to babysit Erin for the weekend, and we went to meet her guy.

Ashley and her dealer gave me the powder and told me how to take it. I couldn't believe I was supposed to snort the meth up my nose. I will never forget the burning or the horrible smell. But the energy was incredible. I felt amazing. I stayed awake for two days straight, binge-watching movies.

After the two days, Ashley and I drove back to the guy's house to pick up more of the drug. While we were there, I looked at myself in the mirror and thought, *Wow, this is what death looks like.* Yes, the energy was great, but the comedown was unbearable. I felt the lowest low I'd ever felt in my life. I couldn't believe what I had done. I was a mother with responsibilities, and I'd left my baby for two days. I couldn't keep doing this. I called Jake from the dealer's house and told him what I'd done and said I was so sorry. He came immediately to pick me up.

That same day, Jake and I decided to leave Utah and move to California. We knew that staying in our small town, especially now that my mom was gone, was taking a toll on me. Jake hated Utah as well and missed California. We both believed we'd do better there.

While we were packing, Ashley called me. I told her we were moving. She said she wished she could do the same. She was having a hard time with her parents and was surrounded by a lot of bad influences. I invited her to come with us. I told her she would need to get a job, but we could share the car and the apartment.

Jake invited his friend Victor as well, and the next day, the four of us, plus little Erin, crammed all of our things into my Nissan Altima and left for Cali. We drove all night. Erin was such an easy baby and slept the whole way. I remember Jake almost fell asleep at the wheel. I rolled the windows down and talked to him to keep him awake. Finally, we pulled up to Mom's new house in Riverside. It was such a relief when we arrived that I almost got out and kissed the ground.

Since neither of us had a good credit score—no credit score, in my case—Jake's dad signed a lease on an apartment for us. All we had was a bed, a crib, and a few other possessions, but we made it work. Jake and Victor took jobs in construction. Mom helped with babysitting, and I got a job at a hardware store to make some money for gas and car payments.

Ashley got a job, like she said she would, but she was still living like a teenager. She started hanging out with the guys in the apartment next door and drinking a lot. I felt like we were growing apart, and I didn't like all of the drinking around Erin. Ashley eventually moved in with one of the neighbor guys and later joined the Air Force, which ended up being a very positive influence in her life.

Jake was working nights again, so I hardly ever saw him. I started to spend more and more time at Mom's. Whenever I did see Jake, he seemed to take no interest in how Erin and I were doing. All he talked about was motorcycles. He missed being able to take off on his bike and ride to Vegas like he used to. It was painfully clear that he didn't want to be a father—or a husband. Eventually, I stopped going back to the apartment altogether, and Erin and I moved in with my mom and siblings.

Looking back, I can see that Jake and I both had a deep father wound, which is probably what attracted us to each other in the first place. At this point in my life, I had stopped communicating with my father. I'd come to the realization that Dad was interested only in himself, and that writing him letters was a waste of time. But that yearning for his validation had never gone away. I'd just started looking to other men to give it to me. Jake had also grown up desperately wanting his father's approval and time. His mother had a chronic illness, and Jake told me that, growing up, his father would spend weeks away from home due to his work as a pilot. Jake's mother was often exhausted from caring for Jake on her own. Jake's dad had very little patience, and when he returned home from his long trips overseas, he blamed Jake for his mother's complaints (and likely for the absence of domestic comforts he expected upon his return) and would take out his frustration on their son. Jake carried a lot of anger toward his father because of that. He also told me that if he wanted to spend time with his dad, it always revolved around what his dad was interested in, which was mostly rebuilding planes. That was how Jake learned to relate to others, too: After we were married, he told me that if I wanted to spend time with him, then we would be doing what he wanted to do, namely rebuilding ATVs, working on motorcycles, and racing. Even though we'd first connected by riding his motorcycle, this did not foster connection for me and was not how I wanted to spend my time.

I wanted, I *needed*, a responsible man to help me raise Erin, but I didn't feel any sense of security or partnership from Jake. To me, he seemed like a boy, not a man. His failure to become the person I wanted him to be meant he was no longer attractive to me. Without realizing I was doing it, I began to look for something new.

One day, Ashley and I went to a hair salon down the street from my mom's house. As we were leaving, the girl at the front desk asked if we would be interested in meeting the owner. I guess he had seen us come in and wanted to ask me out but thought it would be safer to have his employee ask, rather than approach me directly. I said I would be willing to meet him.

The owner, whose name was Julian, arranged to have a limousine pick Ashley and me up outside the salon. He took us out for the fanciest night I had ever experienced in my life. We went to Yamashiro and sat outside near the fire pit. I tried sushi for the first time and ordered lots of expensive drinks I'd never tried. It was so much fun.

Julian called me a week later and asked if Ashley and I would be interested in going to a Dodgers game. We were thrilled. We had a great time watching the game and ordered beer and hotdogs. The Dodgers won.

Ashley and I continued seeing Julian for about a month until finally he asked me out on my own.

We had a lovely evening. He took me to a beautiful French restaurant called Le Chêne. I tried escargot and thought it was delicious. Julian had a way of convincing me to try new things. He always told me that I would like it, and he was usually right. We flirted and smiled at each other for most of the dinner, and then sat outside and watched the sunset.

Julian was such a gentleman. He was fifteen years older than I was, so that scared me a little, but I felt safe with him. We talked for hours. He told me he was originally from Cuba. His father worked for Fidel Castro for two years—a period of time that was terrifying for Julian's family, especially his mother and two younger sisters. When Julian was eight, his family immigrated to the United States. He didn't know any English, so his teachers at school ignored him. I'm sure it was very stressful and traumatic for him to go through those experiences. Julian and his family had to build their lives from nothing. But they did well for themselves, and Julian was very proud of his family and heritage.

Julian knew that I had a little girl. He told me he was going through a divorce and that he had two young girls of his own. I ended up meeting them that night, and we all got along really well.

After our date, Julian said he was interested in exploring something serious with me. What I found attractive was that he *wanted* to be a father and he wanted to take care of me and my daughter.

What I didn't know at the time, but what I have learned since, is that people tend to look for characteristics in their romantic partners that feel familiar; in other words, they subconsciously look for characteristics that they witnessed in their parents growing up or that mimic wounds they experienced in childhood because that's what they identify with love.

ABOVE: Dad, age 11, outside the Lafferty home in Spring Lake, Utah, on a Sunday morning.

LEFT: Dad in 1966, during his two-year mission to Scotland.

Dad and me (at about six months old) in our home in Glendale, California.

TOP: Me in my high chair, age two, looking at my dad. **ABOVE:** My brother Johnny (age two) and me (three) at our home in Glendale, wearing Mom's shoes. We would play together for hours. (You can see we've tipped the piano bench upside down; we used to pretend it was a boat.)

LEFT TO RIGHT: Me (five), Johnny (four), and my sister Rachel (three), wearing clothes made by Mom, c. 1981. We are playing in our "sandbox"—a pile of sand Dad dumped in the corner of our yard in our Salem home, which we called "Pond Town Fort."

A view of the backyard of Pond Town Fort. On the other side of the fence is the stone monument to the old 1856 fort that was located on the site, as well as the pond where Dad threw our toys. This photo was taken from the tree I loved to climb.

Dad riding in a Fourth of July parade during his 1982 campaign for sheriff of Utah County. His platform: "No man is bound to obey an unjust command."

Dad and me (age six) when we lived at the farmhouse in Orem, Utah. I'm sitting on our cow Daisy, who supplied our family with milk, butter, and cheese.

TOP, LEFT: Rachel (five) and me (seven), 1984. This photo was taken in Idaho when we went to visit Gwen. Mom always dressed us in identical outfits. ABOVE: Visiting Grandpa Lafferty's grave, 1984. Left to right: Johnny (six), Rachel (five), Christopher (three), Mom holding Brian (one), and me (seven). LEFT: Dressed for Sunday dinner at Grandma Lafferty's, 1986. Back row: Johnny (eight) and me (nine); front: Brian (three) and Christopher (five).

TOP: My school pictures from fourth grade (top left) and sixth grade (top right). **ABOVE:** Me, age eleven, holding our cat, Chee-Chee, in the front room of our Pond Town Fort home.

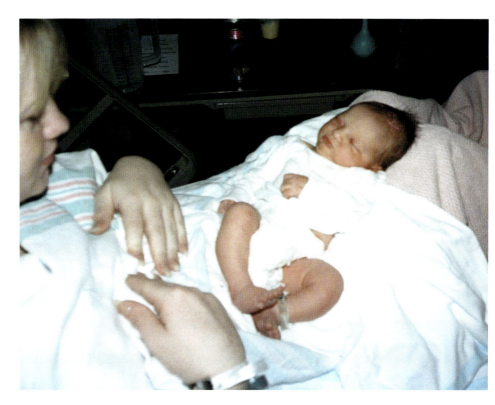

TOP: In the hospital after giving birth to my daughter, Erin, 1996. **ABOVE, LEFT:** Me, right, and Kristi Strack, 2006. **ABOVE, RIGHT:** Grandma Lafferty and me at the Lafferty family reunion in 2009.

It took me a long time to learn how to differentiate between what felt familiar, and thus "safe," and what would truly meet my needs. At the time, the way Julian stepped in and took control (in a way that reminded me subconsciously of my father) felt safe to me. I thought he would be able to give me the love and security I was seeking.

I knew I wanted a partner who wanted to be a father, and that person clearly wasn't Jake. So I told Jake I wanted a divorce. He was very angry. He attacked me verbally and threatened to take Erin from me, but I knew those were empty threats. He wouldn't even know what to do with her. I can see now that he was deeply hurt, so he was lashing out, the way we do when we feel that love is being taken from us.

Jake returned to Utah, and I didn't hear from him for a long time. When he finally contacted me again, about two years later, he told me he'd moved to Las Vegas and was filing for divorce. After I was served the divorce papers, I learned that Jake had met someone new and was planning to remarry. However, after the divorce was finalized, it was still a struggle to get child support from him. The government ended up garnishing his wages a few times. I felt bad about it, but Julian said Jake needed to be responsible for his child.

After he remarried, Jake did eventually show interest in becoming a more involved father for Erin. I thought perhaps he was finally ready to have a family. I later learned that his wife was the one pushing him to see Erin. Luckily, Erin really liked his new wife and always seemed to come home in good spirits, and that's all that really mattered to me. Jake and I eventually figured out a way to co-parent amicably, and we all get along well today.

My relationship with Jake taught me that you can still love someone who wants different things than you do and that love can remain even when you drift apart as a couple. He really was a wonderful friend to me, but the problem was that neither of us felt a strong desire to build a life together. We both wanted different things and found ourselves going through the motions of a relationship based on what was expected of us. And that's okay. We were young, and we were learning. It took me some time to accept that. I thought it was my job to convince him to want what I wanted. In my mind, if we wanted the same things, it meant that he loved me. Once I accepted that wanting different things didn't make either of us wrong, I was able to release my anger and frustration and reach a place of neutrality.

I can see now how not only was I a bit self-righteous in dictating what Jake should want, but I was also looking for an easy out. Something new and exciting had come my way, and I needed to chase that sparkly feeling of love and validation. I didn't feel any love or acceptance for myself, so the validation I craved had to come from an external source. It would take many years, and a great deal of heartache, before I understood this.

CHAPTER 18

1997–2004

AFTER LEAVING JAKE, I found a little studio apartment for Erin and me. The state helped, since I qualified for funding as a single mom. Julian would come visit us there and stay the night. Sometimes he would bring his girls on the weekend. (He was living in Pasadena at the time, renting a room from his business partner. I would occasionally stay the night at his place. He let me know that his situation was temporary and that he was looking for his own space.) We would dress all three girls in the same clothes, and when we went out, people would always comment on what a cute family we were.

My family was sad to hear that Jake and I had split, but they could see that I was making better choices for Erin and myself, and they supported that. It didn't take long for them to love Julian. Family was very important to Julian, and he made a real effort to always include them in family gatherings and dinners.

We celebrated Erin's first birthday at Julian's family cabin at Lake Tahoe. Our daughters got along so well; they were just like sisters. Julian became a father to Erin. She loved him, and he loved her. I thought I had everything I wanted.

Julian told me I should choose a career, so I quit my job at the hardware store and went back to school to become a dental assistant. He supported me while I went to night school to get my certification. After I finished school, I got a great job at a pediatric dentist's office. Soon I was able to pay off my car and other bills. I felt as if my spirit was waking up inside of me. I was growing as a person, and life was becoming colorful again. I felt like I had a purpose.

After about eight months, Julian told me he'd found a home for us, just up the street from my mom in Riverside. It was the perfect size for the five of us and met our needs beautifully. It felt like I finally had the life I wanted and that I'd finally found love. *Real* love, with a real man who was willing to step up as a partner and father.

But after about three years together, things started to change. I began to understand that the things that I'd initially loved, like dressing the girls in matching outfits, was less about us doing something cute together and more about Julian wanting us all to play a certain part. He loved parading us around town and thrived on the compliments he received about his good-looking family. He would instruct me to make sure the girls looked a certain way and even tell *me* how I should dress. That level of micromanagement got very old, very fast, and being put on display made me self-conscious. I began to pull back and tried to find alternative things for us to do instead of dressing up and going out, but Julian was insistent. After I met his ex, I realized that the two of us actually looked quite similar. I couldn't help but wonder if that was part of the reason Julian wanted to date me and parade me and the girls around.

Then we began to argue about how to raise the girls. There seemed to be a double standard with the way his daughters were treated versus how Erin, now four, was treated. Julian's parents didn't accept Erin as their granddaughter. We spent a lot of time with them, almost every weekend, and they were constantly spoiling Julian's girls with expensive gifts and trips to Disneyland and so many clothes there was no place to put them. Their generosity, however, didn't extend to Erin. Again and again, she watched Julian's daughters receive nice toys and clothes and go on fun outings, while she was left out. When Julian's parents babysat the girls, Erin was neglected and excluded. Julian's mother would even say hurtful things to her.

Seeing Erin treated this way triggered my own childhood wounds. I felt fiercely protective of Erin, but whenever I tried to voice my concerns,

Julian always shrugged them off. The little girl inside of me felt like she wasn't able to stand up for herself—or her daughter. I didn't know how to resolve this. I started seeing a therapist to help me express myself, but Julian still refused to talk about it. Anytime I brought the issue up, I was made to feel like I was overreacting. He even told me that I was just being jealous, which triggered me even more and brought up memories of how I felt jealous of my siblings as a child. I was concerned about what raising Erin in these conditions would do to her psychological development.

As the girls grew, I noticed them arguing more among themselves. They would have fights that left Erin in tears, but I felt like I wasn't allowed to enforce boundaries with Julian's daughters. He could be Erin's father, but I couldn't be his daughters' mother. It felt like my hands were tied and I was helpless to intervene on Erin's behalf.

Things were strained with Julian's family, too. He spoke on the phone with his mother at least twice a day. Their conversations were always in Spanish, but I was getting better at picking up what the conversations were about. Sometimes they talked about Erin and me. But mostly his mom seemed to dwell on how sad it was that Julian had split from his daughters' mother. She would ask about the girls constantly: What have they eaten today? Are they okay? Was I treating them well? Is he seeing them enough? Is Erin taking his attention away from them? It got to be very emotionally draining for me.

We visited his parents at least once a week. Julian told me not to speak any Spanish around his mother because she would tell me I sounded ghetto. His mom always sent food home with us to make sure his daughters were eating properly, which made me feel like she thought I wasn't capable of caring for them.

I see now that Julian believed he had failed in his first marriage and was dealing with the disappointment this had brought his family, especially his very Catholic mother, who reminded him of it daily, whether she knew it or not.

Things continued to get worse. After a couple of years as a dental assistant, I told Julian I wanted to go back to school and study psychology, but that didn't fit in with his plan. In fact, he said this idea was an inconvenience to him. He didn't explain why, but it soon became clear: Julian was obsessed with paying as little child support and alimony to his ex as possible. His solution was to have his daughters most of the time, but that meant someone needed to be there to watch them. That someone was me. As a result, not only were my own goals sidelined, but I felt like I'd been tricked into becoming the primary caregiver to his daughters—something we'd never discussed. I'd come home from work, exhausted, and have to make dinner and help the girls with homework and get them into bed while Julian was still out, "stuck in traffic." If I ever lost my temper with the girls, I was made out to be the wicked stepmother. To top things off, Julian refused to spend any money on Erin. He was constantly pressuring me to get child support payments from Jake. I felt myself growing angrier and more resentful.

What made things worse was that Julian had utterly charmed my family, so I had no one to turn to for support. My mom was completely taken with him. So was her sister Maisie, and Maisie's partner, when they came to visit from Scotland. Even my grandma Lafferty adored him. Julian really knew how to wine and dine someone, including me. It was deeper communication we struggled with, but that was hard to convey to my family, who only saw Julian's good manners and charming smile.

It all became too much. I didn't know how to communicate what I was experiencing, and when I tried, Julian would shut down or find a way to punish me. Sometimes he would take his daughters and go do something fun without us. It felt like when I was a girl and my father would push me away or send me to my room while he spent time with my siblings. I could sense my heart shutting down the same way it did when I was a child.

Julian refused to go to counseling with me. I continued to go to therapy on my own, and the therapist put me on antidepressants. I became checked out. The medication made it easier to go through the motions of day-to-day life, but I didn't feel like me. I wasn't creative or inspired anymore. I felt like a robot. The drugs also stripped me of my libido, which opened up a whole new set of problems in our relationship.

Whenever things got particularly bad and I felt a sense of resolve to jump ship, Erin and I would stay with my mom for a few days. Then Julian and I would start to miss each other, and he would ask me to come back. He'd take me on a romantic getaway, and all the bad things that had happened would be forgotten. I didn't know at the time that this was the "reconciliation" phase in toxic and abusive relationships. But soon the "calm" phase would end, the same issues would resurface, and the cycle would begin again.*

Whenever Julian acted displeased or did something controlling, I would immediately feel myself closing up. It scared me how quickly it would happen. One moment I'd be fine, happily in love and wanting to give my partner everything. The next, I'd be triggered by something he said or did and immediately planning my escape. The whiplash made me feel like I was crazy.

Later, I would learn about attachment theory and discover that I had an anxious-avoidant or disorganized attachment style.† For adults with

---

* The cycle of violence, or abuse, is a social theory developed by American psychologist Lenore Walker in 1979 to explain patterns of behavior in abusive relationships. The first phase is "tension-building," when stress builds from the pressures of daily life and the abuser begins to feel ignored or wronged. The second is "eruption" or "acting-out," in which the abuser lashes out in some way, either physically or psychologically or both. The third phase is "reconciliation" or "hearts and flowers" in which the abuser feels remorse and showers their partner with love and affection so they won't leave. The fourth is "calm." During this phase, the relationship feels peaceful, until difficulties inevitably arise again and the cycle starts over.

† Attachment theory is an area of psychology, first developed by British psychiatrist John Bowlby, that studies emotional attachments in humans. There are four primary attachment styles: anxious-ambivalent, anxious-avoidant, disorganized, and secure.

this attachment style, relationships are both their greatest desire and their greatest fear. Anxious-avoidants want intimacy and closeness, but they have trouble trusting others. They have a difficult time regulating their own emotions and so will withdraw whenever they sense that they will be hurt. Because their caregivers growing up were a source of fear instead of safety, anxious-avoidants often find themselves in abusive or dysfunctional relationships that they then struggle to leave because they feel like they can't live without their partner.

At the time, I didn't know that the source of so many of my struggles was my attachment style, which, of course, had been formed in childhood in the ways I had attached to my parents, especially my father. Instead, I blamed myself for failing in yet another relationship. I told myself I should be happy. I had everything I could possibly want, so why did I feel so empty? I wondered if I was self-sabotaging and if my unhappiness was my own fault. But the reality was that I was living with a partner who was trying to control me just like my dad had controlled my mom (and all of us kids), and I was responding to him in the same ways I had responded to my father. I was in the very situation I'd sworn I'd never allow myself to be in, but my spirit had been so worn down, I couldn't see a clear path out.

This went on for seven years. Seven years of resentment and fighting and shutting down. But still, I couldn't give myself permission to leave. Instead, I kept finding reasons to stay. I told myself I lived in a nice home with nice possessions, where we never went hungry or had to worry about money. All of my material needs were met. As someone who was raised in poverty, it was incredibly hard to walk away from that sense of security, even when it came at such a steep cost.

One night, I had a dream about a baby boy. I could see him very clearly. I knew he was my son, and I even knew his name. The dream felt so real, I told Julian about it. He was intrigued. He was the only boy in his family, and he liked the idea of having a son to carry on his family's name. But he said we couldn't have a baby unless we were married. He knew his mom would want us to have a wedding in a Catholic church, as Catholics.

Somehow I found myself attending Mass and taking classes to prepare for a Catholic wedding. I knew I wasn't happy in my life, and yet here I was taking steps to attach myself even more strongly to Julian. Marriage. A baby. Bonds that couldn't be undone. I could see what I was doing, but I couldn't seem to find the strength to change course. I didn't even like going to Mass. All of the rituals and terms and conditions reminded me of going to church as a girl—and the reasons why I'd left.

Catholicism is quite different from Mormonism. Mormons don't have stained glass windows or ornate decorations in their churches (which function as meetinghouses for weekly services and activities, and are open to the public), although they do in their temples (which are used for sacred ceremonies and are closed to the public). Latin is not used in any Mormon services, while some parts of Catholic services may be recited in Latin, and Mormons have a lay clergy instead of a paid, trained one. Catholics don't believe in the Book of Mormon or continuing Scripture. Their views on the afterlife are not the same. But in many ways, the religions felt the same to me. The Mormon sacrament is essentially the same as the Eucharist: The first is bread and water, and the latter is a wafer and wine, but both symbolize the body and blood of Christ and his sacrifice. Both churches want tithes and donations from their members, and both churches are extremely wealthy. And in both churches, I sat among a group of people looking to a leader to tell them who God was, what he wanted from them, and how they should behave.

I'd sit there in that cavernous church, the graphic iconography of a suffering Christ surrounding me everywhere I looked. It was confusing to me that we were meant to feel hopeful by focusing on something so sad and depressing. I always wanted to remember Jesus as kind and loving.

His message, I believed, was that God was a kind and loving god and that we were meant to be kind and loving to each other. Wasn't that the Golden Rule? Do unto others as you would have them do unto you? But in both churches, I only seemed to hear about how angry and vengeful God was and how, if I didn't live my life perfectly, I would be cast out to hell.

I think it's a beautiful thing when people come together to worship, and I would try to focus on that when I attended. But I felt I didn't need a church or religion to have a personal relationship with God. All the times I'd felt closest to Him had been outside of church, in moments of stillness and reflection, when I was free to voice my thoughts and listen for His answer. I wondered why I was being so untrue to myself by going to Mass and taking the classes, but I was so conditioned to please other people, I couldn't find the strength to say no.

Then, one evening, Julian told me to go buy a nice dress because he wanted to take me out to dinner. A limo picked us up from the house, just like our first date. The driver took us to an airstrip where a helicopter was waiting for us. I was shocked. The helicopter flew us over Malibu. I was blown away by the stunning views and Julian's romantic gesture.

Julian reached into his pocket and pulled out an enormous, three-carat diamond ring. I gaped at the ring as he asked me to marry him.

This is it, I heard a voice say in my head. *Everything you've ever wanted, right?* But I felt like I was outside my body, watching myself from a distance. It was someone else saying yes, someone else putting that massive ring on her finger. It wasn't me. I wasn't there.

After the engagement, I felt like I was living in a haze. I knew I was heading down a path that would divide me even further from myself, and that if I married Julian and had his baby, that would be it. There would be no turning back.

One day, I was visiting a neighbor and noticed a poem hanging on her wall. The poem was "Footprints in the Sand." It touched me deeply, and after reading its message of hope and God's unconditional love I began to weep and couldn't stop. I realized I'd felt abandoned by my comforting spirit, the one that always seemed to be with me as a child and would soothe me in times of grief and pain. I wondered if I had failed to feed the relationship that had nourished me and given me the inner strength I needed to overcome life's challenges. I'd lost the belief that, no matter what, I would be all right, that my special protector, whether that was God or my own inner spirit, would always be there for me every time I called upon it for help and guidance.

But I didn't need to feel helpless any longer. I could take control of my life and decide my own fate. I didn't have to do what felt inauthentic to me, no matter how much pressure I faced from the people around me. I was beginning to see that my addiction to being in a relationship was a way to try to fill the bottomless void in my heart.

For the first time in a long time, I felt the haze begin to clear. I began meditating and turning inward. As I did, I felt a tremendous peace come over me, a boldness to march forward. One day, after work, I knelt in front of my bed and did a guided visualization. About ten minutes into the meditation, I heard a voice say very clearly, *"You will not complete what you're here to complete if you stay in this relationship."*

I opened my eyes and looked around, but there was no one there. I felt a peace come over me again. I had total clarity about what I needed to do, and, for the first time, the strength to do it.

I called Gwen and told her about my experience. She said she would welcome me and Erin into her home in Idaho if I needed a place to go. I had been stashing some money away for a couple months, so I packed up my little Nissan Altima, and I returned the ring to Julian. He didn't try to argue with me. He barely said anything at all. We never could communicate with each other about how we were feeling, even when it mattered most.

Looking back, I can see that Julian and I simply had different value systems. We both valued family, but our upbringings, which shaped our view of what a family looked like, couldn't have been further apart. We simply had different worldviews and different paths to follow, and that was okay. We were each doing the best we could.

I took Erin and drove nonstop to Idaho. Flight or fight had hijacked my brain. I was in such a trance I don't remember stopping once. My poor girl didn't understand why we were leaving her dad and sisters, and I felt horrible for causing her pain. But I knew neither of us would be able to thrive if we stayed. It was time for us to go.

CHAPTER 19

2003

ERIN AND I ARRIVED IN IDAHO and moved in with Gwen. At this point, I was twenty-six and Erin was seven. We lived with Gwen for about five months. I felt welcomed there and ready to start fresh. I was great at starting over—I'd done it so many times before. I knew I could take care of all the practical things: job, bills, food. But there was still an emptiness inside of me, a yearning for someone or something else to complete me. I didn't know who or what that was, just that it was missing. I didn't realize that, no matter where I went, there I was. In other words, changing my external circumstances wasn't enough. I had to look inward and do the healing there first if I wanted my life to truly change. Until I did that, I would just continue to repeat the same patterns as before.

I was still grieving Julian and wasn't really ready to date other people. But a few months after our arrival, Gwen and her friend set me up on a blind date with a man named Timothy. He was from Grand View, a town almost two hours west from where Gwen lived in Twin Falls. He was a few years older than I. He had never been married and was just starting a new ATV rental business. He was also Mormon.

Timothy called me before our date, and we talked on the phone for a while. I was impressed. He sounded like a sincere and stable person. Despite my reservations, I agreed to go on the date, *if* I could bring Erin with me. Timothy agreed.

We spent the day riding ATVs and had a lot of fun. What caught my attention was how great Timothy was with Erin. He seemed to genuinely like her. We continued to spend time together, and he taught her how to ride a four-wheeler, feed cows, and do other farm-related tasks. As a child, I'd longed for my dad to spend time with me and teach me things, and I wanted the same for Erin. Watching Timothy step into that role melted my heart.

After everything that had happened with Julian, I had a strong desire to have a family that felt whole and secure. The kind of family I hadn't had as a kid. A family that felt like *mine*. Deep down, I had internalized the belief that I needed a man to help me raise my child. In my mind, that's what a family was: a father, a mother, and children. The fact that I just couldn't seem to get it right on my own cemented this idea further.

Things were progressing a little too quickly with Timothy, but I allowed them to move forward because Timothy seemed like the kind of person who could help me succeed as a parent. He wanted to be a father, and he was looking for a wife who could help him build his business and his home. The stability he offered was attractive to me. And, of course, there was that dream I'd had about the little boy I was certain was my son.

However, I was concerned about the role that religion would play in our lives. I had absolutely no desire to return to the Mormon Church. When we first met, Timothy didn't seem very serious about it, either. He smoked cigarettes and we were intimate on numerous occasions— something that wasn't allowed outside of marriage in the Mormon faith. But my past experiences made me wary.

I appreciated that Timothy seemed to show sincere interest and care for my daughter, almost as if she were his own. However, I still didn't quite trust him. I felt very suspicious of his motives and why he was being so kind. I eventually found out that he had wanted a family for quite a while and that he had dated a woman for some time who had a young girl, but in the end, she hadn't wanted anything serious. That hurt Timothy. He had invested a lot of time in them, so the rejection stung. Part of me wonders now if he viewed me as a replacement for this woman, the way Julian had viewed me as a replacement for his ex.

Would I always be just a cipher for other people to project their past trauma and experiences onto? I wondered. *And would they always be the same for me?*

Timothy and I had been dating for about four months when I started to feel sick. I called my mom, and just like the previous times, she knew exactly what was going on: I was pregnant. I had been using birth control. But as before, it hadn't seemed to make a difference.

I was not thrilled about this development, and neither was Timothy when I told him the news. The first thing he said was, "How will I tell my mother?"

I was taken aback by his response. Not only was it lacking in love and enthusiasm, but it seemed to me to be extremely cowardly. It felt like Jake all over again. I thought to myself, *What a wimp.*

To Timothy, I said, "I'll tell her myself."

Timothy's mom and I had already started building a relationship that seemed to be based on mutual respect. I sensed she liked me and my daughter, and I naturally began to feel close to her. I didn't fully comprehend that his mother was a faithful Mormon who would be *very* concerned about how news of an illegitimate pregnancy would be received in their small town. I, on the other hand, couldn't care less. I'd already been the subject of the worst kind of gossip imaginable. After what I'd lived through growing up in Salem, this felt like nothing in comparison.

Later that week, Timothy and I went to his mom's house for dinner. We were all standing in the kitchen when I decided to break the news to her. She seemed surprised but didn't fall over in horror, the way Timothy had imagined. *See how easy that was?* I thought. Little did I know how much that moment would change his mother's perception of me moving forward.

After that, marriage became the main point of discussion, since we needed to get married before it became obvious that I was pregnant—or at least Timothy's family felt that we needed to get married. But Timothy wasn't enthusiastic; he never took the initiative the way I wanted. I don't recall that he even proposed to me. I just remember that we picked out an engagement ring and drove to Oregon to show his sisters and share the news.

I was willing to overlook the lack of romance and intimacy for one reason: Erin. She seemed to be happy about the wedding and about Timothy. He always took the time to buy her gifts and make her feel special, something she'd never experienced before. This really touched me. One day, while I was at work, Timothy picked Erin up and took her to the local Western store and had her fitted for boots and her first pair of Wrangler jeans. Erin was so excited. Timothy's gestures toward her brought me closer to him. I wanted someone to love my daughter. I wanted her to have a father who was attentive and could offer her guidance, especially after all her years of being slighted by Julian's family. If Timothy was able to fill that role, then that was going to be enough for me. I felt like I didn't need romance. I was even willing to overlook my concerns about religion. I thought that if I could be happy in other areas of my life, then I would even be willing to attend church and do the things his family wanted from me.

I continued to check in with that spirit that had counseled me to move from California to Idaho. I sensed that I needed to make a spiritual change, and I thought that maybe Timothy was the solution. Maybe I was being directed back to church? Even though I hated religion in any form, I was willing to do whatever that spirit was guiding me to do. I kept checking in, asking if this was the place I needed to be.

The thought did cross my mind that I didn't have to marry Timothy. I could have an abortion. I could leave. But I wanted to be brave and do what I thought was the right thing. For Erin and for me.

Timothy and his mom planned most of the wedding. I expressly did not want a big wedding, as I told Timothy many times. I already felt remorse over my first wedding and guilty for the lengths my family had gone to in order to make it a beautiful day, only for the marriage to last less than a year. I wanted this to be a small affair. Something private to the point of being invisible.

My requests were ignored. Timothy was the firstborn, so his getting married was a big deal for his family. I felt a little frustrated, but since his family was paying for everything, I let them make it the way they wanted, which meant an elaborate, formal event. For many girls, this would be a dream come true, but I wanted nothing to do with the fancy clothes and decorations. I didn't want to choose flowers or wedding colors or a cake. I hated that hundreds of people I didn't know were being invited. I didn't want to be seen by anyone, let alone strangers.

Everything felt wrong to me. Once again, it was like I was outside my body, watching from a distance as I was swept along by the current. I didn't know how to communicate what I was feeling. I felt powerless to stop the tide. So I just kept my mouth shut and went along with whatever Timothy's family wanted, ignoring the voice inside of me that was trying to get my attention.

A day before the wedding, my family arrived from out of town. Even though I was pregnant, my brother Christopher and I decided to go for an ATV ride. I suppose I just wanted to do something exciting, to find some small way to rebel.

The speed was exhilarating, as was being out in nature. I felt a thrill knowing my brother was driving behind me. I wanted to show off a bit and let him know that anything he could do, I could do, too. Maybe I was catering to my need for validation.

As I was speeding down the hill, I noticed a large trench up ahead. I immediately let off the gas and hit the front brake at the same time that I hit the trench. The abrupt stop threw me forward. I felt my body rise into the air and sail over the top of the four-wheeler. In what felt like slow motion, the ATV rolled alongside me down the hill.

Oh God, save me, I thought.

When I finally stopped moving, I tried to slowly sit up. I was very dizzy and noticed that my left arm felt numb and tingly. I had the thought that I'd dislocated it, so I attempted to snap it back in place by moving it around and felt myself losing consciousness. I began to pray that I wouldn't black out and that everything would be okay.

At that moment, I had the distinct feeling that I needed to call off the wedding. Something in me knew that I didn't want to go through with it, just like I'd known before I married Jake. But then I thought about all the people who were showing up for me, the distance they had traveled, and how much of an inconvenience it would be to everyone if I backed out. So I just stuffed the feeling down deep and turned my focus back to my body and my concern for the baby I was carrying inside me.

Christopher finally caught up to me and saw me sitting on the side of the trail. Panic-stricken, he quickly picked me up and took me back to the house. Timothy rushed me to the hospital. He kept trying to comfort me, but I just wanted my mom. I asked for an ultrasound to make sure the baby hadn't been harmed. They confirmed that everything looked normal. However, I had broken my clavicle and was told that I would need to wear a brace until it healed. I felt so angry at myself. Why had I done something so risky? I'd put my baby in danger, and now I had to wear a brace at my wedding.

You could still call it off, said a voice in my head. I wanted to talk to my mom about my doubts, but just like last time, I didn't think I had a choice. I set my fears aside and went through with it.

It was a beautiful wedding, but everything felt surreal. I was still a little loopy from the narcotics in my system, and I couldn't quite shake my doubts. It was someone else walking down the aisle, smiling and pretending to be happy.

The worst part was that everything was so lovely. My entire family was there, supporting me, and Erin looked radiant in her flower girl dress. Johnny walked me down the aisle, and I was so grateful for his love and support. But then I looked at Timothy and wondered what the hell I was committing myself to. I immediately felt ashamed of these thoughts. What was wrong with me? Why couldn't I just be happy? Everyone was here for me, and I didn't want to let them down.

After the wedding, Timothy and I rented a place in Mountain Home, a small city about halfway between Boise and Twin Falls, while he worked on building a house for us. We went to church a few times, even though I wasn't really interested in attending. I would frequently get triggered by the way someone would look at me or the questions they would ask about who I was. The leadership wanted to give me a calling (a volunteer position in the church), but I wasn't sure I wanted one. I was asked to be a visiting teacher* to a few of the women in the congregation, and I thought, *Sure, I can go and visit*. But it was short-lived, as my companion always seemed to have something come up.

What reassured me the most was that Erin seemed to be thriving. She was fitting in well at church and at school. She'd made lots of friends and was so excited about everything in her new life, even chores. She was thrilled to become a big sister and have a family that was all her own. I felt a sense of peace knowing that at least I had given her the childhood I didn't have. Maybe I'd finally made up for my mistakes.

At my twenty-week visit, the doctor told us we were having a boy. I felt a rush of emotions. This was the boy I'd seen in my dream. I just knew it. I hoped that meant everything would be all right.

Six months into the pregnancy, Timothy asked me out of the blue, "What if our son has special needs?"

---

* All adult members of the LDS Church are given assignments as a visiting teacher (for women) or home teacher (for men) and are paired with fellow teachers known as "companions." Teachers are expected to visit two to three of their fellow members each month to share a Gospel message and provide support where needed.

I looked at him in shock, confused about where this question was coming from. Timothy's brother had epilepsy, but it was something that had developed later, after puberty. I wasn't sure why Timothy was worried about this, and he never told me.

In retrospect, this would have been the perfect moment to open a dialogue and communicate our expectations to each other. If our child did have a disability, how would we feel? What would we do? What would our lives look like? What would our lives look like regardless? I realized at this point we hadn't had any discussions about how we would approach parenting.

But I said none of this. I still wasn't capable of communicating openly. Years of punishment and suppression as a child had made me physically unable to voice my thoughts, let alone my fears or needs or desires.

"We'll figure it out," I said. That was always my approach: jump in and work out the details later. I never planned ahead. I acted only on instinct. I didn't know at the time that many of these instincts—the panic rising in my gut—were trauma responses. Fight, flight, or freeze. That's all I knew.

I had the sense that if I sat still for a moment and planned ahead, the truth would catch up to me. I might change my mind and choose another course, and that scared me.

I see now that my spirit was trying to talk to me, but I wasn't letting it in. Instead of sitting in stillness and really listening to my inner self, I just kept forging ahead. That was the reason I constantly felt fearful, isolated, and unprepared, like life was always just coming at me. Because it was. Because I was meeting it that way.

If only I had stopped charging ahead and simply stopped to listen and *feel* everything that my body and soul were trying to communicate to me. My spirit was trying to show me the choices available to me, to give me opportunities to prepare for what was coming. But I continued to ignore it.

After this conversation, I decided to go see a psychic to ask about the baby. I wasn't comfortable listening to my own inner guidance, so instead I had to seek advice from somewhere else. The psychic received some kind of premonition about the baby's spine and told me to make sure the doctor didn't use forceps during the birth. I also talked to her about my dad, and she recommended the books *Feelings Buried Alive Never Die* by Karol Truman and *You Can Heal Your Life* by Louise Hay. I went home and immediately ordered the books. However, the moment I started to read, I got really fidgety, almost like I wasn't in my body. I became dizzy and nearly fainted a few times. I was experiencing so many emotions and trying to apply what the books said to my own situation, but it was too much to process. I had to stop reading.

Instead, I focused on preparing for the birth and discussing with Timothy what I wanted. Based on my conversation with the psychic, I wanted to avoid as much physical trauma as possible. I had a doula to support me, and I told Timothy that I didn't want our son to be circumcised. I thought the procedure was unnecessary and too traumatic for a baby, but Timothy did not agree with me. He said our son would be teased when he was older if he wasn't circumcised. I finally gave in, even though I was angry at him for not supporting my decision. As we planned the birth, I continued to feel unheard and unsupported. I believed I had to let Timothy have his own way for there to be peace.

A few months later, the day after Thanksgiving, I stood up to walk into the living room, and my water broke. We quickly grabbed our things and drove forty-five minutes to the hospital in Boise. After six hours of heavy labor, Nathan was born. He was a beautiful baby, weighing in at seven pounds and seven ounces—exactly the same as Erin.

I was so happy to have Nathan. But from the beginning, his birth was overshadowed with challenges. Luckily, the doctor didn't use forceps. However, there were some issues. Even though I was contracting regularly, I was not dilating. The doctor checked me and said I had some scar tissue. He forced my cervix open, which broke my amniotic sac. A huge amount of fluid gushed out, sending Nathan into distress.

Timothy didn't respect my wishes to not circumcise Nathan, and he was also unwilling to cut the umbilical cord, even though I told him it would mean a lot to me. He said he wanted nothing to do with it.

It seemed that I was overturned at every step. I was, however, determined to breastfeed Nathan, even though breastfeeding was a foreign concept to Timothy, and his whole family thought it was weird. "What the hell do you think breasts are for?" I wanted to shout at them.

The challenges continued as Nathan grew. At nine months old, he still was not able to hold his head up for very long and refused tummy time. I noticed that when he was in his bouncer he wouldn't rest his weight on his legs. I was still nursing him and thought maybe the antidepressants I was on might be affecting him, so I stopped taking them immediately. I thought physical therapy might help, so I took Nathan to the doctor.

The doctor took one look at Nathan and then stepped outside the consulting room. I could hear him speaking quietly with some of the other physicians in the hallway. Finally, he stepped back inside and, handing me a piece of paper, told me I should take Nathan to get a CT scan. Shocked, I asked why. He said it looked like Nathan had hypotonia or "floppy baby syndrome," a symptom of spinal muscular atrophy (SMA) type II. He told me not to Google anything, just to take Nathan to the hospital.

I scooped my baby up and rushed out of the doctor's office. I immediately called Timothy and told him what had happened. He hurried home, and we talked about what the doctor had said. I was in complete denial. I refused to accept that anything was wrong with my child. But I was scared. I did exactly what the doctor had told me not to. I Googled "floppy baby syndrome" and found a video of a baby who made the exact same arm movements that Nathan did in his high chair. Reality started to sink in, and I began to cry. Sobbing, I called my mom. She tried to reassure me that Nathan didn't have SMA because it's a genetic condition and Nathan had good genes. But after seeing the videos online, I couldn't deny it any longer.

Timothy and I got a referral to Primary Children's Hospital in Salt Lake City for an evaluation. A neurogeneticist whose research was instrumental in the diagnosis and treatment of SMA happened to be there the day of our appointment, and was able to see us. She walked into the room, looked at Nathan, and then turned to me and said, "He has SMA type II."

I felt myself going numb as she explained what that meant. Nathan would only live into young adulthood. We would need to buy special equipment to support him, and he would need twenty-four-hour care and assistance for the rest of his life. The doctor said that Nathan would be able to participate in a new study with a drug they believed would slow down his atrophy.

Next, they had us meet with someone who walked us through the equipment Nathan would need and the procedures he would have to undergo. She explained that we needed to schedule a surgery to have a MIC-KEY button placed in his stomach for feeding and that he would need to have his esophagus wrapped around his stomach to keep him from aspirating and dying from secondary pneumonia. He would also need a cough assist machine and a BiPAP ventilation machine to help him sleep at night. In the near future, he would also need rods put in his back so that his spine wouldn't collapse and pinch off his air supply.

I sat there, white as a ghost, clinging to my sweet baby. *This has to be a nightmare*, I thought. *This can't possibly be happening right now.* It was a struggle to breathe. Somewhere inside of myself, I felt a part of me die. Where was that source of inner strength I'd felt before? I'd never felt so afraid in my life.

There was nothing I could do to control what was happening. I couldn't protect my son from all of the struggles he was going to face. I couldn't save him.

I felt like I had failed as a mother.

After the appointment, I called my mom and numbly relayed what the specialist had told us. This time she was the one who cried while I sat there, dry-eyed. I told myself that I needed to keep it together. I needed to be strong for my son. But really, I was disassociating. I was suppressing my emotions as deeply as I could because the reality of what I was feeling was too terrifying to face. Instead, I moved forward on autopilot, disconnecting from the pain of my situation.

Nathan's fundamental needs were overwhelming. He had sleep apnea, which made it hard for him to get enough oxygen. He slept in bed with me so I could monitor him during the night. He had to be turned over almost every hour; otherwise, his little body would get sore. That meant I got very little sleep. He was one year old at this point, but caring for him was more challenging than caring for a newborn.

We started taking regular trips to Primary Children's Hospital, driving about four-and-a-half hours each way. Timothy and I both felt stretched thin. Timothy grieved in his own way, mostly by keeping to himself. He would leave early in the morning, and I wouldn't see him until dark. I would know he was returning home because his dog, Toby, would start barking as soon as Timothy pulled into the driveway. Meanwhile, I felt like I was drowning under the weight of our family's needs, with no time or means to take care of myself. I'd once again found myself back in the same place I always seemed to end up in my relationships: alone.

I desperately wanted to make things right. I wanted to be a good wife and mother. I wanted to have the perfect *Little House on the Prairie* family—the thing I'd never had as a child. With every part of me, I wanted this. This was my opportunity to finally create it, I told myself. Even with Nathan's condition, I could rise above this challenge. I could be the perfect mother to him and Erin, and the perfect wife to Timothy. But there was something inside of me preventing it. Every time I tried to step into that idealized role, a part of me started to buck like a wild horse. In my childhood, I'd been conditioned to believe that being a good wife meant being an obedient wife, and nothing triggered me more than those words: "an obedient wife." It would immediately spark memories of my mother lying on the farmhouse floor while my dad choked her, screaming at her to be an obedient wife. It would unearth other memories, too—of being confined in my high chair, of being called a liar and a bad kid, of Dad beating me until I learned to obey.

When I got triggered that way, I immediately felt the urge to run. I'd put on my Rollerblades or sneakers and take off, sometimes running for eight miles or more. Part of me wanted to just keep running and never go back. Because I never, ever wanted to be trapped the way my mom had been trapped. I never wanted to suffer at the hands of a man who was supposed to love me and provide for me. I could sense how close I was to suffocating in my situation, and all I wanted was to escape.

I believed that God wanted me to be a good wife and mother. I just didn't know how. *What is wrong with me?* I wondered. *How am I ever going to heal this pain, this dysfunction I'm always running from?*

Healing seemed impossible, so I broke my promise to God. I stopped seeking out my inner spirit. I wanted to lean on my spirit for support, but I couldn't. I couldn't open myself up. It was easier to stay numb and shut down, to keep plodding along in the dark and focus on surviving. That, at least, was something I knew how to do.

We finally got the equipment Nathan needed to help him breathe and sleep better. The state helped us with funding for all the equipment and therapies he required. It was a godsend. I could finally sleep again.

As my energy returned, I made a renewed effort to improve our situation, to lift it above survival mode. There had to be a way to salvage my relationship with Timothy and find a balance in our dynamic that felt good to me. To be a better mother to Nathan.

I began reaching out to other mothers who had children with SMA and started building a support network. I tried to make our monthly trips to Primary Children's as light and happy as possible.

My efforts began to make a difference. After one weekend of tests and evaluations, I remember Timothy said to me, "You know, at times, I feel like things are so heavy and that our problems are so great, but when I see all the other parents and what they're going through with their children, it makes me feel better about our situation because at least we can manage this."

I felt like, maybe, there was hope for us.

Not long after this, I came across a book about mothers who were also powerful businesswomen. I loved the idea that a mother had permission to run a company and be seen as a leader, that she could have money and resources and power and not be dependent on a man. As I read the book, an empowering energy began to rise up inside of me. I wasn't sure what it meant. Was it a call to start my own business? I brushed the thought aside. I didn't know the first thing about starting a business. Besides, I had a child with disabilities who needed me 24/7. But the thought persisted.

I sat down on the couch and continued reading until I reached the end. It was as if I could see myself as this woman. I was intimidated by the thought, but also excited and inspired. I had no idea how it would be possible, but decided I could start by getting a job. It would at least get me out of the house and give me some financial independence.

I can see now that, even though the ideas in the book genuinely resonated with me and I do have an innate drive to be self-sufficient and successful in business, in this particular moment, I was really just seeking a way to escape my current situation. But God knew my heart and that I needed to feel like myself again. I still wasn't reaching out to my inner spirit, but the spirit world was supporting me and sending me clues that would allow me to eventually gain more illumination. We always have free will, and no matter whatever decision we make, there is always a path forward.

I told Timothy that I wanted to start working again, even if it was part-time.

His response was: "Who will take care of Nathan?"

I told him we could get a babysitter. I knew the perfect person I would trust to watch my son, a woman named Hailey who was married to one of Timothy's friends. She had two boys of her own, just one and two years older than Nathan.

Timothy finally relented, and we hired Hailey. I was right about her. Hailey cared for Nathan like he was her own, which brought a lot of peace to my heart.

I applied for a job at a local dental office, since dental assisting was something that I knew how to do well. They hired me right away.

Being around other people and doing something useful helped me feel less constricted at home. I felt guilty for "leaving" my children, but it also gave me a purpose beyond motherhood. I wanted to serve in other ways.

The energy I felt from working again propelled me forward. I found I was growing more and more antsy whenever I was at home. I needed more outlets. One day I came across a YouTube video of a father who ran marathons with his son in a wheelchair. I felt moved by the video and wanted to show Nathan his limitlessness.

I asked Timothy if this was something he would be interested in doing. He said no. He had no desire to go on a jog or a hike, let alone run a marathon. I decided it was up to me. This freaked Timothy out, but I was eager to try it. Idaho winters are long and cold, and I was sick and tired of being stuck inside. At the first sign of spring, I bought a jogging stroller, with some help from my mom. Then I strapped on my Rollerblades and took off with Nathan. I bladed for sixteen miles and didn't want to stop. I could have kept going for hours. It was exhilarating!

Nathan enjoyed our runs at first, but eventually I realized it was my dream, not his. I was the one who was still desperate for an escape. So I gave up on the marathon idea. However, I continued to look for other ways to make the best of my situation.

Meanwhile, Timothy was growing steadily frustrated with my new interests. He never talked to me about how he was feeling, but I would hear him rant on the phone to his mom and sisters for hours about how I was reading "evil" books and getting worldly ideas in my head. As a result, Timothy and I began to grow distant again. I felt infinitely frustrated. Why couldn't God make Timothy see that my ideas were the perfect solution for us?

I started losing it. I was back to feeling sleep-deprived, overweight, unsupported, and confined. I couldn't believe that once again, I'd ended up in the very situation I'd tried so desperately to avoid. It felt like I was living the definition of insanity: repeating the same thing over and over, expecting a different result.

Things reached a tipping point when Timothy's beloved dog, Toby, who he'd had for fourteen years, passed away. Nathan's diagnosis and surgeries. Toby's passing. My determination to find work and interests outside of the house. It all compounded for Timothy. He began to fully check out. Unfortunately, neither of us knew how to communicate what was in our hearts. What could have brought us closer only drove us further apart.

CHAPTER 20

2006

WHILE I LIVED IN IDAHO, my communication with my dad was infrequent. There was too much happening in my life for me to think much about him. We were still in touch, but I only heard from him a few times a year.

One day, out of the blue, I received a letter from him. He said he was excited to share with me that a new person had come into his life: a woman named Kristi. Dad told me they'd met under significant circumstances and wanted to know if he could connect us. He told me Kristi was younger than I was, and married with five children all under the age of nine.

Who is this person? I wondered. Why would a mother of five kids suddenly be so compelled to seek out this connection with my dad? I was curious about her fascination with him, and more than a little suspicious of her motives, but I agreed to meet her. I figured if I spent time with her, I'd be able to identify her angle.

Kristi lived in Springville, Utah, so during one of our trips to Primary Children's, I arranged a meeting with her in Salt Lake City. The plan was that she would come to the hospital and we would ride back to Idaho together, where she would stay with me for a weekend. This would give us ample time to learn about each other.

When Kristi arrived, I thought she seemed like a nice girl, though there was something a little off about her. She had long blonde hair and definitely looked younger than me. But she had a very friendly and familiar aura to her. She knew a lot about my dad and had much to share.

Timothy drove Nathan home, and I rode back with Kristi in her minivan. On our drive, Kristi explained that a few months ago she'd had a dream. In her dream, my father came to her and said, "My name is Dan Lafferty. Will you please help me?" After she woke up, she searched "Dan Lafferty" on the Internet and almost fell out of her chair when she found my dad. But she took her dream as a sign from God that she couldn't ignore. She contacted the prison and got my dad's inmate number so she could write him a letter. She described her dream to him and asked if they could meet. My dad agreed, and she began to visit him every week.

Kristi believed she'd been called by God to help my dad. She shared with me some of the stories that my dad had told her about his childhood. One that stood out to me was the story of his baptism. The day after he was baptized, Dad was punished for teaching his brother to roll cigarettes from hay. My grandfather smelled his breath and told him he needed to go to his room and pray for forgiveness and wait for him there. Dad told Kristi he couldn't remember the details of what happened next; he seemed to have blocked the trauma from his conscious memory. It's likely he was beaten. The part of the memory he clung to the most was how disappointed his mother was.*

---

* Dad recounted the event to me as well: "I knew my baptism was an important event and my dad was so careful to make sure I was prepared, showed me how to hold his wrist with one hand and my nose with the other so I wouldn't get water up to my nose. . . . It was more of a fun thing getting baptized, at least for me, but as I was coming up out of the water, Grandma was there waiting with a towel, and I was a little taken aback at how for her it was apparently much more significant. She said something like, 'There, you have done it,' like I had just gotten into heaven or something. And here comes the curious part. The very next day I was teaching my brother Mark how to make a cigarette out of [hay leaves]. . . . Grandpa must have seen the butts and told me to let him smell my breath, and I was busted. I don't remember if I got the belt or spanked . . . but I do remember he sent me to my room to pray, and I was worried about what might be coming next. . . . It's more funny to me now, except to think about how disappointed Grandpa and Grandma must have been. But that doesn't really bother me anymore really because I believe everything is predestined and Grandpa and Grandma died and went to paradise to rest from being here in hell before volunteering to play another part and come back. During that time in paradise where we see the big picture again and can study the script of the next part we get to play . . . they probably were able to see the script of the part I am playing, which would give them some consolation about some of the things I did that made them confused. I'm sure they would get a laugh about the smoking hay leaves incident."

Kristi shared other details about Dad's childhood with me; however, since Dad shared them with her and not me, I don't feel comfortable disclosing them publicly. At the time, I didn't want to know these details. However, it did begin to explain why Dad had done some of the things he had, including why he had treated me so harshly as a child.

Kristi told me that my dad loved me very much. She said he missed me the most after we left the farmhouse and that my absence had affected him deeply. I was surprised and a little touched to hear that, though as a child I never would have guessed that was the case, and as an adult I was wary.

My dad also talked to Kristi about the day he murdered Brenda and Erica. It was the first time I'd heard any of the details, since no one in my life had ever wanted to talk about it and I'd been too scared to ask him directly. It was easier to hear it from Kristi. However, she was very emotional about it, and I could tell it was affecting her. But she was determined to keep the connection going. She believed Dad needed someone to help him see that what he had done was wrong. She told me she did a therapeutic process with Dad, asking him to see himself as a child and to view the things he had done from that perspective. She said it was profound to hear him admit that he'd done a terrible thing.

I didn't know how much to believe or what to make of Kristi. She shared some pretty intense things from her own life, namely that she was addicted to pain medication—she was popping opiates like candy while we talked—and that her sister had died from a heroin overdose. Kristi seemed to manifest chaos everywhere she went. On our drive, we experienced a string of wild incidents. Kristi didn't like to wear her seatbelt and said that if it was God's will that she die, then why would she stop it by wearing her seatbelt? That logic sounded all too familiar to me. It was the kind of reasoning I'd heard from my dad growing up. Kristi also had a hard time holding still and seemed to drive erratically at times, which scared me. (I made sure to wear *my* seatbelt.) At one point, we were driving next to a semitrailer when out of nowhere, a huge rock hit the windshield right in front of her. Another time, a bird flew in front of the minivan and ended up getting lodged inside the grill. On a separate trip to see me, Kristi said that she drove off the road and into the ditch near my home but somehow got out and was able to make it to my place safely.

Even though Kristi seemed a little off-kilter, it was clear that she had a lot of compassion for my dad. She seemed to truly want to help my family heal, and she was convinced my father needed my love and support to change. She believed she was helping him atone for what he had done. Kristi told me that she'd encouraged my dad to write letters to Brenda's family as well as mine, asking for forgiveness. I saw the letter Dad wrote to Brenda's parents, which Kristi hand-delivered, but I never received a letter. I don't think my mom or siblings did either.

My dad also viewed his connection with Kristi as divine intervention. He admitted that Kristi had helped him make sense of his past. However, he interpreted Kristi's appearance in his life as confirmation that he was on the right path and that God was guiding him. He believed it meant that he'd be getting out of prison very soon and that Kristi was going to play an important part in his next role. He described it as God "holding a carrot in front of me."

Kristi came to visit me three times, and I began to think of her as my friend. On her third visit, her husband and kids came to stay as well.

At her urging, I decided to visit my dad. The trip was an ordeal. First, I had to drive all the way to the prison. Then I had to go through the involved security process and deal with the rude treatment from the officers and the inmates banging on the windows to get my attention. It was very stressful. When I finally made it to the visitation booth, seeing Dad again was surreal. It had been at least eighteen years since I'd seen him in person. There were a lot of nerves for both of us, and I felt such a jumble of emotions. But he was so excited to see me, which made the trouble of going through security worth it. He kept noticing my hands and commenting on how they looked like Grandma's. He had so much to share that it all seemed to want to come out at once. Listening to him speak, I was overcome with emotion. I was excited to see him again, but angry as well. It wasn't just my old anger rising to the surface—anger over my childhood, over the deep trauma he had caused our family and others through his crimes—I was also angry that he had been so forthcoming with Kristi, a total stranger. He'd shared all of my personal information with Kristi, yet he was protective of her privacy. It confirmed to me that he didn't see me as my own person. I was just an extension of him. Maybe I felt some jealousy too. Why was he so warm toward this unknown woman but not his own daughter?

But after we talked more, my heart began to soften. I could see that my dad truly did want to have a connection with me, in his own way. My eyes filled with tears, and this made him emotional as well. He didn't like to cry, so he tried to keep the conversation really light.

After that, I began visiting my dad twice a month, even though the visits continued to be a challenge for me. On a couple of occasions, the officers refused to let me in—once because I was wearing a bra with an underwire and another time because my address had changed and I hadn't been cleared on my dad's visitation list. The time always went by quickly, and I remember feeling sad when I had to say goodbye but also relieved as I pulled out of the prison parking lot, after showing my driver's license for the fifth time and popping my trunk to have it examined, just to make sure I wasn't helping anyone escape. The way the officers threw my license back at me always felt so horrible, as if I wasn't welcome there. I felt so angry that they were treating me this way, like I didn't deserve any respect just because I was visiting an inmate.

One time I took Timothy and the kids with me. Timothy didn't really interact with my father; he just paced around the room with Nathan in his arms while Erin and I talked to Dad. He never went with me again. Before we went to see my dad, I explained to Erin why he was in prison. She was quiet after I told her and seemed a little apprehensive, but she was still open to meeting him. During our visit, Dad mentioned that he had done God's work and would soon be getting out. This confused Erin, since she knew why he was there. She asked, "What if you don't get out?" Dad laughed at her innocence. He thought her question was precious. He told her he believed he would be released. Erin shrugged and said, "Okay." Dad loved visiting with Erin—he called her "Flash"—and she enjoyed getting to know him. She didn't seem uncomfortable visiting the prison, the way Timothy did. Erin made an effort to maintain a relationship with him, writing him letters and sending him cards for some time afterward. But he wasn't very good at replying to her or asking her about her life, and they eventually fell out of contact.

Most of the time, I went with Kristi. She wanted to be a witness to the healing process between my father and me. Plus, she wanted to see him. The times I went with her were interesting because I saw a side of my father I wasn't used to seeing. He was very flirty and giggly with her, commenting on the letters and conversations they'd previously had, and mostly ignoring me. I wondered why I was even there. It was then that I began to see that they were having an affair, which made me extremely uncomfortable. Kristi was married, and Dad was twice her age. Their relationship seemed inappropriate. However, Kristi's husband, Benjamin, knew about her relationship with my dad and also visited him often, so I figured if everyone involved was consenting to the relationship, it was really none of my business. Kristi loved Dad, and he loved her. I wanted them to be happy, so who was I to judge? My dad to this day still talks about how wonderful it was to be loved by her and all the things they shared together.

Kristi really believed that things were moving in a certain direction— I think she thought she could single-handedly reform him—so she would get frustrated when my dad would revert to calling himself a prophet and talk as if he were God's puppet. I wish I would have just told her that Dad was never going to change.

Timothy was scared as hell by all these developments. He didn't like me visiting Kristi, and he definitely didn't like me visiting my dad.

My mom shared Timothy's reservations about Kristi. She thought it was suspicious that this strange girl would just show up out of nowhere and take such an interest in our family. She didn't like Kristi and refused to interact with her.

Additionally, my father was up for parole, which added further stresses to my family's life. His parole, however, was denied. I'm not sure what he said to the parole board, but they clearly didn't think he was fit for release.

After a few months of rising tensions, Timothy put his foot down and insisted I stop visiting my dad. He wanted me to stay home and "be a family." He essentially told me I had to choose between him and my dad. I was confused and conflicted. Yes, my dad had done horrific things, but he was my family, too. My visits had helped me see him in a different light. Kristi was the bridge between us. She acted as a sort of buffer, filtering and softening our communication. Dad shared things with her that he would never have shared with me directly, and Kristi was able to convey that information in a way that was more palatable for me to hear. I could see that she truly loved and had compassion for him. I thought to myself: *If a total stranger can love my dad, why can't I?*

My reconciliation with my dad made me wish Timothy and I could also rebuild our relationship. More than anything, I longed to be understood and seen and heard by my husband. But it seemed as though Timothy wasn't able to hold that space for me. Instead, he just complained to his mom and sisters about what I was doing. I decided to hide my interactions with Kristi and my dad from Timothy, which made me feel dishonest. But I felt I had no other choice. I knew Timothy would never understand.

On top of all this, Timothy was a workaholic. I hardly ever saw him, except late at night. I longed for connection and presence, but he was exhausted and had none to give me. We never went on date nights or had real alone time, let alone deep and meaningful conversations. He just wanted to gossip and complain about work. I missed the intimacy that Julian and I had shared and was frustrated that Timothy didn't have a romantic bone in his body. I'd thought I could live without romance, but I was wrong. There was no passion in our sexual lives, either. Having been raised LDS, Timothy had a lot of internalized shame around sex and intimacy. He treated sexual desire almost like a disease.

As time went on, I saw only the things that weren't working, the things Timothy was doing wrong. But if I'm being honest, the truth was I had developed an obsession with Kristi and the work she was doing with my dad. I had become more intent on "saving" my dad than I had my own family, and this rightfully terrified Timothy.

In retrospect, I can't believe the shit I put Timothy through or how selfish I was. I was so intent on healing my own pain, it became impossible for me to see the pain I was causing him. It was unfair of me to expect him to be happy with how I was changing the terms of our relationship, especially when my behavior was so manic and unpredictable. I felt like I couldn't be the wife Timothy wanted or the mother Nathan needed. It seemed like too big of a gap between who I was and who I thought I needed to be, and I felt guilty for depriving Timothy of the kind of partner he wanted. This cycle of guilt and shame and self-loathing made it impossible for me to find a healthy path forward.

One day, in the spring of 2006, I reached a breaking point. The impulse to run hit me stronger than ever before, and making a sudden decision, I packed up the kids and the things we needed and loaded all of us into Kristi's van while Timothy was at work. We drove six hours to Kristi's house. I didn't tell anyone where I was going. I had Nathan's equipment, and I knew what he needed and how to take care of him.

It's so clear to me now that I was unconsciously re-creating my childhood by running from Timothy the way my mom had run from my dad.

Timothy was nothing like my father, but in my mind, he was filling that role—the husband controlling my life and limiting my freedom, telling me who I had to be. It was easy to make him the villain, the way my dad had been to my mom, while ironically, I was the one choosing the literal "villain" (my dad) over my imaginary one (my husband). Our inability to communicate and the growing hurt between us compounded to create a situation that I couldn't see a clear path out of.

However, after four days, the reality of what I'd done started to sink in. I'd left Timothy without a word of explanation, just like I'd left Jake and Julian whenever I got triggered. I was living my childhood and past relationships all over again. The difference was that this time I wasn't being abused. There was no danger. But the sense of being trapped, of not having my voice heard, had triggered me so badly, the only thing that felt safe was to run.

I saw how much Nathan, who was three now, was missing his dad, and as I looked at Erin, I suddenly had a glimpse of all the shit I'd dragged her through. This wasn't fair to my kids, but I didn't know what to do. I felt like a lost little girl. I knew I needed help to deal with my trauma in a healthy way. Otherwise, I was afraid I would keep repeating this pattern for the rest of my life.

I called Timothy. He was so relieved to hear my voice. He'd been worried sick. I apologized for scaring him and told him where we were. He left immediately and drove the full six hours to come pick us up.

After we were reunited, Timothy broke down and said that he never wanted to experience the fear of losing us again. We both cried and held each other. But even then, there was a part of me holding back. I didn't know how to express everything I was feeling inside. I only knew how to reassure him and placate him so he felt safe. Yet my true self was yearning for something bigger than that sleepy little town that stank of stagnation and small-mindedness. Going home felt like going back to prison.

I couldn't yet see that I was continuing to repeat the same pattern with Timothy that I had in all my relationships. I was attaching myself to a partner far too quickly, without taking the time to get to know him. Hell, I'd jumped so quickly from relationship to relationship, I hadn't even taken the time to get to know myself! But the wounding and emptiness at my core demanded to be filled with external validation. I was so codependent, so desperate for love, for someone to tell me I was worthy, that I didn't know how to live on my own. I would jump into a lifelong commitment, only to change my mind and run the moment I got triggered—which was inevitable, since I hadn't taken the time to heal any of my childhood wounds.

Even today, I recognize in myself that if I feel trapped in any way, real or imagined, I will look for a way to escape or run. I've dedicated so much time to healing this wound inside of me, but I know there is a part of me that will never feel truly safe. The impulse to run is one of my biggest regrets and failings as a mother. But I've learned that shaming myself is not the answer. The only way forward is through self-compassion and forgiveness. God knows my heart and how hard I have tried.

In Grand View, however, the intent of my heart was not known. I couldn't find anyone to connect with there. Everyone seemed to have already made up their minds about me, no doubt due to Timothy's family, who wielded a great deal of influence in the town.

Not long after I returned home, the girls I worked with at the dental office called Timothy's mom and told her that I was having an affair with one of the patients. This was patently untrue. I have no idea why they said this. I suppose I must have spoken with a little too much enthusiasm to one of the patients. Or maybe they were curious about my recent disappearance and wanted to spread nasty rumors.

Timothy immediately confronted me. I was shocked and told him they were lying, but I couldn't convince him. It felt like I couldn't win for losing. It was like I was wearing a scarlet letter. No one wanted anything to do with me.

I don't know why Timothy's mom and sisters hated me so much, but they formed their opinion of me early on. All of Timothy's sisters lived near each other in Oregon. They were all active Mormons and stay-at-home moms. I, on the other hand, was the exact opposite: When I met their brother, I was a working single mom who had been divorced. Divorce was still stigmatized in the LDS Church, and divorced women in particular were viewed as failed wives and mothers. And then, of course, there was the fact that Nathan had been conceived before Timothy and I were married, and that I was no longer Mormon. Timothy's family also *hated* that I drank coffee. Add to this the scandal attached to my family, and I think it was too much for them.

The Thanksgiving after Nathan was diagnosed, we went to Oregon to visit Timothy's sisters. On Black Friday, I went shopping with all the women. The only time I'd ever gone shopping on Black Friday was with my dental office coworkers in California—the dentist would treat all the hygienists to a shopping spree. While we were out shopping, I grabbed a pair of pants for myself. Timothy's sisters, in contrast, bought items exclusively for their husbands and children. They seemed shocked that I hadn't done the same. I think they truly believed I was a horrible person for not putting my husband's and children's needs above my own.

Timothy's mother displayed photos of all the grandkids in her home. After that trip, Erin's photo was taken down.

On another occasion, we attended a family member's wedding. I approached Timothy's sisters, and they all physically turned their backs to me. I kept trying to make conversation. One of Timothy's sisters had recently had a baby, so I said, "Oh my goodness! She's so precious. Can I hold her?"

"No!" his sister spat and walked away.

I was stunned by her reaction, but I tried hard not to show it. I struggled through the wedding for as long as I could, weathering everyone's cruel glares, until it felt like I was disassociating. Finally, I found Timothy and, crying, told him I wanted to leave.

Instead of supporting me, he said, "You need to apologize to my family."

I think the fact that Timothy wouldn't stand up for me was what finally drove us apart. His mother and sisters treated me unkindly right in front of him—on countless occasions—and he never said a thing in my defense. He took their word over mine, and if he ever had issues with something I'd said or done, he complained to his mom instead of coming to me.

I'm sure Timothy's family thought I was selfish for working instead of staying home with Nathan all day. Or maybe they could see how unhappy Timothy was. Whatever the reason, they couldn't relate to what I was going through and refused to welcome me, or Erin, into their family. I felt like an outcast.

The image that came to me very strongly at this time was the archetype of the witch: the woman who lived on the fringes of society and did things differently. She challenged patriarchal authority and tradition, so she had to be accused of wickedness and removed.

I just wanted to be around people who loved me for who I was, and the only people who seemed to be capable of doing that at the moment were Kristi and my dad.

Even my mom didn't seem to be on my side. She didn't understand my wanting to leave Timothy—just as she hadn't understood when I'd left Julian or Jake. I thought she, of all people, would be able to relate to my situation. However, I think my mom considered Timothy to be a loyal partner who was providing for me and my children. She couldn't comprehend leaving what to her appeared to be a safe and stable environment. I struggled to express to her that the price of that security was my freedom and very identity.

Once again, I felt like I was on my own.

In a last-ditch effort, I convinced Timothy to go to couple's therapy. He agreed, and we found a counselor in town. At first the sessions seemed to give me a safe outlet to voice my emotions and finally feel heard. But Timothy was unable to open up. He continued to blame me for how he felt, and whenever I tried to express my needs, his response always seemed to be, "Yeah, but . . ." and then he'd turn the issue back on me. I was beginning to regret having ever married him. Timothy was a good father and had helped me raise Erin for almost five years at this point, but I was resigned to the fact that things just weren't going to work out.

We continued the sessions for a while without making much progress. We were never able to say the things we truly felt. I longed to look Timothy in the eye and say, "Look, Timothy, I love you, and what I want is something different than what you want. But we have a child together, and I will show up. I want to create a positive life together. Are you willing to co-create that with me?" But I couldn't. Because, deep down, that wasn't what I really wanted. I wanted freedom. I wanted to live! To experience joy, excitement, romance. But my life had none of those things. I felt more closed in and depressed than ever.

The therapist asked me to make a scrapbook of my life, explaining that this had been a very powerful tool for his other clients in their healing journeys. I agreed to make one. As I was looking through pictures of my childhood, I came across a photo of my parents as newlyweds. When I looked at the photo, so many memories and emotions flooded in. I didn't know how to deal with the sadness, the anger, the loss. I felt desperate for a source of assurance and support, someone who could fill the role of a loving parent or mentor and help me process everything I was going through, but I had no idea where to find such a person.

I returned to *Feelings Buried Alive Never Die* and read the whole thing. I was finally starting to see how I was reliving my trauma over and over. I knew I needed to let these patterns from my past go for good. I also came across Sylvia Browne, a psychic who caught my attention when I saw her on *The Montel Williams Show*. The moment she opened her mouth, I was drawn in. She was answering the audience's questions, and her presence awoke something within me. I bought her book *Past Lives, Future Healing*, and couldn't put it down. In these books, I learned about sitting in stillness and using visualization techniques to evoke healing on a subconscious level. It was also the first time I learned about hypnosis. This technique fascinated me.

Timothy saw the books I was reading and said they were evil. He made it very clear he was very uncomfortable with me reading this type of material. He said it was witchcraft and that his religion warned against it.

I stared at Timothy in disbelief. I couldn't believe he'd literally called me a witch. It was the strangest confirmation of the feelings I'd had earlier. Timothy, his family, and the community really did see me as a witch. I was a wicked woman. A bad mother. A corrupting influence.

Instead of being triggered, I leaned into this label. I embraced it. I felt powerful. I told Timothy no one was going to tell me what I should and shouldn't read. It wasn't like I was forcing him to read the books, too.

But Timothy wouldn't let it go. He asked if I would be open to listening to the plan of salvation, which is Mormonism's explanation for the purpose of life (where we came from, why we're here, and where we're going). I laughed at him. The church was the first place I'd ever felt like an outcast, like a witch—wicked and impure. I knew the church leaders would try to control me and tell me how I should and shouldn't live my life, that I should be an obedient wife and stay home with my children and not seek any knowledge beyond the bounds of what they approved. No, thank you. The church had already failed me. The times I went to church were some of the darkest in my life, and not a single member lifted a finger to help me or my family.

I didn't want anything to do with Mormonism, or any religion. I preferred the personal experiences I would have whenever I managed to get very still and quiet my mind, like on the long drives from Idaho to Utah and back. In those moments of silence, I felt like I was able to have a conversation with God. He spoke to my heart and told me my path wasn't going to be easy, but that I needed to keep showing up and that He would be by my side the entire time, lending me strength.

1983

"You embarrassed me in Oregon!" Dad screams at Mom. "In front of John and the whole commune!"

We're standing in our small kitchen. Dad, Mom, my uncles Ron and Watson, and me. My siblings made themselves scarce the moment my dad stepped through the door, but I was cornered in the kitchen with Mom, where she was boiling water in her enormous pot so we'd have hot water to do the dishes.

"Apologize!" Dad demands.

Mom puts her hands on her hips. "I won't," she says.

Dad slams his hand into Mom's face. She staggers back. I stare at Dad in fear and disbelief.

"Say you're sorry," he screams.

Mom looks him dead in the eye. "I refuse," she says, raising her chin. "You'll have to kill me before I say sorry for that."

Dad swings his arm angrily and knocks the giant pot off the stove, spilling boiling water all over the floor. Before I know what's happening, Mom scoops me up and flings me through the air onto the couch we keep next to the kitchen table. I land in a daze and slowly register that Mom has just saved me from being badly burned.

Somewhere in the room, I hear Christopher and Rachel start to cry. From his cradle, Baby Brian screams.

Dad drags Mom out of the kitchen and throws her on the living room floor. He pins her arms down with his knees and hits her in the face again. "Here's how you handle a disobedient wife!" he shouts to his brothers.

Ron is watching Dad with an eagerness that terrifies me, but Watson steps back uneasily.

Mom's skirt has flipped up over her knees, and I can see black-and-blue marks up and down her legs. The marks are in the shape of handprints.

Dad wraps his hands around Mom's throat and squeezes.

"Stop, Daddy!" I want to shout. "You're hurting her." But I can't. Because I don't want him to hurt me, too. Tears stream down my cheeks, and my whole body shakes.

"Apologize," Dad snarls. "Repent for being a wicked wife."

"No," Mom rasps.

Dad keeps choking Mom. Soon, she can't speak. She can barely breathe. I stare at my mother as her face slowly turns blue. I realize then that she's going to die.

"Dan," Ron says calmly. "You're killing her."

His brother's voice snaps Dad out of his trance. He releases his grip and climbs off Mom, who rolls onto her side, gasping for air. Dad paces around the room, fuming. He looks at me, and I recoil. The man staring back at me is not my father. He doesn't seem to recognize me or even know where he is.

Dad looks back at Mom. "You must be punished." His voice sounds strange and distant. "You are banned from this house until you learn your place."

"What about Brian?" Mom asks hoarsely. Mom gave birth to Brian only a few months ago and is still nursing him.

"He's staying here."

"But I need to feed him."

"Then you should have thought about that before you decided to defy me!" Dad shouts, spit flying from his mouth. "A woman's place is in the home, supporting her husband in all things. *I'm* the priesthood holder. I wield God's power on earth. 'Neither was the man created for the woman; but the woman for the man.' Now get out."

"The kids . . . dinner . . . "

"I said get the fuck out!"

Mom climbs slowly to her feet. She reaches for a shawl and then hobbles out of the house.

"And don't come back until you're ready to be obedient!" Dad screams after her, slamming the door shut. He turns around and looks at me. I freeze, holding my breath, afraid to move.

"What are you sitting around for?" Dad snaps. "Get in the kitchen and make us dinner!"

CHAPTER 21

2007

I THREW MY BACK OUT from dealing with Nathan's nightly tossing and turning (he was still sleeping in bed with me), so I scheduled an appointment with the local chiropractor, a man named Bill Martin. He was so kind and genuine. As Bill worked on Nathan, Erin, and me, he acknowledged my struggle, and my strength. He made me feel seen.

Bill told me that his wife knew a woman in Salt Lake City named Darla who did angel readings. He said that maybe she could provide me with some comfort or clarity. He must have sensed my pent-up emotions, ready to spill over like a broken dam the moment a kind word or gesture was thrown my way.

I took Darla's number and called to schedule a phone reading. Her next available session was about a month out, but I was willing to wait. I wrote down all my questions regarding Nathan, my dad, and what my life would look like if I were to stay where I was.

When the day of the call arrived, I was a little nervous but mostly excited. Darla asked me a few initial questions then took a deep breath to connect to the spiritual plane. She asked me what questions I had for her. I asked her about my father, and she told me that deep down he was a good man, but he was dealing with what was called a split, which occurs when a child experiences trauma. She was the first person I'd met, apart from Kristi, who didn't see my father as a monster. She also confirmed that Kristi had come into our lives to help us and that her intentions were good. She told me to be her friend but to not try to save her; she had her own battles, which were not mine to take on.

I told Darla that, as a last resort, I'd been thinking about going to the temple to be sealed to Timothy, that maybe that was the answer to saving my marriage. Even though I hated the church, I was at my wit's end, and I knew getting sealed in the temple would placate Timothy and his family. (Mormons believe that marriages end at death unless you are sealed in an LDS temple. However, you can't go to the temple unless you are an active, believing member who pays a full tithe and keeps all the rules of the church.) I also thought that maybe God was withholding my happiness, and once I agreed to this, I would experience the deeper love in my relationship I was yearning for.

Darla said to me, very gently, "Rebecca, you will get to a point in the temple ceremony where you will be asked if you believe that everything they teach is true, and you will not be able to lie. You cannot be untrue to yourself."

Her response rocked me to my core. Up until that moment, no one had ever given me permission to just be myself. It's difficult to explain how powerful it was to hear someone tell me that I wasn't going to go to hell or lose God's love just by being me.

Darla told me that I needed to learn a healing modality. She knew that I needed to break the cycle of self-abuse I had created within myself, especially my negative thoughts and self-deprecating language. She had a way about her that snapped me out of my story of the past. She refused to relate to me as a victim. She reminded me of what I could be, if I just believed it was possible. She saw my potential, despite the limiting beliefs I had imposed on myself. She didn't buy into those beliefs, not even for a second. She taught me how powerful our minds are and that whatever we focus on we create. I knew that what she said was true, but I didn't perceive how much I'd been creating a negative reality for myself. She showed me how to access the tools within myself to change my patterns of thinking.

Darla told me that my angels said I would be very good at ThetaHealing. I had no idea what that was, but I soon learned that it is a

modality that some believe has the ability to reprogram negative or limiting beliefs in a relaxed, meditative state of mind where you can access
the subconscious. It's not enough to change our conscious patterns of
thought. It's the subconscious mind that's running the show, so to affect
permanent change, we have to make those changes on a deeper level.*

Darla said ThetaHealing would be beneficial for Nathan, too. She told
me to work on improving his diet as he wasn't getting all the nutrients he
needed, and to do work with him on a subconscious level to reaffirm for
him that he was strong and resilient. She also mentioned some additional
things that confirmed for me that she was getting help from the spirit
realm. There was absolutely no way she could have known them otherwise.

There are some people you are automatically drawn to; you can just
sense that they are nurturing and kind. They have a way about them, an
energy, a confidence. That was Darla. She had no desire to have authority
over me, nor was she working an angle in order to get something from me.
Her words seemed to carry a higher consciousness, and the peace I felt in
her presence spoke volumes. She related to me as my own authority and
was the closest thing I knew to an angel. I received all the answers I'd been
looking for and validation that left me feeling hopeful for my future.

Our session was so accurate and reassuring that I immediately
arranged another reading with her. Since Darla lived close to Primary
Children's, I thought it would be nice to meet with her in person and
have some time dedicated to my healing, away from the criticism and
judgment I received from people in Idaho.

I was so excited to meet Darla in person. I think it bothered Timothy
that I was looking forward to seeing her more than our visit to the hospital. I'm sure he felt abandoned. But my spirit was calling me in that

* Darlene was obviously approaching healing from a spiritual perspective, but the concept of
rewiring our beliefs is consistent with the principles of neuroplasticity and epigenetics. The
brain, which is often rewired during times of stress, can be rewired intentionally to create
new, more beneficial neuron pathways.

direction, and I had to listen. I couldn't be held back by his fears. *Why is he being so difficult?* I wondered. I was getting through things the way that my spirit was showing me. I would have supported him in doing the same. So why couldn't he support me?

The day of the appointment came, and I arrived at Darla's office building fifteen minutes early. I had butterflies in my stomach, anticipating what I would experience with her and what she would look like. While I waited in my car, a refined woman with blonde hair, approximately five foot two, walked past me. She was wearing a business suit, her shoulders were rolled back, and she held a phone to her ear. She exuded total confidence. I was in the parking lot of a business complex filled with office suites and working professionals, but I *knew* it was her. She was the very image of professional success and confidence I wanted for myself.

I waited until the time of my appointment. Then I walked into the building and found Darla's office. The moment I stepped through the door, I was met with the calming smells of essential oils and the soothing sound of a water fixture burbling in the corner. It felt like being in a spa or sanctuary. I sat down and soaked in the serenity. My body immediately relaxed in a way I hadn't experienced in years. Darla stepped into the waiting room and introduced herself. I was right; she was the blonde woman I had seen from my car. Her voice was so reassuring and comforting. She handed me a clipboard and a paper with questions to fill out, and then told me to follow her.

Darla led me into another room that seemed to welcome me the moment I sat down. She had me fill out the papers while she worked on intuitively receiving information about me. Then she began to ask me questions, and I spilled out answers. Our connection felt like magic. It was almost as if I had stepped into another time or realm.

After a bit, I started asking Darla questions. Her responses made me feel like she was someone not from this world—someone who knew a lot more about what was out there than I did. My mind opened like a sponge, and I wanted to absorb as much as she would share. I felt bigger than I knew myself to be. I felt understood, forgiven, loved, and that anything I said would be heard and respected.

Just being in Darla's presence, without her even having to say anything, brought incredible clarity to me. It was as if she was such a clear channel that my angels/guides/higher self were finally able to speak to me, and I was finally able to hear. I heard the words come out of my mouth, "I just want healing for my family, but what I am realizing is that I need to heal myself." That was a huge breakthrough moment.

Darla did a process with me that helped me release deep sadness. I was then able to piece together emotions that I had stuffed down or disconnected from. I was more alive and confident. For the first time, I believed that I could create anything I wanted for myself and that I wouldn't be punished for wanting those things, that I was *meant* to grow and expand. She gave me exactly the kind of love and support that I was starving for.

My session with Darla was truly a paradigm shift for me. I would never be the same person after our visit. Her life and energy felt in total alignment with what I wanted for myself. What choices had she made that had brought her to this serene and confident place? I wanted to know.

I was so excited after our session. I bought Darla's manual and began practicing her therapeutic techniques on Nathan and myself. I would hold Nathan and tell him how strong and resilient he was. Then I would move us into a Theta state to work on the subconscious level and reprogram our limiting beliefs. This practice allowed me to start shifting my thoughts in a more positive direction.

I was lit up by this work, but felt like I needed to keep it a secret from Timothy. He made it very clear to me that he didn't approve of my visit with Darla, even though I felt so happy and peaceful afterward. To him, anything that dealt with spiritual matters outside of Mormonism was witchcraft and of the devil. What he didn't understand was that Darla was helping me create a better relationship with myself so I could show up more fully in my relationships with him and the children.

After a few months, however, I could feel myself slipping back into that dark, lost place. It was hard to keep up the momentum on my own. I knew I needed to talk to Darla again, so I scheduled another session.

During our next visit, Darla and I did a hypnotherapy session. That was when I knew for certain that the healing Darla did was powerful. I felt nothing but peace and acceptance for myself and those around me. I felt like I received answers on a soul level about what I needed to know and do. For me, it all came down to love and forgiveness. I needed to forgive and love everyone in my life, including my dad.

I wanted to share with my family what I had experienced, but they weren't really interested. They didn't trust the process. My siblings, of course, wanted nothing to do with Dad, and my mom told me she'd already forgiven him, even though my entire life I'd heard her express her regret that she'd married him and had "all you kids" with him. I'd internalized her regrets, and I was repeating that same pattern in my own relationships.

I couldn't force any of my family members to reach out to Dad, so I just kept walking my own path. I continued to communicate with Kristi and to write letters to my dad and occasionally visit him. Kristi assured me that my efforts were helping my dad heal. She shared some of the progress he was making. I imagine it was heavy work, holding that space for my dad's feelings. Kristi was a true angel for shouldering that burden. I saw that my father had deeply repressed emotions from childhood that were still running his life, just like I did. I felt a lot of compassion for him.

On one of my visits to see Dad, right before they moved him from maximum security to general population, he acknowledged that living with him must have felt like living with a monster. He said, "I wish I would have taught you how to ride a bike."

That was the first time I ever saw my father fully cry. I couldn't believe it. I hadn't realized how much I had longed for that acknowledgment from him, for a sincere apology for the way he'd treated me as a child. I broke down and wept alongside him.

I wanted to make more progress on my healing journey, so I contacted Darla again. She offered to let me stay with her in Salt Lake for a few days. My mom flew in from California to help with Nathan while I experienced the first rejuvenating weekend I'd had in years. I think I slept for twelve hours straight. Sleep deprivation had become my new normal, and chronic pain was manifesting in my shoulders, almost as if someone were stabbing me in the back with a knife.

Staying with Darla felt like visiting a temple. She had a way of offering total comfort. She was so generous in the way she listened to me and validated me. She would let me talk and talk and talk as I released all my pent-up emotions. She showed me kindness in a way I'd never experienced before. She had the patience of a saint, and not one judgmental word ever came out of her mouth. Her eyes shone with understanding and intelligence. This beautiful woman fascinated and inspired me on a soul level like no one ever had.

Darla was going to be teaching a course in regression and hypnotherapy certification. She said I should consider taking the course, not just as a tool for myself, but so I could learn to be a facilitator for other people's healing journeys. My first impulse was to reject the idea. I felt so broken that I didn't see how I could help anyone else. But Darla told me that it was precisely because of what I had been through that I could be of service to others. My life had given me experiences and wisdom that could bless other people because I understood suffering and the devastating effects of trauma firsthand.

I could tell that Darla's intention for me was pure and empowering. She shared with me her own story of adversity and how she was able to be where she was now, which made me love and respect her even more. She introduced me to other women who were similarly empowered and who had had their own experiences with trauma. Each of these women was determined to play a bigger role in life than being a submissive housewife. To be clear, I am fully supportive of a woman's decision to be a housewife. Doing domestic work and raising children at home is an undervalued and extremely demanding job; it was the submissive part that I struggled with—as have many other women before me. I knew I wanted a different path for myself, and I was tired of being made to feel like I was wrong for wanting something else.

As I thought about the idea, I began to feel at peace. It was both exciting and scary because I was charting unknown territory. But I recalled how years ago I'd wanted to go to school to study psychology, and this felt like I was finally on the right track, moving in a direction that matched my authentic desires. I was fascinated by the way the human mind works and the ability we have to take control of our situation and move beyond our limitations. I was ready to learn more and to help others, if I could.

I rushed home to share this idea with Timothy. Taking the course would require me to visit Salt Lake on the weekends, so I told him my vision was to live part-time in Salt Lake, where I was becoming part of a community of supportive women—people with whom I wanted to grow and create—and then spend the rest of the time in Idaho with our family.

Timothy was already livid that I had gone to visit Darla for the weekend. The idea that I would continue to make these trips every week infuriated him. He shot down my plan immediately. The course was going to cost a couple thousand dollars, and Timothy said we couldn't afford it. I told him the course meant everything to me and I would work full-time in order to come up with the money. He said he needed me at home more, not at work.

"That's not what a mother does," he yelled. "That's not what a family is."

I asked him what he wanted from me, and he said he wanted me to quit working entirely so I could take care of Nathan full-time. I told him I wasn't a person who could do that. We needed a nurse to help with Nathan. I couldn't give up my dreams and ambitions to be a full-time caregiver. I loved being a mother, and I loved being *Nathan's* mother, but I couldn't devote every moment of my day to caring for his needs. My needs mattered, too.

I tried to find a compromise with Timothy, but he wouldn't hear another word on the topic. Instead, he ignored me and spent hours ranting to his mom, recounting all the "evil" things I was doing. It felt like he didn't want me to be happy or to grow as a person. The only thing I was good for was staying at home, cooking and cleaning and taking care of the kids. In Timothy's view, a mother who wanted to create something outside of the home was shirking her duties and running away. However, I really believed I could have it all. I wanted to form a team with Timothy and find a way to meet everyone's needs. But he wasn't willing to think outside the box of the traditional gender roles he'd inherited growing up.

The next time Timothy and I went to therapy, he mentioned the books I was reading and expressed his concern that I was checking out of the marriage and failing our family (aka my duties as a mother). I couldn't believe it. I told Timothy I couldn't see our relationship lasting if he was unable to support me in my growth and healing.

I knew with every fiber in my being that I needed to take the hypnotherapy course, so I decided to enroll. Darla worked with me to set up a payment plan, and my sweet and selfless mother agreed to leave her life in California to come help me with Nathan. It seemed like it could work: Timothy would have the support and help he needed with our son while I was in Salt Lake.

I left to attend the first weekend. It was incredible. I made the best connections and formed incredible relationships. The people at the workshops saw me in a different light. They lived from their heart space, and

I felt unconditional love and support from them for who I was. I was beginning to understand just how important it was to create a community of support that would assist me in my healing journey. I could feel my whole being changing. I was becoming someone completely new.

I was excited to come home and share the progress I had made. But when I returned, Timothy had a packet of papers waiting for me on the table. My heart dropped.

"What's this?" I asked.

"This is not a family," Timothy said. "I want a divorce."

I felt as if someone had sucked all the air out of me. I stood there, deflated and speechless. What was I going to do now? How was I going to support myself and the kids? I finally felt like I was on the right path, but once again the rug had been pulled out from under me.

My mom said that Timothy was using the divorce papers as a scare tactic to get me to do what he wanted. But I knew I couldn't back down. I told him that I wanted a life with him in Idaho and a life in Salt Lake where I could continue my growth and healing. I needed both. He refused to allow it. It seemed that his family had been in his ear, telling him that I was a mother who was abandoning her children. I told Timothy I wasn't abandoning anyone. I was planning to take the kids (and my mom) with me on my trips to Salt Lake.

He said, "Absolutely not, and I will fight you for it."

I was shocked. I told him I wanted to find a peaceful solution, a win for both of us. But he was just too damn stubborn; he refused to cooperate or compromise. Our relationship was truly over.

I remember lying on my bed and praying to God. I told Him I was sorry that I was breaking my agreement to be married and walk this path with Timothy, but I just couldn't do it anymore. I asked if He would forgive me. I got the message that I was free to choose my own path. I could end my marriage if I wished, but whatever decision I made, it was not going to be easy. I knew that even though God would love me and support my choice, not everyone would agree with it, especially Timothy. In fact, I had the distinct feeling that Timothy was going to make things difficult for me. I heard the message that I would have to deal with a lot of inner turmoil.

I asked, "How long will it be hard?"

The answer I received was, "*Years.*"

I thought, *Well, as long as I don't have to be married to Timothy anymore, it will be okay.* I felt that I was being given the strength to face things one step at a time.

Looking back, I realize now that Timothy was dealing with immense pressure to keep our family together, and I probably could have done more to see his point of view. Even though the relationship needed to end, I could have approached it differently. But the only way I knew how to handle conflict was to pack up and leave.

This time the price for my decision was going to be much steeper.

CHAPTER 22

2007–14

WHILE I FIGURED OUT HOW I was going to transition out of the marriage and provide for myself and the children, I started seeing a new therapist. This therapist was a woman, and I thought perhaps she might be a better fit for me than the marriage counselor Timothy and I had seen, who was a man. However, the opposite was true. I couldn't connect with her at all. I felt like I was constantly trying to explain myself and justify why I was doing things the way I was doing them. I just wanted encouragement to be myself. Instead, I was met with confusion and judgment. She looked at me as if I weren't speaking English, and I didn't feel any validation from her. I would start to open up about my authentic needs, but the second I felt her judgment, I would switch back to saying whatever I thought she wanted to hear.

One day after my second session, the therapist called the home phone and left a message. In the message, she expressed her concern that I might have borderline personality disorder. I was furious. Not only was this behavior highly unprofessional, but it was also not the kind of help I needed. I refused to let one more person give me a label. The moment I sensed she wanted to give me a diagnosis, I decided to stop seeing her. She kept contacting me, but I refused to return her calls. I'd lost all trust in her, and her refusal to leave me alone troubled me. A part of me wondered if she had even conspired with Timothy, since so many people in this town seemed to be in cahoots with his family. My fears in that regard only increased once I learned that Timothy had heard her message on the answering machine. I wondered if he was going to use this against me in the divorce. If nothing else, it gave him yet another reason to blame me for the pain he was experiencing.

The therapist's "diagnosis" wasn't the only weapon in Timothy's arsenal. I didn't know that he was talking to my family behind my back, telling them that I was crazy and unstable and that I was abandoning Nathan. He called them almost every night, crying his heart out and telling them how much I was hurting him.

One by one, my family members turned against me. I called Gwen and asked her if I could live with her while I got through the divorce. She said, "I'm sorry, but I can't let you." It was clear she disapproved of my choice to leave Timothy, and this was her way of letting me know while not so subtly pressuring me to do the "right" thing. At the time, Gwen was going through her own struggles. She'd recently given birth to a daughter whose brain had never fully developed and who had only lived a few days. This was understandably very traumatic for her, and I think perhaps she was projecting her situation onto mine: I had the chance to keep my family together and continue parenting my child, while she did not.

Rachel didn't support me, either. She made a trip to Idaho to see Nathan and never even reached out to me. I was crushed and felt abandoned. Even my mom said I was making a mistake by leaving Timothy. She said if I left him, my relationship with her would never be the same. This scared me. I tried to explain what it was like for me, but all she could tell me was that I needed to sacrifice more and be less selfish, that I needed to be obedient. There it was again. That word. I felt so angry and frustrated, I could scream. But at the same time, I knew that if I were to express my true emotions, I'd just play into Timothy's narrative that I was mentally unstable.

Despite my family's disapproval, I knew I couldn't stay in a marriage where I wasn't allowed to be my true self. I would just have to figure out a way forward on my own. I prayed for answers and worked on things one day at a time.

The first challenge was finding a way to provide for Erin. She was doing really well in Idaho. She had friends there, and she was taking guitar lessons. I hated to take that away from her, but I knew I didn't have a choice. Timothy said I should leave her with him, and I said hell no. He was already insisting on maintaining full custody of Nathan; I wasn't going to let him have Erin, too. I realized this was an opportunity for Erin's father to show up for her. She'd been going to stay with Jake every summer since she was four, and she was close to his wife, Kaitlin. Jake and Kaitlin had recently bought a brand-new home in Herriman, Utah, and seemed to be doing well financially. This felt like the best option for Erin. So I contacted Jake, and he came to get her. It was hard to let her go, but I knew this was just a temporary separation until I could get back on my feet. I felt at peace about it. She was twelve at the time.

The next challenge was finding a job and a place to stay in Salt Lake. I was still moving forward with the hypnotherapy course. I wanted to work on improving my life and helping others do the same. The women in the course were a great support to me. One of them invited me over for dinner and let me know she was there if I needed anything. Another woman introduced me to some people who were renting out their two-bedroom condo. It was a beautiful place at the perfect price.

Next, I found a job as a dental assistant. It felt like everything was lining up for me, like God and the universe were supporting me in my decision. I was getting all the green lights.

I rented the biggest U-Haul trailer that my Dodge Durango could pull. I filled it up and said goodbye to Timothy and Nathan and headed to Utah. I left before any sadness or regret could set in. I didn't want to second-guess my decision, so I pushed my feelings down—something I was good at doing.

As I approached Salt Lake, it felt like I'd entered uncharted waters. I knew I wanted to become a hypnotherapist, but I didn't know the first thing about running my own business. I told myself to just take things one step at a time. I needed to focus on building a solid foundation for myself, and then I could grow from there.

Despite the confidence and surety I seemed to exhibit in moving forward with my new life, I was scared shitless. I would wake up some nights in terror, disoriented and missing my children. I was still making trips on the weekends to see Nathan, and Timothy was bringing him to Primary Children's for his visits. I would meet them there, and Nathan and I would spend the weekend together.

I could see that Timothy was struggling emotionally. My heart went out to him, but I was having a hard enough time trying to figure out my own life. He had started dating again, and I told him I would watch Nathan for him if he needed me to. I wanted him to find a woman he deserved and who had the same vision as he did. I truly wanted us to both get what we wanted. Despite my struggles, I was so much happier in my new situation, and I wanted him to be happy, too. I thought we were doing a great job of getting along.

In the five years since Nathan had been diagnosed, we had had four or five nurses come to help out during the day so Timothy and I could work. But once winter hit, the roads would get snowed over. The nurse always quit shortly after that.

A month or two after I moved out, Timothy told me that he needed more help with Nathan. I asked if his mom could help until I could get there on the weekends, but his mom was done raising kids. She wasn't "that kind of grandma," she said. (The irony wasn't lost on me.)

My own mother felt somewhat responsible for the situation we were in. She had offered to come help me with Nathan but had never been able to make the trip. I think she felt that, had she been there earlier to support me, perhaps I would have stayed. She offered to take early retirement and return as a full-time nanny to Nathan. It was so incredibly noble and selfless of her. Timothy and I were both grateful, and her relationship with Nathan was beautiful.

Of course, even though Timothy was thankful for my mom's help, it wasn't her help he wanted. He wanted a wife. A partner. I can't blame him for that.

Not long after my mom started watching Nathan, Timothy admitted to her that it was his plan to try and get me back. Mom told me he was hoping I would come to my senses and come running back to him.

I was shocked. The next time I saw Timothy at Primary Children's, I told him I was sorry if I hadn't been clear about my choice. I told him I wanted to make things as easy as possible for us to both spend time with Nathan, but I no longer wanted to be married, and I wouldn't be moving back to Idaho.

The moment it was clear to Timothy that I wasn't coming back, everything changed. He shut down any kindness or workability that we had. It seemed that Timothy was going to do everything he could to make me pay for my decision to leave him.

I was told that I needed to sign the divorce papers in front of an attorney. I found one in Grand View, a decision I now regret. Everyone in that town knew Timothy and his family.

I read over the papers in something of a hurry. I just wanted the process to be done. The lawyer, who went to school with Timothy, asked me, "Are you sure you don't want anything from this divorce? No money? The house?"

It felt like the attorney was egging me on, and I wondered if he had his own ax to grind with Timothy, who I knew some people perceived as being somewhat arrogant. (His family was one of the wealthier ones in the community.)

But I didn't want anything from Timothy. I didn't want to be tied to him in any way. All I wanted was my freedom.

Little did I know that by signing those papers, I was signing away my rights as Nathan's mother. The terms of the divorce stipulated that Nathan would reside with Timothy full-time.

When I discovered the truth, I felt so powerless and stupid. I was ashamed that I wasn't more educated. If I was smarter, I would have realized what Timothy had done. If I hadn't been in such a rush . . . If I had just looked at the papers more closely . . . But I'd just wanted to get the process over with and had relied on the attorney to guide me. I don't know whether he was annoyed that I wasn't willing to try to take Timothy down a peg and so deliberately chose not to tell me about the terms of the agreement, or whether he thought I already knew, or whether he was just a bad lawyer. Whatever the case, I'd been played.

It seemed like Timothy genuinely wanted to punish me. He quickly started dating a woman named Melanie. She wanted anything that looked or smelled like me out of the house. She and Timothy packed up everything I had given him or Nathan and put it in a box and mailed it to me. I know it was probably therapeutic for Timothy, and we all need to process grief in our own way, but it still stung.

It wasn't just my stuff they cleared out. The moment the divorce papers were signed, my mom was literally pushed out of the house. It broke my heart to see her treated that way, especially after all she'd done to support Timothy and help him with Nathan. She got an apartment in Twin Falls to try and support me with Nathan when I visited. After this, my mom changed her mind about Timothy. She saw the difficult parts of his personality that she hadn't been able to see before.

During one of my weekends with Nathan, Timothy dropped him off at my mom's apartment. Later, Melanie came to pick him up. She walked in and saw that I had him in the bathtub. Because I was bathing him, his feeding tube was disconnected. She marched in, grabbed the food, and told Timothy to get Nathan. She concocted an elaborate story about how I was an unfit mother who wasn't feeding Nathan and wanted to kill him. I could see I was dealing with someone who was very insecure and possessive. Melanie couldn't have children of her own. It was clear she wanted to be a mother but seemed too threatened by me to co-parent peacefully.

Despite her animosity, I really believed I could convince Timothy and Melanie to collaborate as a team. I found videos of other children with SMA who were doing water therapy. I tried to show Timothy and Melanie how being in the water brought joy and movement to these children's lives. I sent them all the things that inspired me, hoping that they would be moved like I was to create something that would improve the quality of Nathan's life. But they weren't interested in working with me or exploring new ways of doing things. They just wanted me to go away.

Things got worse from there. Timothy and Melanie began doing everything in their power to push me out of Nathan's life. They told me my visits were harming him because he would cry when he had to come home. They also began telling him that Melanie was his mother and that he had to call me Rebecca. To this day, my son refers to me as Rebecca instead of Mom.

Melanie contacted *The Wendy Williams Show* and appeared live to tell her story of how she had "rescued a special needs boy" whose mother had walked out on him. When my mom told me, I couldn't believe it. I couldn't understand why anyone would do something so hurtful and dishonest.

Melanie and Timothy also refused to tell me the dates of Nathan's hospital visits. One time I was on my way to visit Nathan. Three hours into my drive, Timothy notified me that Nathan was being life-flighted to the hospital and I wouldn't be able to see him that weekend. I immediately turned my car around and got to the hospital as quickly as I could. But when I arrived, the doctors wouldn't let me see him. Melanie had told them that I wasn't his real mother and that *she* was his mother and legal guardian.

I couldn't believe this was happening. My son was literally being taken from me! I was living in a waking nightmare. This was worse than anything that had happened to me up to this point. I felt like my heart was physically breaking. I kept praying to God, begging for help. Was I being punished for making the wrong decision? Was it true I was a bad mother? Was it better for me to just walk away, the way Timothy and Melanie wanted? But I knew in my heart I couldn't give up.

I hired an attorney and spent thousands of dollars fighting for my right as Nathan's mother. The attorney said that Timothy and Melanie were supposed to let me know of any and all changes to Nathan's health and doctor visits. But they wouldn't comply, and there was no way I could make them. They tried to deny my visits several times, and I had to bring my divorce decree to the police station and force them to let me see my son.

Timothy and Melanie made a rule that I had to visit Nathan in their home. Melanie supervised the entire visit. She'd sit in the corner, staring me down with what can only be described as pure hatred.

I couldn't understand how my life had turned upside down. Melanie was the one chaperoning my time with my son, when it should have been the other way around! *I* was his mother.

Additionally, I was also scared for Nathan's safety. I didn't trust that Melanie actually loved him and was taking good care of him. How could she be, when she was treating me this way?

I would leave the visit and sob the whole way home, wishing I had someone to comfort me and tell me things were going to be okay. I tried everything in my power to love and forgive them, to find softness in my heart when my heart was literally breaking. All I wanted was to be with my son and to be treated with respect, but they continued to accuse me of trying to harm Nathan and repeatedly claimed he wasn't safe in my presence. That's what hurt me the most.

I let their cruelty get to me. I was so focused on how Melanie was behaving toward me that I lost sight of the precious time I had with my son. My conversations with God on the drive from Utah to Idaho, which used to bring me such peace, were replaced with screaming matches on the phone. I let the injustice I was experiencing build in my mind. I began to fall deeper into negativity and self-focused emotions. I blamed myself for what was happening. I hadn't been a good wife and mother, so I was being punished in the worst way possible. My child had been stolen from me.

This was, without question, the lowest point in my life. I was on the verge of a full mental breakdown. I was diagnosed with Hashimoto's thyroiditis, and my hair began falling out in chunks due to that and to the chronic stress I was experiencing. I almost rolled my car twice driving in the winter months to see Nathan.

Despite this, I continued to try everything possible to see my son. I would have crawled to Idaho if I had to. I asked Timothy if we could arrange video calls or if I could take Nathan so he and Melanie could go on vacation. But Timothy always said no. He continued to find more and more ways to restrict my visits. I began to lose hope.

One day, I attended a self-empowerment workshop in Salt Lake. After the seminar, one of the leaders pulled me aside and said, "Honey, I get that you are doing everything possible to make this work, but you can't force either one of them to play your way."

It was such a profound truth, it left me speechless. I finally saw that I'd been living within the narrative that Timothy and Melanie had created. I'd been so desperate to prove them wrong that, in so doing, I'd given away my power. For seven years I had been trying to prove to Timothy, and the world, that I wasn't a failure as a mother. But *they* were the ones who had been making me feel like a failure.

I went home and lay on the floor of my bedroom. I realized I was done. The battle was over. If I kept trying to fight this war, it would be the end of me. I no longer had an ounce of strength left to continue the way I was going. My health was ruined, and I was on the verge of collapse. I had to accept that my relationship with Timothy was never going to be a peaceful or a loving one, not in this lifetime. I couldn't force another person to be kind. I couldn't force someone to cooperate who didn't want to or make them see that what they were doing wasn't helping Nathan thrive. I was tired of constantly being attacked and mistreated. It was time to lay down my sword.

The warrior in me had been telling myself I had to be unmoving in the face of adversity. But what I learned is that true courage is to know when to surrender. Surrender doesn't mean losing or giving up. It means allowing Source/God/the Universe to show you another, more peaceful way.

I knew I needed to hand my struggle to God and lean on that spirit I'd shut out of my life. That meant opening my heart so I could finally begin to heal.

The first step was forgiving Timothy and Melanie. This took me a long time, but I tried to truly put myself in their shoes and see things from their perspective. What was their actual experience, not just my perception of it?

I saw that Timothy did love his son and wanted to care for him. I saw that he was hurting, too. And I was the one who had hurt him. Continuing to fight him to see Nathan was only making things worse—not just for Timothy, but for Nathan, too. Nathan's peace and happiness mattered more than my pride.

So I surrendered and walked away. I no longer cared what it looked like to outsiders. I felt at peace knowing God was my witness. He knew I wasn't giving up on my son and that I had done literally everything in my power to stay in his life. That was all I needed.

My in-person visits with Nathan were replaced with FaceTime calls. Without the long drives to Idaho and the energy spent on fighting with Timothy, I was able to focus on loving and finding myself again. Where had I gone during these past years? I hardly recognized myself. Why had I allowed myself to be abused for so long?

I realized it was because, on a deep level, I felt like I deserved it—and not just for my mistakes as a parent. For the first seven years of my life, my father's actions had instilled in me the belief that I was bad and needed to be punished. This programming was only reinforced in my preteen and teen years as I saw over and over again that I didn't belong and I could never do anything right. Because something was wrong with me.

My spirit whispered to me that this wasn't true, that I *was* worthy of love and respect, but it would take concentrated work on my part before I would believe it. It was time to show up for myself and prioritize healing and joy.

I stayed in Salt Lake to begin my healing, and my mom went back to California. I will forever be grateful to her for all of her heroic efforts to help me. She is amazing to me. A true angel on Earth. She never once gave up hope. She believed in me and encouraged me to keep going. I love her for that.

I don't know what the future holds for Nathan and me. What I do know is that I can focus on the meaningful time we had together. I can even find warmth in my heart for the good times I shared with Timothy and appreciation for Melanie for caring for my son. I can choose to breathe in and foster this positive energy within myself. I believe Nathan and I are still connected and I can always communicate with him energetically and send him light and love. No one can stop that or take that away from us, and that brings peace to my heart. I am grateful that Nathan is being loved and cared for. That's all that matters.

I've asked myself many times why I had to go through this experience. Why did I continue to repeat the same mistakes when it came to relationships? And why did each one seem to generate more pain and suffering than the one before?

I have since learned that all relationships—romantic and non-romantic—are mirrors. They reflect back to us the things we need to heal within ourselves. The emotions and judgments I have toward other people reflect the parts of myself that most need love and compassion. If I feel hatred, anger, or disgust toward someone's actions, or if someone's words trigger my anxieties, that's a sign that there's something within me that needs to be healed. Every time another person triggers me, especially a partner, I'm being invited to look inward.

We are vibrational beings. What we think creates emotions, depending on what we believe about those thoughts. Emotions are literally energetic waves. They're an indicator of what we are emanating, and what we emanate attracts more of the same.

I continued to invite the same experiences into my life because I was existing in a vibration of low self-worth. I didn't feel worthy of love, so I attracted people who treated me as such.

Of course, I am not saying that victims of abuse attract abuse. I was obviously not responsible for the way my father chose to treat me as a child. However, I *felt* responsible. And that's precisely the vibration that we survivors must learn to shift. Because as long as my subconscious mind continued to loop on the belief that I was a bad person and undeserving of kindness and love, I was going to continue to attract more experiences that reinforced that belief.

In order to heal from my trauma, I had to teach myself that I *was* worthy of love. But first I had to fully feel all of my grief and pain and shame so that these emotions could move through my body. My entire life, I'd learned to stuff down my emotions instead of feel them. When trauma and feelings are repressed instead of expressed, they are stored in the body, where they can create physical ailments. Only by releasing my negative feelings would I be able to create the space to invite in higher emotions such as joy and abundance and love.*

My entire adult life, I jumped from relationship to relationship, looking for a safe place to land, but in the process I was really handing all of my childhood trauma and grief to the other person, hoping they'd

---

* You can release trapped emotions through stillness, prayer, tapping, EFT, somatic experiencing, body work, movement, and other modalities and programs like the Steps to Recovery program.

be able to heal me, when of course they couldn't. It took going through these experiences for me to finally look inward and address the pain that resided deep in my heart. To face it instead of run from it.

I had stuffed my pain down to the deepest parts of my body and soul where I would never have to see it again. Consequently, my experiences in partnership grew more painful and more extreme, because life was forcing me to look into that mirror and see what I refused to.

While another person can't take our trauma from us, God/Source can. I've found that taking my heavy emotions to God allows me to experience the greatest healing possible. He can help me see the bigger picture, not just my own limited perspective, and give me new things to focus on. When I surrender my heavy emotions to him, I can ask to be shown what love and worthiness feel like. And then I can focus on those feelings instead. I can find the blessings and lessons in my experiences and focus on those, rather than the pain.

After separating from Timothy, I was ready to take my healing more seriously. However, I hadn't yet fully integrated these lessons, which meant more mirrors awaited me.

CHAPTER 23

2007–11

AFTER THE DIVORCE FROM TIMOTHY, while I was struggling to regain my rights as Nathan's mother, I continued my training as a hypnotherapist and tried to move forward with my life in Salt Lake City. During this time, Erin was still living with Jake and Kaitlin, whom she adored. She would come to stay with me on the weekends. But most of the time, I was alone. My life felt very isolated and lonely, especially during the battle for Nathan's custody.

I came across a book called *Conscious Loving: The Journey to Co-Commitment* by Gay and Kathlyn Hendricks. This couple inspired me because of the intimacy they had created together. I wanted what they had. I read all of their books and then attended a few of their classes. I loved the idea of creating a beautiful relationship filled with intimacy and connection as well as autonomy, and wanted to know everything there was to know about what made relationships work for both people. I wanted to learn how to express myself in a way that felt safe and create that same space for my partner.

While attending one of these classes, I met a man named Simon. He was fifteen years older than me, just like Julian, but he was kind and playful. We talked for a bit, and he invited me over for dinner. During our date, we couldn't stop talking, especially about spiritual concepts. We both loved learning about Jesus—who he actually was, and the radical way he lived and taught—beyond the construct provided by organized religion. There was a spiritual bond between us that I hadn't experienced before. I'd never been able to have these kinds of conversations with

Timothy, or any of my past partners, so it was very fulfilling. I thought Simon would be the perfect person to practice some of these communication exercises with.

A few days later, Simon dropped a book off at my doorstep with the sweetest note inside and a little cartoon picture of him smiling next to it. This was something my father would do in his letters to me, so I immediately felt a connection to him.

Even though I was still raw from my divorce from Timothy, there was something very healing and loving about Simon's energy. I found myself spending a lot of time with him. He was very understanding of my frequent trips back and forth to see Nathan in Idaho and offered me a lot of comfort.

The apartment I was renting wasn't working out, so Simon offered to let me move in with him until I was able to save some money and pay off my debt. He worked out of his home, so he made it clear that this was a temporary solution.

I moved in and continued working on my certification. As time passed, we grew closer, and soon our temporary solution became permanent. Living with Simon was great, at first. He gave me my own room and office space so I could get my business off the ground. I was so grateful to him. A year after I moved in, I finished my certification and was finally ready to start practicing hypnotherapy. Simon allowed me to work out of his home and encouraged me to start seeing clients.

As soon as I began advertising and holding classes, things really started to progress. I was seeing four to five clients a week, and I felt safe that Simon was around when I would see male clients. This was all so new to me, but it was so rewarding. I was making a difference in people's lives, and it felt good.

I thought back to the book I'd read about mothers who were successful businesswomen and the empowering energy I'd experienced while reading it. I was amazed at how far I'd come. Here I was, doing the impossible. I'd actually managed to start my own business. It felt like my life was finally getting on track.

After a time, however, my dynamic with Simon shifted. Simon had a lot of stuff, and he demanded that I clean his home in exchange for living there. I was happy to help, but Simon expected me to do everything, including dusting and organizing all the items he'd collected over the years. He would frequently tell me the house wasn't tidy enough. Meanwhile, he didn't clean at all, and it was his things that were cluttering up the space! I spent most of my time cleaning, and eventually became resentful that I was cleaning his place and not my own. But the thought of getting my own place felt like too much of a jump at the time, so I stayed and cleaned for him in return for space.

Simon and I would go out and do things together as a couple and with friends, which was a great stretch for me. I enjoyed meeting all the creative people he introduced me to. My world seemed so small compared to his, so this was a wonderful experience for me to step outside my comfort zone and expand. However, when I was gone too much, visiting Nathan, etc., Simon seemed to feel neglected. He would have parties while I was gone and see other women. I felt angry about his lack of commitment to me. He said it wasn't a big deal and that I was just jealous. This was one of my biggest trigger points, so it hurt deeply when he said that. He never lied to me about seeing other people, but it was still incredibly painful. And his dismissal of my emotions felt like salt in the wound. However, I wasn't secure enough to stand up for myself and my boundaries. Instead, I made myself feel like I was in the wrong for wanting a committed relationship with someone I could trust.

It's obvious to me now how much Simon was like my father, down to his interest in spiritual topics (finding the "hidden truth"), the cartoons in his letters, his demand that I perform domestic labor, and his insistence on having multiple sexual partners.

This is of course exactly why I was drawn to him.

We tend to attract partners who embody the traits of the caretakers who raised us, especially the caretaker we had the least secure relationship with, which in my case was my dad. This happens because our subconscious minds believe that we'll be able to heal our unresolved childhood pain and trauma through this other person. In other words, we think our partner will make us feel whole when the truth is they're just mirroring back to us the wounds that we need to heal within ourselves.

Even though it wasn't clear to me at the time how Simon was yet another stand-in for my father, I was still able to make progress with my healing. I signed up for some courses through Landmark Education. One of these courses was about self-expression. The instructor had us select a project that was close to our hearts and would affect our community of choice. I set a goal for myself to become better at expressing my true, authentic self and to stop hiding who I really was. I also wanted to find a way to bring healing, forgiveness, and closure to my family.

To do that, I knew it was time to stop running from my past and finally face the demons that had been chasing me for thirty years. I needed to confront the truth—the full truth—of what my father did in order to release his hold on me.

2009

I open my closet door. There's a stack of boxes in the back corner, where they've sat unopened and untouched since my move from Idaho. A mausoleum of shame.

I reach for one of the boxes and tear off the packing tape. I dig through the painful reminders of my past until I find the most painful reminder of all. I pick it up and look at the image of the hacksaw mountain on the cover.

I take a deep breath and open the book.

"Almost everyone in Utah County has heard of the Lafferty boys."

My body shakes as I read. I get to the part about Allen finding Baby Erica, "slumped over in her crib in an odd position, motionless" and almost put the book down, but I force myself to keep going. I can't hide from this any longer. I need to see my father for who he is if I'm going to see myself.

I start to cry as I turn the pages, but I don't hold myself back. I let the tears come in gasping, heaving sobs as the emotions that have lain stagnant in my body for decades finally come to the surface.

For the first time in my life, I face the full details of my father's actions. As I gain the context that had been missing from my younger self's perspective, some of the confusion starts to clear.

What's left is raw, unfiltered pain.

PART THREE

WITHIN

CHAPTER 24

July 24, 1984

AFTER READING *Under the Banner of Heaven*, I was finally able to come to terms with the reality I had been pushing away my entire life. I spent days, weeks, and months ruminating over my dad's choices. I had so many questions, but I was afraid to voice them. It wasn't until ten years later, while writing this book, that I finally found the courage to ask my dad the questions that were still eating away at me. Here, to the best of my knowledge, based on Dad's answers and Jon Krakauer's research, is what happened that fateful Pioneer Day in 1984.

After Dad's surprise visit to our house on July 23, 1984, he hitchhiked to Provo, where he met Ron and two of their associates, Ricky Knapp and Chip Carnes, at Grandma Lafferty's home. The next day was Pioneer Day—a state holiday in Utah, with parades and fireworks to rival the Fourth of July. Dad and the others were considering going to Salt Lake City to watch the spectacle, but Ron said that God had other plans for them. According to him, Pioneer Day was the appointed day to act on the removal revelation.

Why Pioneer Day? I wondered when I first read about these events. Did my uncle hope that the fireworks and festivities would provide a good cover for the murder? Did he feel like a holiday commemorating the Mormon pioneers' arrival in Utah was an auspicious time to act on "God's commandment"? Or, now that they had returned to Utah, did he just need a firm date to latch onto in order to follow through with his plan?

Dad told me that he knew Ron was getting bloodthirsty when he visited us the day before, but he had no idea that he was planning to carry out the revelation on Pioneer Day. He never mentioned anything about the revelation to my mom or grandma.

I asked Dad how he felt when Ron made his intentions clear. In a letter from June 2022, Dad told me: "All I can say is that I just listened to him, and I can't say that I really had any particular feeling about it. For quite some time, he had been implying that the time was getting close. The only thing I did was continue to pray to know if I should continue to be with him and follow the things he was saying and doing, and I always got that I should."

As Dad was praying, he received a "revelation" that they should use a knife rather than a gun.* I've tried to imagine what was going through my father's head during this time. How was it possible for a man to spend time with his five small children, the youngest barely one year old, and then the very same day contemplate murdering an innocent baby? Dad's answer is always, of course, that God commanded him. He'd had so much practice putting aside rational thought in order to do what he thought God wanted him to do, that he didn't even question it.

I, obviously, reject the idea that God would command my dad and his brother to murder anyone, let alone an innocent woman and her baby. The only explanation I can find is rooted in utter delusion and fanaticism, as well as a lifetime of indoctrination and unquestioning obedience.

Dad's associates were less convinced. Carnes asked Ron why they needed to kill Erica. Ron's response, like Dad's, was that God had commanded it, and that Erica was a "a child of perdition" and thus had to be removed; besides, after they killed Brenda, Erica would no longer have a mother, so it would be a blessing to kill her, too. The level of delusion required to believe this is astounding.

---

* When I asked him why a knife, he said, "That is a question that would require more information than I can possibly do justice to at this time. It is a good question, and I'm sure I will be able to explain the answer later." He has yet to explain it.

The next morning, despite his intention to use a knife, Dad woke up and, after praying, felt "prompted" to saw the stock and barrel off the 12-gauge shotgun he'd been keeping in Grandma's garage. The men also loaded several other guns into the car, and then went to my uncle Mark's house and asked to borrow back the 20-gauge shotgun Dad had lent him several years ago, which Mark reluctantly gave to them after they claimed they were going hunting, even though no game was in season.

"What are you going to hunt?" Mark asked.

"Any fucking thing that gets in my way," Ron replied.

Afterward, the four men drove to a gravel quarry to "sight" the guns (adjust the sights), but then realized they didn't have the right ammunition for one of the rifles, a .243 caliber. They went back to Mark's to see if he knew where Ron's .243 caliber was; he told them he thought it was at Allen's.

Dad then drove the men to American Fork, where Brenda and Allen lived. Ron got out of the car and went up to the house. He held the shotgun barrel that Dad had sawed off to use as a club and a ten-inch boning knife in his boot. He knocked loudly on the door.

While he was waiting in the car, Dad prayed to God and said, "I hope this is what you intend, because if it isn't, you better do something right now."

No one answered, so Ron returned to the car. Dad told me, "I felt a great sense of relief because I felt that it was a test of faith, kind of like Abraham when he was told to kill his son Isaac, and I was thankful to think that I had been faithful and obedient even when it wasn't really meant to be."

If only Dad had accepted that idea and returned to Provo. However, in another contradictory move, as he was driving the car, he had a strong feeling that he needed to turn the car around and go back to the house. He tells me, "I didn't decide to turn the car around. God did it. That's about the only way I can describe it. I was as surprised as everyone else in the car. I kind of had an out-of-body experience, and they said, 'Why are you turning the car around?' And I said, 'I don't know.' And from that point I was just led by the spirit as I fulfilled the revelation." Dad had the thought that maybe they hadn't been successful because *he*, not Ron, was the one who was supposed to act as the arm of the Lord.

Dad drove back to Brenda's house and walked up to the door. This time, perhaps because Dad's knocking was less violent than Ron's had been, Brenda opened it.*

According to Krakauer, Dad asked if Allen was home, and Brenda said he wasn't. He asked if she knew if Allen's deer rifle was in the house. Brenda said no. Next, Dad asked if he could use the phone. Again, Brenda said no and asked him to leave. Dad pushed past Brenda and entered the house. Brenda snapped at him, saying she knew he was going to take things too far. Then, perhaps reading the violent intent on his face, she started to apologize for angering him and influencing Allen.

However, Dad tells me, after Brenda opened the door, "I just went in. I didn't really do or say anything as I can recall. I just went in like I belonged there, and I was rather taken aback as she immediately began blurting out this rather lengthy apology, saying she was sorry for doing things that I didn't really know what she was talking about."

In Dad's own words, he thought to himself, *You are a bitch.* Then he pushed Brenda to the ground and sat on her back, holding her wrists behind her.

What happened next is difficult for me to comprehend, to write, to witness. It's hard to believe that my own father could be capable of such a horrific act. What makes it more difficult is that Dad has always been willing to talk about what he did and always speaks so calmly about what happened. He wrote to me in a recent letter, "The only thing I can say about what happened from then would be to read the explanation I gave to Jon Krakauer, that he wrote in the book in chapter 24, I think it was. But there are more details I could give you if you want when we can talk. But

---

* Dad told me, "I was a bit surprised when Brenda answered the door at my first knock, especially after Ron had stood and knocked for quite a while, until he was satisfied that no one was home."

it all was just a continuation of what made me turn around the car, and I would describe it as being led by the spirit."

Despite Dad's insistence that he was being led by God, I can't help but wonder if his taste for violence had grown—or if his capacity for empathy had dulled—after abusing my mom and us children. If it made him feel powerful to hurt someone who wasn't as strong as he was. I don't know how else he could have so easily hurt another human being like that.

Fifteen-month-old Erica began crying for Brenda from her bedroom, and Brenda begged him not to hurt her baby.

At this point, Ron entered the house, and the two men proceeded to beat Brenda. Ron let all of his pent-up anger out on Brenda, calling her a bitch and a liar. "Because of you, I don't have a wife anymore," he shouted.

Ron and Dad hit Brenda in the face, over and over, until she was bloodied beyond recognition and Dad had to stop because his hand hurt. They released her, and she slumped into a corner.

At this point, Ron came to his senses. He got scared and told Dad they needed to get out of there. Dad told him he could leave if he wanted to, but he was going to finish what they started. Hearing this, Brenda got up and tried to flee. Ron did nothing to stop her, but Dad lunged for her and grabbed her by the hair, dragging her down to the kitchen floor.

Dad, supposedly praying about what to do next, told Ron to grab something he could tie around Brenda's neck. He wanted to make her pass out so he could take care of Erica first. Ron grabbed the vacuum cleaner cord and tried to tie it around Brenda's neck, but, according to both men, an unseen force pushed him away from her, again confirming their belief that Ron was not the one who was meant to do the killing. Dad took the cord from Ron and wrapped it around Brenda's neck tightly until she lost consciousness.

Once Brenda passed out, Dad took Ron's knife and walked down the hall to the baby's room. He opened the door and saw Erica standing in her crib. She seemed to calm down upon seeing him. At this time, both

Dad and Allen had beards and their voices were similar, so, according to Dad, Erica likely thought my dad was her father.

Dad closed the door behind him and spoke to Erica. He told her he didn't understand why he was being asked to do this, but he had to do what God had commanded him. He then took the knife and, closing his eyes, slid the blade under her chin, all but decapitating her.

I still can't believe my father did this. He knew exactly what he was going to do to that innocent child, and he never wavered for a moment. It was as if there was no compassion, nothing human, left in him. The fact that sweet Baby Erica thought he was her father makes it even worse.

After taking the baby's life, Dad walked to the bathroom and washed the blood off the knife. When it was clean, he walked back to the kitchen and straddled Brenda. He removed the cord from her neck and, grabbing her by the hair, drew the knife across her neck. He recounts that he again closed his eyes, but this time he could hear the blade cut through her trachea and spinal column. He washed the blade a second time, and then announced to Ron that they could leave.*

They returned to the car, blood-soaked, much to the horror of Knapp and Carnes, who later reported that Ron said, "Thank you, brother, for doing the baby, because I don't think I had it in me."

---

* When I asked Dad if he was afraid he would be caught (he didn't wear gloves) or if he'd ever stopped to think about how his actions might affect us, he wrote the following: "Let me answer a question that you didn't ask, that is a normal question that some ask, which I think would be meaningful at this point; I have been asked why I carried out a revelation from my brother, who I say I believe is a child of the devil as opposed to a child of god, and my answer, as I understand it now, is that I wasn't fulfilling Ron's revelation from the moment God took over and I turned the car around. I didn't wear gloves when I carried out that revelation. You ask if I was afraid I would get caught, and I think it would be helpful in understanding my answer that no, I wasn't afraid of being caught. If you read Samuel 1:15, which is the story of Saul the first King of Israel after the children of Israel got to the promised land. This story was in my mind, and I wasn't concerned about being caught or what any of the people you mentioned might think. My only concern was to do everything I could to be sure it was the right thing to do."

Dad replied, "It was no problem."

After they left Brenda's house, Dad changed into a clean shirt he borrowed from Carnes, and the four men drove to Highland. There were still two more names on their list of victims: the next person to remove was Chloe Low (see page 81). Dad tells me, "Driving to Chloe Low's house, my only thought was that if it was God's will, it would also work out like it did at Brenda's."

Ron was shaken by the murders and said he didn't think he could follow through with killing Chloe. Dad, however, remained eerily calm the entire time and reassured Ron that he would be the one to do the killing. My understanding was that Dad was fully convinced that if he removed Brenda, Erica, Chloe Low, and Richard Stowe (see pages 81 and 250) as the Lord had commanded, the path would be cleared for them to build their city of refuge. However, my dad recently told me that he "wasn't thinking about building a city of refuge or anything else at that time." He just wanted to make sure he was carrying out God's will: "All of my energy was being focused on making sure I was doing what I was supposed to as far as staying with Ron and following the things he was saying to do. He had received a revelation that said he was the mouth of God, and I just didn't want to fuck up and piss off God like King Saul did."

The four men reached Chloe's house, but nobody was there, as the Lows were away at their summer home. Instead, the men decided to loot the house, stealing jewelry, a watch, car keys, and $100 in cash. Ron also destroyed Chloe's collection of porcelain figurines, purely because he knew they held sentimental value for her. In my mind, this is just more proof that the men were being led by their delusions and warped self-interest. If they were truly convinced God wanted them to kill Chloe, why bother looting her house and damaging her property? The answer, I believe, is that Ron was acting purely on resentment and bitterness and had never been given the tools to process his emotions. The only outlet he had was patriarchal rage and the justification offered by his religious beliefs. (Interestingly, in Dad's account to me, he attests that they did not trash the house.*)

After raiding Chloe's house, the men set their sights on Richard Stowe. However, on the way there, Knapp missed the turn. At this point, the July heat was stifling their will and enthusiasm to fulfill God's commandment. They debated about whether they should turn around to go back to Stowe's house, but Carne begged Ron to forget about it, arguing that if the Lord had wanted him to kill anyone else today, it would have already happened. Ron agreed and told Knapp to keep driving.

"After Chloe wasn't there," Dad writes, "Ron was in a pretty flustered state. Ricky was driving, and Ron was telling him where to drive. By the way, Ron was directing everything and we were just doing what he said, including going into Chloe's house! But when Ricky missed that turn, Ron said, 'Let's just drive to Wendover.'"

Had the men decided to go back to Stowe's house, they would have found him. He was there all day, working on home repairs with his son. Luckily, the four men were too hot and tired to continue their murdering spree.

I can't be the only one who thinks that the hypocrisy of these men is too much to bear. They claimed to be doing God's work and then

---

* Dad wrote, "We didn't have any money, and when no one was home, Ron cut the wire to the alarm that was going off, and we went in. I had the idea come to my mind that her husband probably had some cash that he could use if he needed it in a hurry, and I went straight to his dresser drawer and found a hundred-dollar bill which we used to buy gas to get to Wendover and some food. . . . We didn't trash her house. The only damage . . . other than Ron cutting the alarm wires, was when Ron and Ricky Knapp were looking for guns and they were breaking down a rather flimsy door that was locked that they thought was perhaps the door to a room where guns might be. I learned later that that door was to the room where there were guns, and I thought it was rather interesting that when they had nearly broken that door down, they just stopped trying to get in there. . . . I figured that it was just God that stopped them because it wasn't part of the plan?"

decided to give up because it was too hot. It seems like whatever they happened to do that day was simply "God's will."*

From there, the men drove to Salt Lake City and then on to Nevada. The entire time, my dad held a shotgun in his lap in case they were stopped by the police. Clearly, his willingness to kill wasn't limited to the people named in Ron's revelation.

The four men reached the Nevada state line around 6:00 p.m. and rented a motel room in Wendover. Around 11:00 p.m., Ron announced they needed to get going. They packed everything up and got back on the freeway.

Shortly afterward, they were pulled over by a Nevada highway patrol officer. The men held their shotguns at the ready, prepared to open fire. However, the officer didn't realize they were fugitives. He just told Knapp he needed to replace a taillight and then let them go. The men replaced the light, but the fuse blew out again, so they returned to the motel to wait for daylight.

While Ron and Dad got some rest, Knapp and Carnes went out to buy cigarettes. They were shaken by the encounter with the officer and decided they needed to bail on my dad and uncle. As soon as Ron and Dad were asleep, they took the car and drove to Wyoming, dumping the murder weapons en route.

Dad and Ron woke the next morning to find themselves stranded, with no car or money. They decided to split up and hitchhike separately to Reno.† They managed to lay low in Nevada for two weeks until they

---

* My dad said, "You ask what our plan was, and I'm not sure if Ron had a plan as such. He just seemed to be trying to receive guidance on what to do and was giving directions as we went along."

† Dad wrote, "We checked into a hotel in Wendover, and that night while Ron and I were sleeping, the other two guys took the car and went to Wyoming to the family of Chip Carnes, where they were caught a couple days later I think. But Ron said we should make our way to Reno separately and meet up at the Golden Nugget Casino where we had briefly visited earlier, which we did."

were found by the FBI.* (During this time, we were staying with Laura Richardson and living in the rental house, hiding until Dad was caught.)

Dad and Ron were arrested and tried for their crimes. After his competency hearing, Ron tried to hang himself in December 1984, resulting in brain damage. He was held at the Utah State Hospital, where he underwent psychological testing. The doctors found him competent to stand trial. He was tried, convicted, and sentenced to death in 1985. However, the Tenth Circuit Court of Appeals overturned the verdict, finding that the competency ruling was in error. Ron was sent back to the Utah State Hospital. Three years later, he was again found competent and in 1996 was retried for his crimes and found guilty. All of his appeals were denied. In 2019, he elected to be executed by firing squad. However, he died of natural causes in November of 2019, at the age of seventy-eight, before his execution date.

Dad opted to represent himself at his trial. He was not given the death penalty because one of the jurors, whom Dad supposedly flirted with through eye contact, voted in the negative. Instead, he was given two life sentences.

Dad has always taken full responsibility for murdering Brenda and Erica; he has never once tried to deny it. He wrote the following to me:

> For years, while going through the trial and everything, I didn't really talk about it. I always just said that it was God's business and didn't feel like I should answer people's questions, but at Ron's retrial and when

---

* Dad recounted, "We stayed two weeks in Reno when Ron said we should go over to a part of the city we had been avoiding because we had been there before, and when he said that, I told him that if we did, and went to Circus Circus where he was suggesting, that I was sure we would be arrested. He didn't really respond to my comment; he was just deep in thought . . . like he was trying to get a revelation or directions on something. So I said that if it was that time then I guess it was that time, and as I was sure I was still supposed to stay with him and follow what he was saying to do, we went to the Circus Circus casino where we were arrested, and I was okay with it."

talking to Jon Krakauer I felt like it was time to explain what it was all about and that is when I confessed or actually just explained what happened. Again it was just another case of doing what I felt God wanted me to do and no, I didn't let myself be distracted by any other thoughts about how it might affect others. King Saul let himself think about what others said or thought about what they wanted him to do, which is what made him do something other than what God wanted, which is why God told him that he was no longer God's King and kicked him off the throne and David became the new King of Israel. And God loved David because he trusted and obeyed God. And always in my heart I had and still have the assurance that having always tried to determine what God wanted and not being afraid or letting myself be influenced by anything anyone else might think; in the end, it would have good results and it would also be best for everyone else and that God would take care of any of the people I loved who may have wondered why I didn't take their feelings into consideration.

While I do believe that God is always watching over us, that in no way absolves my father of his actions or his decision to abandon us. That choice was his and his alone. Tragically, for our family and Brenda's, Dad's decision to follow Ron's "revelation" did not turn out "best for everyone else." And for a long period of my life, I felt certain that no one was taking care of any of us.

Facing the truth of Dad's actions left me feeling raw and vulnerable. But for the first time, the wound inside me felt like a clean cut, rather than a festering sore. I was no longer denying or hiding from my reality. Mark Wolynn writes in *It Didn't Start With You*: "When we try to resist feeling something painful, we often protract the very pain we're trying to avoid." That was exactly what had happened to me. I had avoided the truth for so long that the wound had developed into an infection, infiltrating every aspect of my life.

Reading the book inevitably changed my perception of my father. For the first time, I saw him for who he really was—or at least the parts of him I'd been too afraid to see before. But instead of internalizing his treatment of me, I was able to view him as a flawed parent and human being. I could see now that none of it was my fault. There was absolutely nothing I could have said or done that would have changed things. This realization felt like an enormous relief. I could finally stop punishing myself for something I hadn't done.

This was a huge and crucial step in my healing journey. But the human psyche is a circuitous labyrinth, and there is no direct path or shortcut to wholeness. I had taken the first step into the maze, but there was a great distance still to travel.

CHAPTER 25

2009

AS I FOCUSED ON MY GOAL of freer self-expression and healing, I knew the next step was to open lines of communication with the Lafferty family again. It had been decades since I'd spoken to most of them, not since I was a child. After they'd turned their backs on my family (as I'd perceived it), I'd closed my heart to them and had no desire to initiate contact. But I knew I needed to continue the work of facing and integrating my past instead of running from it.

My brother Johnny, who was still in touch with the Lafferty side of the family, told me about an upcoming family reunion. I knew this was the perfect opportunity to reconnect with my family members. I was scared to see them again, these people who had rejected me as a child, but I gathered my courage and went to the reunion. Simon came with me as support.

The reunion was held in my cousin Tiffany's large barn, which she had built for such occasions.* The first face I saw when I stepped inside the barn was my grandma's. I immediately started crying. The resentful

---

* Tiffany is my aunt Cynthia's oldest child. My dad's sisters, Cynthia and Catherine, were never included in his schemes. Dad had a rather competitive relationship with his brothers-in-law. (Cynthia's husband always seemed disgusted by my dad and apparently believed my dad was going to kill him.) We visited my aunts when I was a kid, but I had no comprehension of the adult dynamics playing out. I just knew that Cynthia's kids always had the best toys. I liked tagging along with my older cousins, who were always talking about makeup and teenage girl stuff. My aunts are beauticians and hairstylists. I remember thinking as a kid that they had the same hair as my grandma. Catherine, in particular, looked a lot like my grandma Lafferty.

feelings I'd been harboring just melted away. All I felt was love. I gave her the biggest hug, which she eagerly returned.

Cheerful music played as we arrived and greeted each other, and there was an enormous table filled with food. Everyone had brought their best dishes, and it was all phenomenal. My uncle Mark had made a delicious tapenade and served it over a large wild Alaskan salmon he'd caught himself. My aunt Heather was there, too. I tensed when I remembered how she hadn't wanted to associate with my family in the past, but she was all smiles.

My uncle Allen was also there. I was nervous about talking to him. Of everyone there, he had the most reason to harbor bad feelings, but he gave me a huge hug.

It was a little more uncomfortable to connect with some of my other family members, but I just kept breathing through it, finding consolation in the fact that healing was happening. Once the initial awkwardness was over, I began to relax into being back with my family.

No one blames me, I realized. I could see now how I'd created that narrative in my head as a child, when the truth was my family members had their own lives and stories that were different from mine but equally important. I was able to let them be who they were, and they were able to let me be who I was. No one blamed me because they knew it wasn't my fault. How could it have been? I was a child when it happened. They knew I'd been hurt just as much as they had. We had all suffered together.

Everyone asked me about my mom—how she was doing and where she was living. I hesitated to share too many details, because my mom is very private and no one had reached out to her before. But everyone seemed sincere; maybe they hadn't known how to contact her or what to say, just as I hadn't known what to say to them.

I was able to reconnect with my cousin Rachelle, whom I hadn't seen since we were in primary school together. It was easy to talk to her. We picked up right where we'd left off. I learned she was the mother of two beautiful children. We shared what we were doing with our lives and what our kids were up to. Simon took photos of the two of us out on the grass. In the pictures we looked like we were playing together, as if we were children again.

I was able to catch up with some of my other cousins as well. Everyone seemed genuinely happy to see me. My brother Johnny and his family were also there. Johnny had made his peace with what happened a long time ago, so he was far more comfortable being there than I was. I was grateful for his safe, smiling presence.

Attending the reunion was incredibly healing for me. I was able to start rewriting the narrative I had been clinging to about my family and my place in it, and I was able to view the past from a new perspective and step outside my own suffering. These were all huge steps for me. I felt like I was making great strides in my goals.

At the end of the reunion, I mentioned to Grandma that I had been visiting Dad. Her face lit up, and she said, "I want to go with you."

I arranged to take her with me that same day. It was as if God and all his angels made it possible for that visit to occur. For one thing, Grandma wasn't on the visitors' list. For another, it wasn't even a visiting day. It was also over an hour's drive to get to the prison from where she lived. So the odds were against us from the beginning, but the way she looked at me, combined with all the training I'd had about being unstoppable and believing that something good would come from going to the reunion, propelled me to get into the car and drive. I didn't allow one bit of resistance to creep into my mind.

When we arrived, the guards allowed us into the prison without a problem. I couldn't believe it. I thought of all the times I'd been turned away from the prison for something as small as wearing an underwire bra. It was truly a miracle.

It was difficult to see my father after finally reading the full extent of his crimes. But at that moment I felt it was important to cultivate love and forgiveness in the present by bringing my dad and grandmother together. I think it brought up a lot of emotions for my dad. My grandma was very old at this point, and she seemed a little confused about why Dad was there. My father tried to explain it to her, which was difficult for all of us. Finally, he stopped himself and just stayed quiet and listened. Grandma was almost deaf and could barely make out what was being said. But the love was there between them.

That was the last time they saw each other before she passed away. I was so grateful I'd taken her to see him. It felt very much like I was being supported by the spirit world to foster healing in my family.

Shortly after the reunion, I had the first inkling that I should write this book. For as long as I could remember, other people had been telling and interpreting my story for me, and I'd accepted those stories as my own. I'd lived under my father's shadow for so long, I'd allowed his story to define mine. But the reunion had shown me how many other stories there were, and that my story—my real story—was just as valid. Maybe, I thought, it was time for me to reclaim my voice.

Through Landmark Education, I met a woman who had written about her struggles with suicidal ideation and now helped other people write their stories of trauma and healing. When I told her who I was and what had happened in my life, she said, "We need to write your story."

This felt like a confirmation. I was excited about it and agreed to work with her. Our collaboration went well for a while until I realized we didn't quite share the same vision for the project, and we parted ways. But I still felt the need to write the book, so I kept opening my laptop and writing for an hour or two, here and there, just letting whatever came to mind flow onto the page.

I worked on the book in my spare time, eager to express all that I was learning and experiencing. Mom gave me her journals to read through, and the Laffertys said that I was welcome to visit them anytime.

I connected with my cousins on social media. My uncle Watson was very supportive of my writing the book, and gave me a personal letter from my grandmother to include. Uncle Mark made a compilation of home movies from his childhood—all the siblings growing up together—and hand-delivered it to me. This was such a beautiful gesture.

My uncle Allen and I also visited and talked about working with medicinal plants and essential oils. He told me he was open to answering any questions I had. I was so grateful for his generosity and sat down with him to hear his story. He was incredibly gracious and took the time to open his heart and tell me things he regretted and lessons he had learned. It was very emotional and very sacred. Allen told me he'd visited my dad in prison and that he had forgiven him.

It felt as if my family was giving me permission to be who I was, outside of any particular religion or worldview. For the first time, I felt free to be myself.

Shortly after this experience, my mom called me and told me that her mother had had a stroke and was in a care center. She knew she needed to see her soon before she passed away and asked if I would go with her to Scotland. I, of course, agreed.

It was a beautiful trip. I was able to be present with my mom and grandmother. Nanny wasn't able to talk, but she could understand what we were saying. It was hard to see her so helpless. The bitterness I'd held on to from my childhood experiences with her melted away. I thought about the joy and support she and William brought my mother in the darkest moments of her life. I thought about that long car ride to Idaho, and how Nanny had let me rest my tired head on her shoulder. I thought about that first sip of delicious tea.

Tears filled my eyes as I held Nanny's hand and told her how much I loved her.

Mom and I went to visit her almost every day. It was special to see my mom get to spend that time with her mother and a reminder that the past remains in the past. All we have is the present moment to be with the ones we love. My heart felt so full from the strides I'd made to release the past's hold on me and move forward with forgiveness and love.

All of these were massive steps for me. Facing my past, instead of hiding from it, and taking action to move forward allowed me to find greater confidence and belief in myself. I learned that I was still lovable, even if others didn't agree with my choices. No matter what I've been through or what other people say about me, I am still a good and loving person.

These experiences also helped me understand that Timothy and his wife had their own stories. They shared different views than I did about what we believe is best for Nathan, but that didn't mean that they didn't love him as much as I did. That was a hard lesson for me to learn, but there was so much peace that followed once I was able to accept it. Unconditional love means allowing others to be where they are. I reminded myself that my son was safe, and he was getting the care he needed, even if my mom and I weren't the ones to give it to him. This brought great peace to my heart.

CHAPTER 26

2010

ONE DAY IN 2010, after three years of being with Simon, I felt sick and thought I had the flu. After a few days, however, it became clear that it wasn't the flu. I was pregnant again. I don't know how it happened; Simon already had two boys in their late twenties and had gotten a vasectomy. It shouldn't have been possible. But it was.

This was the fourth time I'd experienced a surprise pregnancy. I was worried that I was repeating the same pattern I had in the past, getting attached to a partner through an unplanned child. I felt very stressed about it. I was hitting a groove with work, and I figured there was no way Simon was going to want to become a father again at his age.

Part of me did want to have another baby. But then a voice in my head would kick in, telling me I was being irrational. *You've already screwed up with the last two. What makes you think you can handle another one?* I figured maybe I wasn't fit to be a mother. And the thought of being attached permanently to Simon, along with anticipating how upset he would be at this change in his life, weighed heavily on me. I believed not having the baby was the most responsible decision I could make. An abortion is not an easy thing to accomplish in Utah, but I began taking steps toward having the procedure.

When I was about six weeks pregnant, I went to visit Nathan in Idaho. I was holding him on my lap, when out of the blue, he cuddled in close and said, "Aww, baby!"

It was as if my heart suddenly burst open. For the first time, I allowed the thought of going through with the pregnancy to enter my mind. It was as if I'd been looking at a screen in black and white, and the moment I thought about having the baby, colors began to flood in. As soon as a doubt arose, feelings of peace and assurance would immediately replace it. This continued for about five minutes. It felt like someone was communicating with me, and I had the very clear sense that this baby wanted to come into this world.

Maybe I'm not just blindly repeating the same pattern, I thought. *Maybe I'm being offered a chance to do things differently.*

I started sobbing and called Simon. I told him that I was going to have the baby and hoped that he would support my decision. He said he would. I drove home with the light of my spirit shining. I knew I was making the right choice.

When I got home, Simon told me that he wanted to make our relationship work. He was ready to commit to me fully and raise our child. His reassurance was a huge comfort to me. Even though I was certain I was making the right choice by keeping the baby, I was still feeling vulnerable and nervous about bringing another child into the world, especially by myself. I leaned into the sense of security he was providing.

We decided to get married and asked our friend Anita, who was an ordained minister, to officiate our wedding. I loved spending time with Anita. She was old enough to be my grandmother, which was probably why I enjoyed her company. She was born in the South and spoke with that lovely Southern charm. I felt so comfortable having her marry us.

We held the wedding in the living room of Anita's tiny two-bedroom apartment. It was a small and sacred gathering with just a few friends. Anita served punch and a small carrot cake and another of our friends played the banjo and sang some songs. It was intimate and delightful. We visited for a couple of hours and then wrapped things up. It was short and sweet, just how I wanted it. It was truly a lovely experience, and I felt happy knowing Simon was committing to our relationship for good.

I knew that when it came to raising this baby, I wanted to do things differently. When I'd had Erin (barely more than a child myself), I hadn't done much to prepare for pregnancy or the birth, let alone raising her. And when I'd had Nathan, I hadn't felt free to pursue the birth options I wanted. This time around, I read a long list of books on childbirth and parenting, especially about how to foster a positive environment for your child's unique spirit and how to create a structure in which they can flourish and grow. I was clear from the beginning that I wanted a midwife and a water birth at home. I wanted immediate skin-to-skin contact after the birth, and I also wanted to allow the placenta to finish its job before cutting the umbilical cord. Finally, I insisted that the baby not be circumcised. To my relief, Simon was fully supportive of everything. At my next appointment, the ultrasound confirmed it was a boy.

I quit working so I could stay home and get the rest my body needed while carrying this beautiful baby. I was worried that when I'd thought about having an abortion that perhaps my son's little spirit had felt that, so I wanted to make it very clear that he was wanted. I would talk to him all the time and tell him that I couldn't wait to meet him and love him. I would rub my belly and say mantras like, "You are going to be such a healthy, strong, little spirit. You are so loved. You are so wanted." My entire focus was on loving and nurturing this baby growing inside me.

I felt at peace throughout my entire pregnancy. This time, I had the help of friends and a partner who loved me and supported me. I felt supported by my family as well. I was still making trips to Idaho to see Nathan, and when I was there, I would stay with my mom and my brother Brian, who had an apartment a few houses away from Gwen. Mom and I were back on good terms, and she was excited about my pregnancy. I was also able to mend my relationship with Rachel. She had just had her first child a year and a half before this, and when she found out I was expecting, she was delighted. My relationship was better with Gwen, too. She was no longer acting like my second mother, as she had often in the past. We were able to relate to each other as sisters and peers.

(Johnny was living in Oregon at the time, finishing medical school, and Christopher was in California.)

I felt so tuned in to my body throughout the pregnancy. My midwife gave me a due date, and as the date approached, I asked my dear friend Amy to stay the weekend with me. I had always been on track with my due dates, so I wanted to be prepared. I had been reading stories from the book *Spiritual Midwifery* by Ina May Gaskin, and it struck me that the women who struggled to dilate were the ones who didn't feel like they had been able to nest properly. (That had certainly been my experience with my previous two births.) The moment they nested, boom, the baby came. I wanted to feel fully ready so the labor could proceed smoothly.

Amy's company was so soothing. We talked and caught up, and she weeded my garden for me while I assembled the crib. My other friend Mary also stopped in to check on me, and Erin, who was a teenager now, stayed the night to be close by as well.

The stage was set. All the details were covered. My birth plan was rehearsed. Now I just had to wait.

I woke up around seven o'clock the morning of July 18, 2011, to use the bathroom. Suddenly, whoosh, I felt the pressure of the baby's head. The contractions began to intensify pretty quickly, and I asked my friends to call the midwife. She was over an hour away, but her apprentice arrived in no time. Amy was very calm and steady. She filled the bathtub with water, and I got in immediately. The warm water helped soothe the contractions.

I do remember being frustrated with Simon because he'd decided to take a bath shortly before this and had used up all the hot water. Consequently, my bath was warm, not hot. I felt like Simon was a little bit in his own world, but I was happy that Amy was there. She rubbed my back exactly where I needed it and kept telling me I was strong and doing so well. I was able to use hypnosis as a tool to guide me through labor. Then the midwife arrived, and fifteen minutes later, Baby Max was born. He came out a bluish purple and gave only a faint cry. The midwife took

him immediately and sucked out his mouth so he could breathe. Then
she gave him back to me.

After another contraction, the placenta was out. I held my precious
baby on my chest and let him find his way to my breast. We waited for
the umbilical cord to stop pulsing before we cut it.

The love was so full in that room, almost as if a doorway to heaven
had been opened beside us. Simon and I both wept with joy. The experience couldn't have been more beautiful. It was everything I'd wanted
with my previous births but hadn't been able to have and was incredibly
healing for both of us.

I realized that all of my children were miracle babies. Each of my
birth experiences had been vastly different, but all three children had
been conceived miraculously—despite the pill, despite other birth control
methods, and even despite a vasectomy. It was as if their spirits had been
determined to come to earth, no matter what, and I was honored to be
their mother.

As I settled into a routine with Max, I couldn't help but reflect on my
recent experiences with Grandma Lafferty and Nanny Burns. The healing
I'd shared with both of them, as well as my own parents, prompted a great
deal of contemplation on my part about the ways that parenting evolves
across generations. My grandparents had raised my parents based on what
was modeled to them by their parents. My parents then perpetuated that
model to a certain extent when they became parents themselves.

*Can the next generation really make different choices from what was
modeled to them?* I wondered. *Or are we doomed to inherit the sins of our
parents?*

I know that my sweet grandma Lafferty always struggled with this
question. I can't imagine the depths of her pain. I'm sure she wondered
whether she had done anything to cause the tragedy in our family, or
whether she could have at least done something to prevent it. I believe

she thought she had failed as a mother.* With Grandpa gone, this was a burden she had to bear entirely on her own.

"How could Dan and Ron have done this to Allen, their little brother?" I heard her wonder aloud on many occasions.

My precious grandma. I wished so badly to provide an answer that would have consoled her.

For the rest of my grandmother's life, she searched for a way to find peace after such terrible grief. I believe she eventually found it.

In her final years, Grandma stayed in an assisted living center. I went to visit her several times. She and I laughed at how she couldn't wait to get out of there and go do something fun. I would take her to the park and talk. She told me how one time she and Linda, her roommate, went for a walk. Linda lost her balance, so Grandma went to catch her, but instead of helping her stay upright, she fell on top of her. We both laughed about that for a while. She repeatedly said that she was just so grateful to have such a wonderful roommate and how she loved that she could help out by folding laundry. That was just like my precious grandma, always keeping busy and sharing how blessed she was.

I saw her a few months before she passed. We met at the LDS Payson Temple. It was hard to see her in a wheelchair. She'd had a stroke and was declining. She passed away in 2016 at the age of ninety-seven.

A few years before she passed, Grandma wrote her testimony in her journal. Her words touched me deeply. I've included a few of the things she said here:

---

* In the 2022 television adaptation of *Under the Banner of Heaven*, my grandma is portrayed as being supportive of her sons' extremist behavior. I want to clarify that this was a largely fictionalized account of events and that the depictions of my grandmother and other members of my family (many of whom were omitted and/or invented) were not representative of the actual people in any way. The actions of my father and uncle pained my grandmother for the rest of her life.

Heavenly Father has blessed me with an amazing family who are truly my most precious jewels. My children and their spouses and families are where I find my greatest joy, and where I have felt the greatest sorrow.

During what I call the dark ages of my life—after agonizing with what went wrong in the family and wondering how I could have lived differently to influence my children, and not being able to see in my mind what could right all the trauma and heartbreak of the tragedy— I asked the Savior to take my burden. He did, and has, and this is where I found peace.

I learned that the Lord will take our burden if we ask, if we do all we can to help ourselves. I also realized that I had to make the choice to be happy or sink into despair. I chose to find [happiness] and live happily for my family and those around me.

I was so moved by her words that, after reading her letter, I began to sob. I love and miss her so much.

Like my grandma, I realized I, too, could make the decision to choose happiness. I could choose to believe that my father's decisions did not dictate the shape of my life and that I could make different choices than he did as a parent. At the same time, I could accept him for who he was instead of living in the past, hoping desperately to rewrite something that could not be changed or fixed.

In his book *It Didn't Start With You*, Mark Wolynn explains that trauma is frequently inherited. He writes, "The family story is our story. Like it or not, it resides within us." His book, which I highly recommend, explains that family patterns can keep a cycle of suffering alive, generation after generation. But this cycle can be changed. The first step is to face and repair our relationship with our parents. "Regardless of the story we have about them," Wolynn writes, "our parents cannot be expunged or ejected from us. . . . Rejecting them only distances us further from ourselves and creates more suffering."

I began to see that it didn't matter how much my father could or could not love me. What mattered was how receptive *I* was to love. As a child, when I had closed myself off to my father's love, believing I wasn't worthy of it, I had closed myself off to all love. My task now was to open myself back up, to be willing to love without expectation of anything in return, and to accept whatever love the people in my life were able to give, without dictating the terms and conditions for how that love was given.

I decided to start by focusing on the love I was giving (and receiving) as a parent myself. We may inherit the "sins" of our fathers, but we do not have to keep them. Yes, we will likely find ourselves defaulting to behaviors that were modeled to us as children because they feel familiar, but we always have a choice about how we parent our children and how we treat others. It starts with the desire to do better, and we can start right now. All change happens in the present moment.

If we want to see results in any area of our life, we should begin with the awareness that something needs to change. After this initial inquiry, and acceptance, we can create a plan that will help us act on our intention to change. The good news is we don't have to do this alone. There are so many amazing resources out there for conscious parenting.* Books on parenting and inner-child work were a huge support for me as I worked on becoming a better parent. I learned how important it is for a child to feel heard and safe to express their feelings. This was something that was not available to me; nor was it something that was available to my parents, let alone my grandparents. Consequently, it became my primary objective to provide this sense of safety for my children.

I could see in myself how I'd already begun to make a change, beginning with the way I approached pregnancy and childbirth. As I parented

---

* Some books that helped me were Anne Marie Ezzo and Gary Ezzo's *Preparation for Parenting, Preparation for the Toddler Years*, and *Parenting from the Tree of Life*; and Tedd Tripp's *Shepherding a Child's Heart by Tedd Tripp*. See full details on these and more in the resources section on pages 319–20.

Baby Max, as well as Nathan and Erin, I made a conscious effort to allow my children the space to express their emotions. I asked how they were feeling, and then I listened. I let them know that they were always safe and loved, even if we disagreed, and I was quick to apologize for my mistakes or when I did something to hurt their feelings. I encouraged them to follow their hearts and the things that interested them, rather than what I thought they should do, and I gave them my attention and time as I supported those interests. Every night, I prayed with them before bedtime so I could hear them express their hopes and dreams and support them in seeking their highest good.

My simple intention to ask and listen has opened up many beautiful conversations with my children. It makes my heart swell whenever they come to me for advice if they are experiencing conflict with friends or at school—and especially when we're able to find a resolution. This tells me that something is working.

I was not (and am not) a perfect parent, by any means. There were countless times I could have been better. But whenever I caught myself feeling guilty, I'd remind myself that this was new for me, and that change takes time. My intention was to transform myself and my behavior so that my children would have something better to offer their children and so the cycle of trauma could end.

I want all children, not just mine, to feel safe in the world and to be able to tap into their creative potential. When we are afraid or dealing with trauma, the creative part of our brains doesn't work because we're stuck in survival mode. Can you imagine a reality where everyone feels safe and loved enough to be creative? We would truly create a different world.

As I worked on becoming a better parent, I realized I was being given an opportunity to re-parent myself at the same time. After all, I saw my children as precious beings who deserved all the love and safety in the world. Shouldn't I see myself in the same way? I was doing everything in my power to love, support, and protect my children. Surely, I could do the same for little Rebecca, that innocent and hurting girl who was still a part of me.

And so, the more I worked to listen with patience to what my children had to say and give them a voice to safely express their emotions, the more I learned to have patience with myself and to honor and express my emotions. The more I treated my children with respect and viewed them as full human beings with their own individual needs, the more I was able to respect myself and acknowledge my own needs. The more I spent quality time with my children, honoring their authentic interests, the more I began to cultivate my own interests and prioritize quality time with myself.

What helped me the most was taking time to sit in stillness and to communicate with my inner child. I asked her how she was feeling and what she needed. Over time, my inner child became my best friend. Through my time with her, I've been able to experience the love I always wanted. This love hasn't come from an outside source. It has come from me.

It may seem like a strange concept to converse with our inner child or spirit, but we have conversations with ourselves all the time. We just usually aren't paying attention to our self-talk. What kinds of things are we telling ourselves? Are we empowering our spirit or disempowering it? When you talk directly to your inner child or spirit (or your higher self, creator, the universe, whatever fits your belief system), it may seem uncomfortable at first; it was for me. But the insights you glean will create a new awareness within you. Growth can only happen outside of our comfort zone, and being willing to experience discomfort allows us to move to a new level of maturity and understanding.

I've come to appreciate that we are always in relationship with our inner being, whether we are aware of it or not. When we feel bad, we see the situation we are experiencing differently than the way our inner being sees it. This creates a disconnect. There is nothing wrong when this happens. What I have learned is that if I am feeling heavy emotions, this is the perfect time to surrender to my inner being through meditation, intention, and prayer, and ask it to show me a more peaceful outcome. I have found that when I take time to connect with the divine presence that resides within me, and all of us, true healing happens.

My inner spirit always provides me with answers to my questions. The answers don't always come right away, but they do come, and I have been guided to read the books I have needed to read and talk to the people I have needed to talk to. As I've reached out with an open heart, trusting that I will be given the support I need *because I am inherently deserving of love and help*, life has shown me miracle after miracle. I've learned to trust that I am loved and that my inner spirit is not only listening, but helping me to live a good life, to experience peace, and to guide my children to be the best version of themselves that they can be.

In my lifelong effort to be a good parent to my children and to love and support my own inner child, I like to imagine my grandparents looking down on me from wherever it is we go when we transition from this life, cheering me on.

CHAPTER 27

2014–16

PART OF ME WISHES I COULD END MY BOOK HERE, with everything wrapped up in a tidy bow. With my third marriage and third child, I seemed to have finally figured things out. However, the healing journey is rarely linear, and there were still wounded parts of me, hidden deep in the maze of my psyche, that had yet to be uncovered.

After having Max, for the first time ever, life felt truly wonderful, especially as I worked on cultivating a stronger relationship with myself and the people I loved. I thought I had solved all of my problems. But by the time Max turned three, my fatigue from having a new baby still hadn't lifted. I was getting at least nine hours of sleep each night, but I still woke up every morning feeling exhausted. I began juicing and changing my diet to see if that would help, but I still needed several cups of coffee to get me through the day.

Simon and I began sleeping in separate rooms because I was getting up a lot at night to tend to Max, and Simon would act very put out about his sleep being interrupted. We'd gotten along so well when Max was a baby, but now our arguing seemed to be getting worse. I was under a lot of stress trying to manage his frustration. Simon said the apartment was never clean enough, which would trigger a huge outburst almost every morning. He also complained that I wasn't making any money to contribute to the bills, even though I was caring for Max full-time. I felt at a loss as to what to do.

During this time, I was still visiting Nathan and fighting for my right to see him. The stresses from the custody battle and my relationship issues with Simon, along with caring for a toddler and the continual pressure I felt to return to work, were just too much for my body. When things were stable in our relationship and I felt safe, I felt good about staying with Simon. But when we argued, I suddenly felt unsafe and had an overwhelming urge to flee. Despite the progress I had made in my healing, I was still going through the same cycles in my relationships that I always experienced. Once again I found myself at the end of my rope.

Max's legs were covered in eczema, and I was searching high and low for a solution. Nothing seemed to be helping him, and I finally started mixing my own skin creams, using various essential oils, in an effort to bring him some relief.

One day, I met a woman who invited me to a dance symposium. She said there would be a healer there whom she believed could help Max and me. He would only be in town for a few more days, so going to the symposium would give me an opportunity to schedule something with him. I marked the date on my calendar. I remember not knowing what exactly to expect, but I loved dancing and figured if this healer could help Max and me improve our health, then it would be worth my time and effort.

The morning of the symposium arrived. I went to the event with the intention of connecting with Source energy and finding inspiration for the best path forward. At the symposium were speakers who spoke about Native American dance and how nature is its own symphony. It was fascinating to me. A group of girls taught us a type of celebratory dance. We all stood in a circle and waved our arms while holding them up in a type of worship. The energy this allowed me to channel was incredible. I felt so alive!

While lunch was being served, I took the time to walk around and check out a couple of the tables. I looked up and noticed a handsome gentleman in his mid-fifties with dark hair. He had the look of a wanderer with tired but bright eyes. He introduced himself as Daryl, and I realized he was the healer my friend had told me about. I introduced myself as well and said that I was interested in his services and would like to schedule something with him. We talked about Max's eczema as well as Nathan's SMA. Daryl mentioned he also had a son in Idaho whom he wanted to bring home to live with him full-time. His son, a young adult with autism, needed twenty-four-hour care like Nathan; he was nonverbal and showed signs of aggression. Daryl believed this was due to the environment he was in and felt that he would be safer at home with him. I thought that was an admirable thing for him to want.

Daryl said, "I would be willing to go with you to see your son and do some work on him if you are interested?" Just the fact that he would offer to do something like that felt like a gift from the heavens. Here was this complete stranger, offering to support me. I couldn't believe it.

I scheduled a session with him for the next day. Daryl's modality involved kinesiology. I held out my arm while he asked me a series of questions. After each question, he would press down on my arm. My arm would lower or hold strong to indicate either a yes or no from my body. Daryl determined that my tiredness was due to what he called adrenal fatigue. He then did something that my dad used to do with me and his patients: He got really quiet and held his hands over the area that needed treatment, which created a sensation of light, pulsing energy. I could literally feel the healing energy. It only took about five minutes at the most; then the session was complete. I couldn't believe how much better I felt afterward.

As I paid Daryl and got ready to leave, he told me he'd like to show me something. He pulled out a blueprint of a planned community he had created for parents of children with special needs. He made it sound very appealing. My heart opened to him as he talked. I wanted to thank him for all he had done for me, so I told him he just needed someone to believe in him to make his dream a reality.

"It's so easy to talk to you," Daryl said. "Is it okay if I tell you something?"

"Sure," I said.

"When I first saw you at the symposium, I had the craziest thought. I thought, *Wow, that's my soulmate.*"

I blinked in surprise, not sure what to say. Daryl said he could feel a strong energy between us and that he was disappointed I was already taken. He said if I was ever single to look him up.

I should have recognized his overstepping professional boundaries as a red flag, but instead I felt flattered and excited. I, too, felt a strong energy between us. I couldn't put a name to it, but it was something I wanted to experience again.

I got home and told Simon about the session. He was not impressed. He called Daryl a charlatan. I was angry and frustrated by his response. Daryl had done something to help me, and Simon was not able to validate my experience.

I asked my spirit about the energy I'd felt during my session. The answer I heard was, *"Pure, unadulterated love."* I had to look up "unadulterated" because I didn't even know what it meant.

What I didn't understand at the time was that I have a special ability to tap into a frequency of love. I can sit and hold space for other people and feel tremendous empathy and compassion for their situation, no matter who they are or what they've done. As Daryl talked about his son and his desire to help him and other people in similar situations, my heart opened. I was able to tap into a sense of love for him and his vision. Because Daryl was also a conduit of energy, the two of us were able to generate a powerful connection. However, I incorrectly attributed the source of that positive energy to Daryl, when it was really coming from me.

After this, I started to think about Daryl obsessively. I attached the meaning of love to the energy I'd felt between us. I began to believe that I would only be able to experience that kind of love with him. In my spiritual immaturity, I thought that meant I was supposed to be with Daryl, especially since things were rocky with Simon.

Oh boy, here we go again!

This was all the push I needed to end my relationship with Simon. I decided I was done dealing with his lack of support in creating structure and discipline for Max as well as his constant criticism, complaining, and negativity. I'd had enough of that in my previous relationships. Why did everything seem like such a battle? It felt like I was raising two children: Simon, as well as Max, but Simon was by far the more difficult one to manage. It was more than I could handle. I saw that I was back in the same situation I'd been in with Timothy.

This was an eye-opening moment for me. I re-learned, yet again, that I couldn't escape myself. I was still seeking solutions in my external circumstances, when what I needed to do was look inward.

Unfortunately, at this point I was still unable to see how I was repeating the same pattern of seeking a new partner to fulfill my needs while I was in a relationship with someone else. My emotions and wounded inner child were still taking the reins, redirecting me from the person who was no longer meeting my needs (Simon) to someone I thought could (Daryl).

Fortunately, I had reached a point in my growth where I was less codependent and more willing to let my partner go, instead of trying to convince myself to stay, as I'd done with Timothy and Julian. So I calmly told Simon I would be moving out and asked him to please be patient with me while I found a new place to live. It was the most peaceful ending of a relationship I'd experienced yet.

I have no ill feelings toward Simon. Once we got honest with ourselves, we realized we just wanted different things. I followed through on my plan to move out and end our marriage. However, we were able to remain good friends and co-parent our son. Simon has been a great dad to Max, and I think becoming a father again has been very healing for him and has helped him address trauma from his own childhood. The amicable way we were able to transition our relationship felt like huge progress to me.

◆ ◆ ◆

I was still visiting Nathan once a month with Max, so I thought I would reach out to Daryl to see if he would be willing to travel with me to Idaho. He said yes. I was so excited. On the drive, we talked about life and the spirit world and different healing modalities. I couldn't wait for him to meet Nathan.

The visit was a disaster.

I'd told Timothy and Melanie that I was bringing a friend with me, but I hadn't told them he was a healer. I knew they wouldn't be open to that kind of thing; however, I didn't anticipate how badly things would go.

While we were visiting with Nathan, Daryl started to do some energy work on him. Melanie saw him crouching beside Nathan with his hands over his head and freaked out. She yelled at Timothy to grab Nathan while she called the cops. When the police arrived, they said I was allowed to stay but Daryl needed to leave. In retrospect, I can understand why Timothy and Melanie were concerned. I should have communicated better, or left Daryl out of it. I was just trying to help Nathan—and relieved to have an ally for once—but the whole situation spiraled out of control and became very emotionally charged. It was very difficult for me to stay present with Nathan after that.

I visited my son for four hours while Daryl waited in the car. After the visit, I returned to my car, defeated. Daryl walked toward me and put his arms out and gave me a big hug. It was exactly what I needed at the time.

On the drive home, we talked about what had happened. I appreciated that Daryl was someone who could actually relate to me about Timothy and my struggles (Simon never wanted to visit Nathan with me). Daryl shared his struggles with me as well. We were two wounded souls, identifying with one another. When we returned to Salt Lake, we said goodbye, but something in me wanted to see him again.

About a year after I got my own apartment—just down the road from Simon, so we could both raise Max, who was now almost five—I had the impulse to contact Daryl again. He said he was living in Heber City, about an hour southeast from Salt Lake, and that it would be nice to have me stop by for a visit on my way to see Nathan.

Seeing Daryl again was like reuniting with an old friend. There was something so familiar and inviting about his presence. I felt an instant connection. I was starving for a loving and present man who would make me feel safe and validated.

We continued seeing each other and had so much fun together. We would go dancing and rock climbing, which I loved, and our connection on a physical level was phenomenal. I'd never experienced a sexual connection like it. I had a deep core need to be loved by and desired by a man to whom I felt physically attracted; consequently, our connection was like a drug to me—like taking a drink of cool refreshing water after years of thirst—and the wounded child at my core latched on tightly.

What I know now is that the feeling of instant connection and even addiction to someone, aka "love at first sight," is often a sign of trauma bonding. It means your trauma and your partner's trauma are perfect matches for each other. Daryl had a lot of the same wounds that I did, from both childhood and past experiences. And he shared a lot of similar traits with my dad, even more than Simon had. When Daryl would talk about his dreams for his planned community, it reminded me so much of the way my father used to talk. My wounded inner child gravitated to him more strongly than any of my past partners. Daryl's visions were exciting and gave me something to work toward. I utterly fell for him.

There was another crucial similarity between Daryl and my dad: Daryl also believed he was a prophet, specifically John the Baptist. For some reason, Daryl believed that he would die the way the John had (beheaded), which didn't make any sense to me. Daryl surrounded himself with ex-Mormons and religious fanatics, the way my father had. The group he was staying with when I met him had revealed his true identity to him during a collective spiritual experience. This led him to believe he should be able to heal his son, Jack.

Daryl shared this information with me almost a year after we started dating. He was very strange and cryptic about it, demanding I keep it a secret and asking me if I could "see" him, almost as if it were a test to see how spiritual I was. I remember getting that sinking feeling in my stomach that I would get when my dad would go on his long rants about his role as a prophet.

After Daryl shared this with me, I had a moment of absolute clarity. It was so plain to me that I was attracted to this man because of how much he was like my father. It both scared me and kept me attached to him. I knew it wasn't going to be easy to leave, and I knew I wasn't ready to cut ties. I also did not want to hear anyone else state the obvious about the relationship. I knew the truth; it was just going to take me some time to process it.

I recognized that, just like with my father, it would be pointless to question or directly challenge Daryl's belief because of how deeply it was held. I know how powerful the mind is and that we can justify anything if it meets a fundamental need, even a distorted one. Like my dad, Daryl had a deep need to be seen as someone important and special.

I chose not to respond. I didn't want to feed into his delusions. But it saddened me greatly. I knew then that this relationship was based on false beliefs and that it was destined to end.

Even though Daryl and I shared many good experiences, things soon became quite difficult. His son, Jack, came to live with him, and Daryl was trying to get him the care that he needed. But Jack had frequent episodes where he would act out aggressively. It was hard to spend time together while we were always on edge. Max wasn't safe around Jack alone. Sometimes when Max and I were there, it felt like we were all a happy family. Other times, it felt like we were outsiders and under threat.

Now that Daryl was separated from his community and isolated with his son, the light seemed to fade from him. He started to show signs of being abusive, another similarity he shared with my dad. His past failings with his family, marriage, and businesses, compounded by not getting enough sleep and his son not improving, all exacerbated the situation. When I saw how self-destructive Daryl was growing, I stopped trusting him.

Daryl would frequently rant about how his first wife wasn't a virgin. He believed that she'd "stolen" that from him. I was always very perplexed when he said this. For one thing, I couldn't understand why he was still fixated on a past relationship instead of our current relationship. For another thing, why did he think his wife owed him her virginity? As if that were a tangible thing, something that could be given to someone else. It became evident how patriarchal and misogynist Daryl's views were.

As I pulled back, Daryl felt even more bitter and abandoned, and he became more manipulative. He told me that I had a disdain for men. I believed him at first and tried to fix whatever prejudice I was holding on to until I realized it was just another way he was trying to control me.

One time Daryl tried using neuro-linguistic programming (NLP) on me, claiming he'd had a vision in which he saw me as a spiritual shaman from his past life. He wove a big elaborate story around this supposed vision. I saw immediately that he was just trying to appeal to my ego and manipulate me to get what he wanted. It again reminded me of something my dad would do. But I didn't share Daryl's (or my dad's) desire to be someone special, a "chosen one." I believe that none of us is more special than the next person. So all he accomplished was eroding my trust further.

1983

"A man cannot lawfully be placed under the law of the wife, for he is the head," Dad says adamantly. I look up from the couch where I'm holding Baby Brian. Was that directed at me?

There's no one else in the room, so Dad must be talking to me. But he's not even looking at me. He's pacing up and down the length of our small living room.

"Paul said, 'Suffer not a woman to teach or usurp authority over the man, but to be in subjection!'" Dad slams his fist onto the table.

I nod but don't say anything. It's clear that Dad's about to start one of his long rants. I already know he doesn't care what I think. He just wants someone to listen to him. And with Mom banished to the trailer and his brothers gone, I'm the only option.

"That's the problem with society," Dad continues. "Women don't know their place anymore! God created Adam first, not Eve. He made Eve to be a companion to Adam. The wife is under the law to the husband, but the husband is not under the law to the wife!"

Brian fusses, so I shush him and bounce him gently in my arms.

"Who can find a virtuous woman? For her price is far above rubies." Dad's pacing grows more agitated. Suddenly, he whirls on me. "Your mother is not a virtuous woman! That bitch doesn't know her place. She wasn't even a virgin when I married her. She should be grateful that I was willing to take her, but has she ever shown gratitude to me? No. She's just a constant thorn in my side. I'm not even attracted to her, you know that?"

I keep my gaze on my little brother as I focus on tuning out Dad's words. "Shh, shh," I whisper.

"It's my God-given right to have a pure wife! And yet your mother continues to defy me. But I will have my due—on earth as it is in heaven. In the celestial kingdom, I'll have as many wives as I want. All of them virgins."

I grip Brian tightly. *I can't hear you*, I tell myself. *I can't hear you.*

"Polygamy is the true order of marriage, Rebecca. The sooner you understand that, the better. All the Old Testament prophets had plural wives. Abraham, Jacob, David, Solomon. That was God's reward to them. Joseph Smith and Brigham Young understood this. They knew that was the way God organized his kingdom. But the leaders of the church today are false prophets and cowards."

Dad gesticulates wildly, his eyes growing wider and wider as he works himself into a frenzy.

"We've perverted the true order of marriage. It's the source of all that's wrong in the world. It's *my* job to create a new society modeled after God's kingdom. Heavenly Father has given me a special mission and calling. 'Behold I will send you Elijah the prophet before the coming of the great and dreadful day of the Lord: And he shall turn the heart of the fathers to the children, and the heart of the children to their fathers, lest I come and smite the earth with a curse.'"

My eyes glaze over as I hold sleeping Brian close to my chest. Dad continues to rant, but I can't hear him anymore. I've escaped.

CHAPTER 28

2014–16

I NEEDED A BREAK FROM DARYL, so I decided to take a trip to California to see my sister. While I was there, I got a call early in the morning. I answered the phone. It was Kristi. She sounded a bit off, and I was immediately concerned. She told me that another one of her siblings had overdosed on heroin and died. There was very little emotion in her voice when she said it. I think she was becoming numb to losing loved ones to drugs. This was her third or fourth sibling to die from an overdose.

She asked me if I believed this world was real. I told her I thought it was. She wanted to know what kept me wanting to go on. I had never thought about it before, but I told her there is always a better way and there was so much to live for and to look forward to—like seeing her children grow up.

Kristi asked me if I still kept in touch with my dad. I told her yes and that he was doing all right. She said that she had not written to him for over a year, and she'd had to give up the P.O. Box that she'd used to correspond with him. She said she was angry at him for believing he was a prophet and that all the work she had done with him seemed like it was a waste of time. She felt as if he'd pretended to go along with what she wanted to hear but never really believed it.

I assured Kristi that her time hadn't been wasted. She'd helped repair the bond between my father and me, and it was because of her that I'd taken my grandma to see him again before she died. She'd been the catalyst for so much healing. I told her I loved her and that I would love to hear from her again.

That was the last time I heard her voice. I had no idea that Kristi and her husband believed that there was going to be an apocalypse. She had never mentioned this to me.

A year later, in 2015, I received word that Kristi and her husband had committed murder-suicide, taking their three children with them. It was the most devastating news I'd ever received. I kept thinking about our phone call, wondering what I could have said or done that might have prevented this from happening.

After her passing, my dad told me, as he fought back tears, "I loved being loved by Kristi. She was so special." Then he cleared his throat and said that he knew this life wasn't the end and that he believed we would all see each other again.

Kristi's tragic passing made the news, and with it, her connection to my father. Once again, my family was back in the spotlight. The media seemed to focus on the possibility that my father had influenced Kristi and perhaps talked her into the whole thing. In an interview with the Associated Press after her death, Dad said he hadn't spoken to Kristi in years but he believed his "hell-on-earth philosophy" may have influenced the murder-suicides. He is quoted as saying, "My insanity messes with people's lives. It's just the way it is. . . . I'll miss them, but I'm happy for them. I believe they're in paradise now."

Life kept moving forward. I continued working as a dental hygienist; I enjoyed the people I worked with, and the practice was very successful. Erin got a job there as well, and we saw each other every day. She also moved in with me for a while, as she finished her schooling at Westminster University. It was so nice to have that time with her.

After work, my friends and I would go rock climbing together. We would talk and laugh about all the stuff we were going through. We also met up every Tuesday for a study group to read from *The Urantia Book*, an anonymous text that brings together scientific beliefs, philosophy, and religion. It was a beautiful spiritual outlet for me, and I always left feeling close to God again.

While things were going well in most areas of my life, I was still struggling in my relationship with Daryl, which was becoming more strained. We were arguing more and more, and the hour-and-a-half drive to Heber on the weekends was exhausting me. Max hated the drive, and Daryl's son scared him. I told Daryl that I felt that we needed to do something different. We entertained the idea of them moving into my little apartment, but that wouldn't have helped our situation at all, and was a big no. So we replaced most of our visits with phone calls.

As we felt the distance begin to set in, Daryl became suspicious of how I was spending my time, and I became suspicious of him as well. All the phone calls in the world couldn't seem to prevent the inevitable. I started to suspect that he was flirting with other women, based on comments he would make. I saw he was chatting with people online and noticed texts on his phone from various women. I also observed that he would only ever have female clients, and at times he would tell me some of his clients had asked him out. I couldn't help but think about the way he had hit on *me* when I was his client, and I seriously doubted that it was his clients who were making the advances. My trust in Daryl was further eroded. I'd caught him in too many lies.

Daryl's dishonesty triggered my avoidant attachment. When I felt jealous, I would want to make him jealous. I would withhold my love and start looking elsewhere for validation, the way I had in the past when I was hurt or triggered by my partners—and the way I had as a child when Dad would hurt me. I wanted to show Daryl that I didn't need him, but I was just hurting myself more.

In 2016, when I returned home from my aunt Maisie's funeral in Scotland, exhausted from the long flight and my fight with my mom (see pages 146–48), I phoned Daryl to notify him that I'd landed. He immediately began interrogating me, asking me why I hadn't had my phone on the previous night. I told him I'd gone out with my cousins and assured him that everything was fine. He got upset and accused me of dancing with other men. I couldn't believe it. First, my mom and aunts. Now, Daryl? I felt like I was constantly trying to prove myself to the people around me.

But convincing Daryl that I was being faithful was nearly impossible at this point. Then he dropped the news that he was moving to Arizona to stay with his daughter. He thought that would be the best situation for his son. This came as a total shock. Now *I* was the one who felt betrayed and hurt. Why had he kept his plans to move a secret? He must have been planning it for some time in order to get everything lined up, but he'd waited until two days before he was leaving to tell me. In hindsight, I should have predicted it. Daryl is a wanderer and a dreamer, just like me. He was never going to stay.

I then understood that I couldn't make Daryl be different. I was the one who was miserable when I argued with this reality. He was who he was, and I had to accept that. All the dreams I thought we would create together were just that. Dreams.

If my other relationships had been mirrors to my childhood wounds, my relationship with Daryl was like a magnifying glass. He had experienced much of the same pain that I had and was the most like my dad of any of my partners. It was as if the universe were holding up an exact replica of my father, screaming at me to recognize my patterning and wounds and finally make a change.

One thing that helped me recognize this was the way that Daryl seemed to be stuck in a victim mentality. By the way he talked, you would think that all the pain he had suffered after his divorce had happened just a year ago, when in reality it had been over twenty years. And yet he was still revisiting that pain every day, keeping it alive. In almost every conversation, he found an opportunity to blame his ex-wife for something and list all the things she had done to hurt him. If I ever tried to put myself in her shoes and imagine what might have been going on for her, Daryl would say that I was taking her side, and it would lead to a huge argument. He was very angry and refused to consider another point of view. I knew after three years of listening to him and his stories that there was no way he was going to change.

Despite our issues, this was probably the hardest relationship for me to end, mostly because of our sexual chemistry. In my teen years, I'd equated sex and physical closeness with love, and I'd never revised this belief. By giving up my sexual connection with Daryl, I felt like I was giving up love. I didn't want to give up the romance, either, or the fun activities we did together. Watching him leave was like being abandoned by my father again.

I think that, in some measure, connecting with Daryl *was* a healing experience for me. For him, too. Even with all of the challenges, we had many wonderful times, and that was something I desperately needed at that time in my life. I just didn't know how to view our relationship as a temporary thing—something meant for this moment only. Like a child, I clung to it and tried to make it into something more. I fought with reality and tried to convince myself that Daryl would change.

Once I realized that Daryl really only needed a friend and a lover, nothing more, I was finally able to let him go. I didn't need to step into my old codependent role of fixing everything. I was complete on my own. We parted ways, and I felt nothing but love and peace in my heart. I have not spoken to him since, but I wish him and his son the very best.

Daryl's departure, coming on the heels of my tumultuous trip to Scotland, was a clear sign that it was time to dig deeper to excavate the patterns of codependency that were still playing out in my life.

CHAPTER 29

2016–21

EVEN THOUGH I FELT AT PEACE about my decision to leave Daryl, after we broke up, I experienced what can only be described as emotional withdrawal. I was physically unable to sit in stillness or call on my spirit, and started relying on marijuana to feel calm—but I was really just replacing one addiction with another.

Daryl and I had talked often on the phone, and I missed that. I began to think about calling him and letting him back into my life, maybe finding a way to make things work—the way I had with my past partners—but I stopped myself. Breaking up and coming back together was a pattern I knew all too well, and this time I wanted to do something different. I just didn't know what.

I went to a bookstore and browsed the self-help section. I came across a book called *The Breakup Bible: The Smart Woman's Guide to Healing from a Breakup or Divorce*, by Rachel Sussman. It was so validating to read exactly what I was experiencing and to learn about the stages you go through in the breakup phase. Reading about other people's experiences and how they got through the pain and found exactly what they wanted in a relationship, instead of repeating old patterns, gave me hope. What empowered me the most was that these women chose to view their situations as soul growth, a learning experience that made them stronger. If these women could do it, so could I.

I started to seriously analyze the patterns in my life that needed to be healed. Why had I been attracted to each of my romantic partners? Why had they been attracted to me? And why weren't we able to make it work? This was the moment when I finally began to see how, throughout my life, I had (unconsciously) attracted emotionally unavailable men who reinforced my belief that I was unworthy of love. Again and again, my relationships resulted in disappointment, grief, abandonment, and an overwhelming urge to flee.

These patterns, of course, rooted back to childhood. My father's detachment and emotional unavailability, along with his controlling and abusive behavior, especially toward my mother, had created a deeply formed belief inside of me that relationships only led to loss and hurt. Furthermore, when a child is abused or mistreated, as I was, they are unable to express their feelings because there is no outlet for them. As a child, my feelings were not validated. If I was angry or upset, I was punished or laughed at. This taught me that my feelings were just a nuisance that got in the way. So I stuffed them down deep inside of me. This caused me to act out, withdraw, and even become ill. Many times, abused children suffer from chronic earaches. I think back to the earaches I had suffered as a child, and how I was punished for having them, which likely only made them worse and further contributed to my belief that there was something wrong with me, that I didn't deserve love.

I didn't know how to feel love without the approval of another person, so I became codependent. Consequently, I demanded quite a lot from each of my partners. I expected them to fill the hole in my heart that could never be filled by an outside source. It was an impossible task, and an unfair one. But I thought that I needed another person in order to feel whole because I wasn't worthy on my own. For this reason, I attracted partners into my life who mirrored my childhood situation—people I would never be able to please—and then blamed myself when these relationships failed. This continued to reinforce my belief that I was worthless and unlovable.

At the same time, I was constantly on edge in my relationships. I was living in survival mode, the way I'd learned as a child. Every moment I was worrying about what my partner was thinking, if they were mad at me, if I was going to get in trouble. There was a constant tightness in my stomach that never seemed to let up. My nervous system was permanently in a state of fight or flight.

Whenever there was an argument, I would immediately feel the instinct to flee. As a child, I'd learned that fighting and conflict meant I wasn't safe, that I needed to run and hide to save myself. Part of me also wanted to punch back and hurt my partners. I would think to myself, *You didn't appreciate me, so now you'll know what it feels like not to have my love.* I believed I loved them more than they loved me and that I'd tried everything I could to make it work—just as I'd tried to be a good daughter to earn my father's love. And when it didn't work, I turned off my heart, just as I did as a child.

My constant worrying about others—trying to meet their needs and expectations at the expense of my own—took a toll on my immune system, until eventually I became severely ill. The only way healing could happen was if I finally acknowledged and expressed all of the emotions I'd buried deep inside me. My emotions had made my body sick, so my emotions had to be treated in order for my body to heal.

My desire to become whole became the primary focus in my life, but I knew I needed support. I prayed that I would be led to sources that could help me. I knew I needed to do deep work on the subconscious level to truly heal these wounds and change my life. I began listening to books by Jerry and Esther Hicks, who talk about how our emotions create our reality. I also listened to Joe Dispenza's work on rewiring your brain, and enrolled in an online course with women who were dealing with health issues that were similar to mine. I began to ask people around me for help, even though I still had trouble trusting others. It was a struggle, but by spending time reading, journaling, meditating, breathing, asking, listening, attending courses on communicating, and learning to respond from a conscious place rather than blindly reacting, I began to make progress.

As I practiced communicating with my higher consciousness as if it were my best friend, just as I did as a child, my old belief in myself returned: No matter what happened, I knew I would be okay. But I also knew I needed to be fine on my own first before I attracted a partner. I needed to heal the codependency that had been preventing me from entering into a healthy relationship. I was always seeking someone outside of myself to fill the hole in my heart, to comfort me and reassure me. But if I relied on my inner spirit to fill my heart instead, I would finally be able to stop running.

I took a break from dating and focused on finding peace and tranquility within myself. For the first time in my life, I lived alone (except for when I had Max). I knew I needed to recalibrate my body's sense of peace and tranquility and learn what true safety felt like. I got rid of all distractions and focused on retraining my body's response to stress.

I had to remember that when I felt the urge to run or shut down my heart, it was because I was being triggered. My mind was re-creating something from the past that didn't necessarily reflect my current reality. I learned to tell myself that I was safe, and remind myself to breathe, that I have a choice about how I respond and that I am allowed to voice my needs, that my feelings matter. I told myself, "Rebecca, I am here and will listen to you, always." Over time, I learned to reprogram my nervous system to create a healthier, more stable emotional response in times of stress.

The more I learned to self-soothe and take care of my own needs, the more I was able to let others off the hook. I didn't need anything from them; they were free to be who they were, just as I was free to be who I was. I no longer felt that I required their permission to live the way I wanted to. The more I loved and accepted myself, the more I could love and accept others. I learned that real love is an action and is something that I actually enjoy and find great pleasure in. When it comes from a place of genuine care for another person, love is much easier to practice than I thought. I love connecting with people. I especially like to show my love by being present with others and listening to understand.

* * *

As I began to tune into my emotions, I realized something that surprised me: I didn't just have a father wound. I had a mother wound as well.

I began to reflect on my relationship with my mom. When I was a teenager and her marriage with her third husband, Matthew, ended, I swore I would never end up in her situation. And yet here I was, a single mom with children from three different fathers. Three different marriages, ended.

Like mother, like daughter.

I'd spent so much time thinking about and trying to heal the trauma caused by my attachment with my father, I hadn't given as much attention to my attachment with my mother. And yet it was her life I was replicating!

I recognized that Mom had her own abandonment wounds. She'd been abandoned in key moments by her mother, who in turn had been abandoned by her birth parents. I recognized that Mom hadn't always been emotionally available to me, just as Nanny hadn't been emotionally available to her. I was her third child, and I was quickly followed by four more. Not only was her attention divided among seven children, but she'd also spent most of my childhood managing my father's emotions and outbursts. So much of her energy had gone to protecting and providing for us physically—both before and after leaving my dad—she'd had little left to offer us emotionally. I knew she regretted being trapped in her marriage and was forever stressed and overworked because of all us kids, and I'd internalized that regret.

I don't blame my mother for any of this. But I needed to acknowledge and heal the insecure attachment I'd experienced with her, too, if I was going to be able to move forward. I used the same tools I used to heal my attachment wound with my father: sitting in stillness and deep meditation to connect to my inner child and rewire the belief that I wasn't worthy of my parents' time or love.

Digging into my relationship with my mother helped me recognize how much generational trauma there is on my mom's side. I come from a long line of strong and independent women, but these women were also routinely repressed and forced to fit into a mold that didn't feel true to them. Nanny was vehemently opposed to being a housewife. She resented the role she'd been handed and found every opportunity she could to rebel. But in the process, she'd (unintentionally) hurt my mom and her siblings. Unfortunately, without the support or space to be our true selves, none of us were able to figure out how to navigate life in a way that felt authentic and liberated without hurting others around us.

My mom, at her core, is also an incredibly independent and feisty woman. We wouldn't have survived if she wasn't. But her ability to survive came at a cost. When the choice is sink or swim, you don't exactly have time to carefully nurture the emotional well-being of the young children in your care.

That said, I have never felt anything but unconditional love from my mom, even in moments when we fought or disagreed. And the more work I did to release my childhood resentments and forgive her for being human, the more I was able to see what a gift her love was, and continues to be.

I am very much my mother's daughter—independent, restless, rebellious. "You remind me of me," Mom said the first time I left Julian. "Packing up your stuff and leaving. It's the same thing I would do."

But Mom has never tried to change me. When I felt like I didn't know how to be a traditional wife or mother, it was my mom who gave me permission to just be myself. "Stop trying to be something you're not," she said. She helped me see there was another way forward. That meant a lot to me and opened up the door for us to have a deeper relationship.

Over the years, our relationship has grown into something truly beautiful. I think that, because of our similar natures, there's a part of my mom that she feels she can express freely around me. I love that I can be that for her. She's opened up to me about what it was like to live with my dad and has given me her journals to read. I am so touched that she's trusted me with the innermost feelings of her heart.

Mom has always been a source of wisdom for me. When I was dating Daryl, she could see that I was really struggling. I would complain to her how he was still acting a certain way, even though he'd told me he was going to change.

"Well," my mom said, "you seem to be the only one who has a problem with it. Clearly, he doesn't!" Her bluntness helped me see that Daryl was never going to change and I was trying to control something that wasn't mine to control.

Mom has always supported me in my decisions—from having children to leaving marriages to starting businesses. Her faith in me has never faltered. On many occasions she's said to me, "I have this vision of you as a strong, professional, successful businesswoman. I can see you so clearly." I'm so grateful for my mom's unwavering support.

In my healing journey, I have also been supported by my ancestors on my mom's side. Anytime I've gone to a psychic, my mom's grandmother, in particular, has always come through very strongly. After leaving Timothy, I went to see a Romanian woman who is a very talented psychic. I was worried I'd made the wrong decision, and I was looking for reassurance. She told me that I came from a strong line of intuitive women on my mother's side. She said she could feel my great-grandmother's presence. Nanny's mother told me that I had permission to move forward with my life. She told me I have a gift of healing and that I receive joy from holding space for people and helping them have moments of self-realization.

After I left Simon, I went to another psychic. He told me the same thing, that he immediately felt the presence of my maternal great-grandmother. Again, the message from my great-grandmother was to follow my heart and to give myself permission to experience life and to be happy and free. To dance.

Scotland is a land steeped in magic and paganism, and I strongly believe that the women in my family had, and still have, potent spiritual gifts. I would even go so far as to call them witches. My mom has psychic gifts of her own that I believe she repressed after joining the Mormon Church and marrying my father. This realization helped me understand why I felt so triggered in Idaho when I was ostracized by my community, and why I sensed so strongly that I was being treated like a woman tried for witchcraft. No doubt I have ancestors who were accused of and likely killed for being witches, and this trauma and fear has been preserved in my DNA. (I also find it a fascinating coincidence that I was born on the winter solstice, and grew up in a town called Salem.)

Tapping into my maternal lineage has been a source of tremendous power for me. The more I've followed this line of inquiry and opened myself to the spiritual realm, the more I've felt my own gifts come to the surface. Mormonism taught me at a young age that spiritual gifts like medium-ship, tarot reading, and any kind of intuitive ability—such as clairvoy-ance, claircognizance, precognition, and so on—were evil, even though Mormons believe in plenty of spiritual gifts themselves, including healing, prophecy, seership, personal revelation, the ability to speak in tongues, and many more. (The Twelve Apostles are called modern-day prophets, seers, and revelators, and male members are given the priesthood—God's power on earth—and frequently give healing blessings.* Only men can hold the priesthood and give these blessings, although there was a time at the begin-ning of the church's founding when Joseph's wife Emma gave priesthood blessings as well, before Joseph adopted more patriarchal practices and

---

* The Articles of Faith were written by Joseph Smith in 1842. Article 7 states: "We believe in the gift of tongues, prophecy, revelation, visions, healing, interpretation of tongues, and so forth." Many religions, Christian and otherwise, hold similar beliefs. Yet any spiritual practice that falls outside the domain and control of organized religion is viewed with sus-picion and labeled evil. I don't find it a coincidence that the vast majority of alternative spiritual practitioners (such as psychics, tarot readers, and palm readers) are women.

excluded women from leadership.) These restrictions were put in place to prevent women from tapping into their sense of personal power in the same way that the women of the past—who had been the midwives, wisewomen, and healers in their communities—had been accused of witchcraft because they threatened the authority and dominance of male physicians.

Once I was able to drop all labels and preconceptions surrounding spiritual gifts, I found my connection to the spirit world increased exponentially. A few years ago, the local Girl Scout troop asked me to do tarot card readings at an event. I wasn't sure if I was doing it right, but I felt words flowing through me as I read the cards. One of the women I read for started crying and asked me, "How did you know that?"

I'd tapped into my spiritual gifts as a child, before I'd been forced to repress them. As a kid, I would just know things. I remember saying to my dad, "I heard you say this in my dream." My dad would snap at me and tell me not to make up stories. But I remember my sisters exchanging glances with each other, as if to say, *How did she know that?*

When I went to see Darla for the first time, she told me that I was an open channel. For a long time, I resisted what that meant. I was confused and scared by it. But the more work I've done to surrender and stop fighting, the more I've begun to understand about my abilities. I've realized I'm an empath, which means I can intuitively feel other people's emotions. And because I can feel what they're feeling, I'm able to experience pure love, compassion, and empathy for them, regardless of who they are. What I didn't know is that they are able to feel that love from me in return.

The more I've explored this gift and its healing potential, the more I've been able to understand why I entered so many relationships so quickly. My partners could feel a strong sense of love in my presence, which made them eager to pursue a connection with me. I didn't understand the source of these feelings, so I allowed myself to be talked into relationships before I was ready. But the love hadn't come from them. It had come from me. It was always me.

"You are here to love," my spirit told me when I was a little girl. It took me forty years to understand what that meant.

My gift is love.

As I worked on rewiring my body's response to my triggers and filling my life with things that made me feel good and safe, my nervous system and stomach relaxed, my hair stopped falling out, and my health returned. I actually woke up every day happy and excited.

To support my physical healing further, I learned about the role of good nutrition and dietary supplements. In 2021, a friend suggested that I get a part-time job at the local health food store, which I did. I enjoyed working at the nutrition store. It was fun to mix things up a bit and meet people who wanted to talk about health. Plus, it helped me find answers to further support my journey.

It also inspired me to devote more time to working on the skin creams I'd first developed when Max was a baby. I'd been wanting to sell them, but I kept finding excuses, telling myself I didn't have enough time or money to invest in designing the labels and the website. But without a toxic relationship draining my energy, I soon realized I did have the time and money. Developing the creams and serums with organic ingredients was such a rewarding endeavor for me. (It felt like my own little version of witchcraft, making my healing salves and potions.) I'm so proud of the products I created.

As I made progress in all areas of my life, I was inspired to share my story again, so I also returned to working on the book. It felt so good to put my experience into words; it helped me process all the things I'd gone through and to see my patterns even more clearly.

Once I felt secure in myself and fully happy with my life on my own, I decided it was time to call in a romantic partner. I worked on a list of attributes I was looking for. I knew I wanted someone who was fun to be with and who could make me laugh and who was possibly younger than me. (I wanted to shift away from dating older, authoritative men who reminded me of my father.) I wanted someone supportive and encouraging. Someone spiritual, who had his own interests and his own calling in life, but who wasn't dogmatic or controlling in any way. Someone who could listen well and had the desire to communicate consciously. Someone who didn't have children. Someone who was not threatened by who I was and could support who I was becoming. Someone I could grow with.

I got very intentional with my list then let it go, trusting that the right person would come in when the time was right. Instead of actively dating, I worked on being in the right vibration to attract my ideal partner. I focused on doing the things that I enjoyed. I took relaxing walks, went dancing and rock climbing, and laughed with my girlfriends. I spent time with Max and did the things that felt authentically good and fun to me, the things that made me happy in my heart. I allowed myself to get plenty of rest, attended my spiritual classes, and continued reading and writing. I was finally putting my authentic needs and feelings first and, in the process, learning to love myself.

I'd been working at the health food store for about three months when, one night, a customer poked his head around one of the aisles. He had long, curly, shoulder-length hair, a mustache, and a goatee. My first thought was that he looked a little bit like Jesus. He was wearing sweats and a hoodie and emitted total surfer vibes.

I asked him if he needed any help. He said no thanks. Then he looked up and did a double take. "Hang on," he said. "Who are you?"

We introduced ourselves and started talking. His name was Josh. We discovered that we had many common interests and experiences. We had both previously lived in Glendale, California, and he knew the Cuban bakery that I loved and visited whenever I was there. His family was from New Zealand, and he'd lived there for a large portion of his life. My brother Johnny had served an LDS mission in New Zealand, so we talked about New Zealand for a while. He was also very knowledgeable about health and philosophy, as well as the law of attraction. It was so easy to talk to him and such a delight to have a deep but also lighthearted conversation. I really liked how he actively listened to what I was saying. At the end of the conversation, we exchanged numbers and said goodbye.

A week later, I was meditating about who I wanted to spend time with, and Josh popped into my head. I texted him and invited him over to watch a movie. It turned out he only lived a block away from me.

When Josh walked through my door for the first time, he said, "I really like your place." That made me smile. He had a natural optimism about him. I noticed how kind he was and how I felt when I was around him. He was ten years younger than I was, and really brought out the youthful part of me. I'd never dated someone younger than me before, and I loved our playful dynamic. We talked until the early hours of the morning.

Over the following weeks, Josh would come over after I finished work, and we would talk. We loved being together. The way he effortlessly got along with my kids and family touched my heart. He helped me see that life doesn't have to be so heavy and serious all the time.

After about two months of spending almost every day together, Josh said he was changing his living situation and entertaining the idea of moving back to California to look for work there. I told him he should come stay with me since I had plenty of extra space. Before offering, I thought about it, meditated on it, and made certain that I felt it was the right thing to do. He accepted, and we moved in together.

My relationship with Josh has been unlike any of my previous relationships. The issues I experienced frequently in the past—codependency, getting triggered, needing to run—have simply not surfaced. We rarely experience any conflict. We aren't perfect, by any means, but we approach our problems as a team. We work together. We cook and clean together. We spend time together. My kids love him. And with all the support he has given me, I've been able to focus on regaining my health and return to my work as a regression therapist.

Josh also helped me put the final pieces in place for selling my skin care products. Our neighbor took some gorgeous photos for me, and Josh helped me set up a website. I began selling my products online and in local stores. It's been such a fulfilling endeavor for me, and I'm so grateful to have a partner who is supportive of my dreams and business ventures.

I love the time Josh and I spend together; it is fresh and expansive. We give each other the encouragement to be our best. What strikes me the most is how *easy* it is with him. It's been easy since the day he showed up, and it still feels easy, two years later. I never knew a relationship could feel like this, and I appreciate him every day for being in my life.

CHAPTER 30

2021–22

"DO YOU WANT TO HEAR THE SCRIPT I've prepared to announce Jesus Christ's return?" Dad's voice is so earnest and eager.

I close my eyes. "Sure, Dad. Tell me."

Dad reads me his announcement for the Second Coming and the beginning of the Millennium, Christ's thousand-year reign on earth. "Soon I will be out of here," he tells me, "And I'll be able to say, 'That part of our journey is over, so let's get this one thousand–year party started!'"

Then Dad bears his testimony. "Heavenly Father put us on earth so we could prove to Him that we would keep his commandments," he says. "The obedient are the people who will survive the Second Coming and the burning of the tares. God sent us to earth to test us, to see if we would do whatever He commanded."

Suddenly, a lightbulb goes off in my head. I understand now. *This* is Dad's code. From a very early age, he internalized that what mattered most—above love, compassion, empathy, anything—was obedience. Not to other men, but to God.

The last puzzle piece finally fits into place, solving the mystery for me. I no longer need to agonize over why or how or what if. The answer is simple: Dad has *always* done what he thought God demanded or expected from him. Tragically, his view of God's will grew warped over time, influenced by other people and his own mental illness, and it led him to do something unspeakable. And yet, in his mind he truly believes, even still, that it was what God wanted him to do.

Our fifteen-minute window ends, and we say goodbye.

After the call, I sit on the edge of my bed, giving myself a moment to process everything I'm feeling. I wrestle with the conflicting emotions raging inside of me. A daughter's desire to love her father at war with a mother's horror for the things he's done. My inner child's resentment for being neglected and abused battling the compassion I feel now as an adult for the things my dad himself endured.

And then, I release it all. I can see now it's not my job to understand, change, condemn, or exonerate my father—or his father before him, or any of the many links in the generational chain that brought us to this point. I don't have to assume any responsibility for his actions or carry his shame as my own. I can just accept that he is who he is.

A lightness bubbles up in my throat, and I almost laugh. The weight I've carried in my chest since childhood, the crippling sense of shame and guilt, is gone.

I am finally free.

After this conversation with my dad, I knew it was time to finish the book. I was finally ready to face the difficult work that needed to be done.

I felt fully supported as I returned to the manuscript. The words flowed out of me, and the universe aligned to help me find the perfect writing partner, someone who understood and shared my vision for the project and could help me shape the book in a way that best captured my experience.

As I worked on the memoir and delved back into painful childhood memories, I decided I was ready to have a more direct conversation with my father. Never once had I asked him why he did what he did. I was too scared to face the reality of his answer. But now I knew I could hear his response without being overwhelmed by my emotions. His guilt was no longer my burden to bear.

I asked Dad if he'd be willing to answer my questions. He said he was. And so I asked him about everything—from the way he'd treated me as a child, to his decision to take Brenda's and Erica's lives, to his own experience growing up in his family. Dad answered all of my questions. In one of his letters, he wrote, "I like how you said that you wanted to get to know and understand me as the person I really am versus how you saw me through the lens of a little girl, which was all you had to go on before. These are really insightful questions, and I'm happy to answer them as best I can. I will never lie to you, and I want to answer any question you may have."

Even though it was a difficult process and his responses didn't always make sense to me, breaking my silence on the past was hugely cathartic for both of us. We were finally able to give voice to the pain that had weighed us down for so long.

Having these conversations with my father filled me with a sense of grief and compassion. He sacrificed everything, even the people he loved, because he truly believed he was following God's will. And now he was paying the price.

Again, I realized that it was possible for me to love my father without excusing his behavior. Perhaps the two of us could try once again to weave the threads of love between parent and child.

In March 2022, I went on a writing retreat to my birthplace of Glendale, California. It seemed only fitting that I finish my book in the place where my story began.

I didn't anticipate how many memories and emotions the trip would stir up for me. Sitting in the warm California sun, watching the palm trees sway gently in the breeze, I was transported back to my early childhood—days of freedom and innocence, when the world felt safe to explore and life seemed so full of potential.

Even though I've found peace and acceptance in my situation, I still occasionally get overwhelmed by grief. This was one of those moments. It was hard to work on my book and deliver a message of healing when I was being confronted so vividly with a vision of what might have been.

As I had many times before, I couldn't help but wonder: What if we had stayed here in California? What if Dad had chosen to embrace his creative side and open a practice with people who supported him, like the colleagues he met at school who, to this day, recall how brilliant and innovative he was? What if he had felt free to leave the constraints of the church and his father's expectations? How would things have turned out for us kids if Dad had been there for us, instead of in jail my entire life? If we hadn't grown up with the rumors and gossip, the shaming and the shunning? If our family hadn't been shackled with the trauma caused by his actions, the unbearable darkness?

For a moment, I allowed myself to imagine it. Dad, pursuing a fulfilling career focused on healing others. Mom, surrounded and encouraged by independent, progressive women. My siblings and I, free to follow our dreams and be our full selves.

But, of course, that didn't happen. Instead, we moved to Salem, where any potential for self-discovery was abruptly halted. Dad stepped right back into his old family dynamic, resisting at first, but ultimately submitting. Feeling stifled and unexpressed, he needed a voice to follow that was louder and more authoritative than the church or his father, who seemed only to pull him down and discredit his ideas. Like all of us, he longed for a way to shine, to be seen for his unique abilities and gifts.

But it's hard to break free of the worldview and consciousness that surrounds us. For my father, the only path to freedom he could find was in extremism, immersing himself more deeply in church doctrine and ideology than the people who were trying to control him. After all, the only person who had more authority than the church or his father was God Himself. And God, as He is represented in the Bible, is rarely merciful.

Growing up, I blamed my father for the pain and suffering I experienced. But as an adult, I've realized that there was no way I could accurately know what his experience was like. If I had walked in his shoes and experienced the things he had, who's to say that I would have turned out any differently?

I think about the complexities of my father's experience. The way he was repressed and mistreated as a child, and given a worldview that required blind faith and unyielding obedience. Mormons are taught from a young age never to question, never to doubt. "Doubt your doubts before you doubt your faith" has become one of their modern proverbs.

I think about the way Dad in turn mistreated us as children, imposing the same dogma and discipline on us. I think about the way our family has been caricatured, ignored, and misrepresented in the wake of his crimes. I think, too, about the way many of my family members don't understand why I continue to talk to him.

Many people, hearing my story, are quick to deliver judgment or tell me how I should feel toward my father. It's easier, I suppose, to focus on the shocking nature of his crimes rather than take a closer look at the actual people involved, to ask yourself how or why this could have happened, or who else was hurt in the aftermath.

To be clear, I am in no way defending or justifying my father's actions. Far from it. The pain he caused our immediate and extended family—the pain he caused Brenda's family—is immeasurable, and the responsibility for his choices lies on his shoulders alone. But hating him is not the answer. Healing can never come from hatred or bitterness, only more suffering. Trust me. I hated my father for a long time, and it only magnified the pain.

Whenever I feel anger or bitterness creep in, or whenever I get caught up in a spiral of "what ifs," I remind myself that I'm grateful to be alive, to be here now. I ask myself how I can be the best version of myself today. How can I help others?

The answer is the same it's always been, the message of reassurance I felt in my closet as a four-year-old child, the message I hope I've been able to convey with this book:

It all comes back to love.

◆   ◆   ◆

We are all born with the desire to love and be loved. However, when time showed me how dark life could be, I began to think that love wasn't for me. For most of my life, I felt rage, sadness, shame, confusion, resentment, guilt. Everything but love. I was convinced no one could love me. That I was broken and unwanted. That I didn't deserve love. But *everyone* deserves love.

Over the course of my life, I tried to find solace in so many places: drugs, therapy, religion, relationships. But nothing worked because, deep down, I didn't love myself. As a child, I'd come to believe that I wasn't worthy of love, and so at my core, I felt irreversibly flawed. It was as if, no matter what I did, I would never be enough. My self-loathing ran so deep that I even blamed myself for the horrible events that devastated my family. Maybe, I thought, if I had been better, things would be different and my family would still be whole.

I carried this self-loathing with me throughout my life and into every relationship I entered. As a result, I wasn't capable of loving another person or finding a healthy partnership until I first learned to love and forgive myself and those who had hurt me.

Despite my father's choices, I love him and choose to see the good in him because I love and forgive myself for my own choices. I've learned that you can still love someone unconditionally, even if you do not agree with or condone their actions.

In *The Urantia Book*, there is a passage that reads: "You cannot truly love your fellow by a mere act of the will. Love is only born of throughgoing understanding of your neighbor's motives and sentiments." It's incredibly difficult to surrender the blame and judgment we hold toward others, but when we try our best to understand, that's when healing can finally happen. Forgiveness doesn't come easily, nor does it excuse what has happened. However, it *is* necessary in order for our souls to grow. Anger, blame, and resentment only poison our hearts and keep us from the very things we desire.

In a regression session I did with Darla a few years ago, I was taken back to a time before my incarnation into this life. I learned that I was *not* a victim of my circumstances and that my experiences in this life were meant to help my soul grow in specific ways and with specific people. Everything I went through supported my growth as a person and has now allowed me to help others who have suffered. I believe part of my purpose here on earth is to teach others that the love we seek is waiting for us at all times.

The struggles I experienced throughout my life were real. But I can see now that wishing they had never happened is counterproductive. What matters most is how I respond to them.

It makes me think of the lines from Garth Brooks's song, "The Dance." Life really is a dance, with twists and turns as well as repeating patterns. We would not understand or appreciate joy and love without the struggles and heartache. Through all the ups and downs, the spirit world is there to lend us strength, if we want it.

Many of my struggles, especially within relationships, happened because my energy was vibrating at a level of low self-worth. The universe wanted to show me where I needed to heal—it provided me with mirrors so I could see my wounds. But for such a long time, I refused to look into those mirrors. Instead, I blamed my problems on my dad. I blamed my partners. I blamed all the people who had hurt me. I told myself I was the victim and I was broken beyond repair. So many times in my life, I'd say to myself, "If Dad would only do this or if he'd only say that, then I would be happy." Or I'd tell myself if it hadn't been for my uncle Ron influencing my dad, none of these bad things would have happened. But this kind of self-talk is disempowering. None of those thoughts or beliefs helped me heal or attracted more good into my life. The truth is I am the one who determines my happiness, just as we all are.

I believe that we are the authors of our own inner experience. No matter what we have suffered, no matter what limiting beliefs we have internalized, there is always a way to heal. I also believe we do not have to struggle alone. Even in my deepest moments of pain, I have *never* been alone. There has always been a loving presence with me, guiding me and supporting me. Whenever I have prayed and asked for help, I have received it. Conversely, the times I believed I had everything under control and didn't need spiritual guidance, my life ended up being messy and confusing. It was only when I embraced this presence and asked for its help that I was finally able to find healing.

I want to feel good. I want to feel joyful, happy, and peaceful. I want to feel love. That's what I have been searching for my whole life. The experiences I went through taught me what works and what doesn't work in the journey toward love. In order to find love, we must be willing to let go of the things that are not serving us, take accountability for our own actions, and forgive those who have wronged us. Then we have to do the difficult work of looking inside and healing our own wounds and insecurities.

It's much easier to blame our unhappiness or misfortune on God or another person rather than accept the responsibility for our own actions. We have no idea what others' lives and upbringings were like, how they were disciplined, what things they were taught, what they witnessed, and what heartaches or pain they experienced. All we can do is forgive them for hurting us and focus on creating the life for ourselves that we desire. *The Urantia Book* states, "[Jesus] taught that God *has* forgiven; that we make such forgiveness personally available by the act of forgiving our fellows. When you forgive your brother in the flesh, you thereby create the capacity in your own soul for the reception of the reality of God's forgiveness of your own misdeeds." The more I was able to forgive the people who had hurt me, the more I experienced true peace.

Regardless of how it may appear, the universe is an unconditionally loving place. But holding on to grudges, resentment, envy, and other negative emotions creates a feeling of lack inside of us and keeps us looking for external solutions to our problems. Once we release these negative emotions—through stillness, communion with our inner spirit or God, breath work, movement, bodywork, tapping, EFT, somatic experiencing, and other modalities—we can create space for more positive emotions to take their place, and we can begin to foster a sense of oneness within ourselves. When we look inside ourselves and ask, "How am I creating this experience, and how can I create the experience I would like instead?" a shift takes place. This allows us to move from blame to accountability, which, in turn, allows us to relate to others in a deeper and more meaningful way.

What has been fascinating for me to discover is that as I work on creating my own optimal inner experience, I forget about wanting to change others. The more you become in tune with your own feelings and thoughts, the more you release your expectations for other people. You realize that, after all is said and done, you are not responsible for changing anyone but yourself. Some experiences are just a part of living in this world. Ironically, as you focus more on improving yourself and worry less about changing others, you begin to have a greater impact on the people around you. When we lift ourselves, we lift the people around us. I've seen this to be true.

In sharing my story, I hope I've been able to point people toward their inner guidance system. The answers are already there, inside of us. My whole life, I searched for something outside of myself to anesthetize, hide, or treat the pain. I felt incomplete and broken, so I thought I needed something external to fix me. Sometimes I turned to negative sources (drugs, toxic relationships, other addictions); sometimes I turned to positive sources (therapists, healers, workshops). But always it was outside myself, when what I really needed to do was go inward. In *It Didn't Start with You*, Mark Wolynn writes, "There's . . . something about the action of searching that blocks us from what we seek. The constant looking outside of ourselves can keep us from knowing when we hit the target. Something valuable can be going on inside of us, but if we're not tuning in, we can miss it." Learning to sit in stillness and communicate with God was the most important part of the healing process for me. Everything I needed to know was already inside of me.

Once you turn inward and pinpoint the problem there, you'll be shown additional tools that can help you in your journey toward self-improvement and wholeness. One tool I've found to be particularly helpful is regression therapy. I recommend it highly to anyone wishing to heal childhood trauma. Returning to and reframing past events reminds us of our own individual source of strength and allows us to align with our personal meaning of life and thus experience more joy. Regression therapy has changed my life, and I've witnessed how it's changed the lives of so many others. I feel so happy with who I have become, precisely because of the things I've gone through. My love for myself and my family has only gotten stronger because of my challenges, and I know with all my heart that this shift can happen for anyone.

The perspectives I've gained through regression have also helped me to better understand what life is really about. I've come to recognize that the spirit world has supported me and guided me my entire life, from the time I was a child, and that our separation from the spirit world is just an illusion; it is real and there to assist us at every moment. In my opinion, this is crucial to understand in order to heal our deepest wounds.

After my negative experience in the Mormon Church, I rejected my connection to Source/God through religion. I didn't trust the church or the people in it. They all seemed to have an agenda. I'd lost that feeling of the love I'd experienced as a child when I sang "Jesus Wants Me for a Sunbeam" or when I looked at a beautiful picture of Christ embracing the children. It felt like every time someone mentioned Jesus, it was about how he died for our sins and that God loved him so much he had to sacrifice him. None of that resonated with me and, in fact, it reminded me of my father's own twisted logic. To me, Jesus's message was about sharing the good news that we are all children of God, that Heavenly Father is a kind and loving father, and that the kingdom of heaven is within us. The love Jesus demonstrated was bigger than a single church or religion. Christ Consciousness is about finding a never-ending well of love and peace within. Up until his death, Jesus lived what he came to earth to teach: forgiveness and mercy.

Some people believe that life is predestined, and that we are spiritual beings having a physical experience—maybe multiple times—on this planet. Others believe that we're here by pure chance, and this one life is all we've got. I don't have the answers to these big questions. All I know is that we're not here alone. I believe we all have the divine within us and our connection to that divine power is the most important relationship we will ever have. Once we truly recognize our divinity, and the divinity in others, everything changes.

"Love thy neighbor as thyself," Jesus told his followers. The more I've tapped into this message, the more I've come to understand how healing it is, and how powerful. Just as Christ taught, I have found that true happiness comes from compassion and service to others. We are all divine. We are all worthy of love. God has shown me this time and time again through beautiful messages.* Sometimes these messages are spoken directly to my heart. Other times, these messages come through other people's experiences.

Recently, I watched a documentary about the murder of Chandra Levy, a young intern at the Federal Bureau of Prisons in Washington, DC. At the end of the documentary, and after years of painful suffering, Chandra's mother said that she learned which things are important in life and which things are just trivial. She said that she and her husband

---

* I believe that we each have spirit guides who help us on our journey. Their purpose isn't to help us avoid difficult situations, but rather to grow and learn from them. They will only ever be friendly and comforting and for the greater good. These spirits will never ask us to do anything that will harm anyone else or is destructive in any way. (If we are receiving destructive messages, they are not from our spirit guides.)

choose to focus on celebrating their daughter in unique ways. She shared that when they were in a remote place in Mongolia, a ladybug showed up and stayed with them for quite a while. Chandra's secret name was Ladybug. When Chandra's mother asked the people around her if ladybugs were common in the area, they said it was the first time they had ever seen one. Later, in Russia, Chandra's parents saw a girl ride by on a bike who looked just like their daughter. All of a sudden, Chandra's father saw a big ladybug sign on a passing bus. To them, this was evidence that their daughter was communicating with them and sending them peace and love.

After watching this, I thought to myself, *If Chandra can communicate with her parents, then maybe some of the people I've cared about who have passed on can communicate with me.* A few days later, I went outside and noticed an adult ladybug and a baby ladybug walking across the top of my car. I felt a tingling sensation throughout my entire body. A feeling of peace washed over me, and I instantly thought of Brenda and Erica. I believe with my whole heart that this was the sign I'd been looking for.

I shared this experience with Sharon, Brenda's sister. It touched us both deeply.

EPILOGUE

IN 2021, I HEARD THE NEWS THAT *Under the Banner of Heaven* was being adapted for television. I had a feeling this was going to stir up some emotions for my family, and I was particularly worried about my mom. She told me she was sick of hearing about my dad and didn't want to think about him anymore. My siblings also didn't like the idea of being seen in that light or having attention brought to them in a negative way. But for me, I felt like this was another sign that it was finally time to share my story, rather than allow one more person to tell it for me.* I wanted to fully liberate myself from the skeletons in my closet by shining a light on them instead of pretending they didn't exist, and I wanted to show myself and everyone else that I wasn't a victim of my circumstances: The past, while always a part of me, does not define my future. More than that, I felt strongly that sharing my healing journey might help someone else, the way I'd been helped by reading about the experiences of others. That is my deepest wish.

As I reach the end of this project, I feel so much gratitude for the progress I've made. I have so much more awareness about my patterns and wounds. I have greater self-love and understanding for myself and my past. I'm better able to process my triggers so that I respond differently instead of reacting from my wounds, and I can hold space for my partner, children, and family members to do the same.

---

* As mentioned previously, the television series was largely fictionalized. My older sisters are depicted in the show, but my younger siblings and I are not. FX invited me to the Salt Lake City premiere on April 25, 2022, which I attended. I watched the first two episodes at the premiere but did not finish the series. I appreciate what the filmmakers were trying to accomplish, but for me, watching the show was a difficult experience.

It's been so exciting and rewarding to see my children grow up and become their full selves, with their own likes and dislikes. Their own life paths.

Erin is twenty-six now. She lives in North Carolina. She is on her own spiritual journey and practices and teaches yoga and stillness to people in her community. We enjoy spending time together, just talking and laughing. Erin knows me better than anyone. I can be my true self around her, and I hope she feels the same about me.

Nathan is eighteen. He is able to use a wheelchair and is doing well. Timothy and Melanie keep me updated with photos, and I FaceTime with him regularly. I hold him close in my heart and treasure the time we would lie on his table and play with Thomas the Tank Engine for hours.

Max, who is twelve now, is a very happy kid. We like to ride our bikes to the park and play on the swings. He loves tag and the thrill of being chased. We enjoy laughing at the silly videos we make together and going to the library, where he reads to me in our special circle chair.

Often, when Max and I ride our bikes together, I think back to the time my father handed me a bike but then refused to teach me how to ride it. I think about how I finally taught myself, about the long hours I would spend biking all over Salem, tasting true freedom for the first time. I think about Dad's words, bringing us both to tears. "I should have taught you how to ride a bike."

I suppose I'm just doing my best to be the parent I always wanted.

I'm so grateful for all my children. My only desire is to be there to support and encourage them in whatever it is they want to do. I'm also grateful to be on good terms with their fathers and that we've all found a way to work together toward a common goal.

Occasionally around the holidays, I get a message from Julian, wishing me and my family the best. I have nothing but good feelings and love for a dear friend.

The rest of my family is doing well. I love each one of them and admire my mother and siblings for their strength and resilience. Despite their many trials, my siblings have been very successful in their careers and relationships. Because of what we've gone through as a family, we are all very close. The bond is thick, and the love is strong. We are truly miraculous.

For years, Mom talked about how she felt responsible for the choice she made to marry my father. She has always been private about our past, and when journalists have contacted her to ask her perspective on any of the events that took place, she has always been quick to retreat and say she will not talk about it.* She blames herself for the suffering we kids had to go through and the hardship Dad's choices caused all of us. It saddens me to hear her say such things. I tell her that she did her best and that there is a reason for everything we experience in this life. My mom is the strongest person I know. She's my hero. She protected us and did her absolute best with what she was given. That's all any of us can hope to do.

For the most part, my older sisters keep to themselves. They've changed their last names and have stayed as far away from the media as possible. They have asked me not to mention them by their real names or share details of their story for them, and I have respected their wishes. I love them deeply and wish them nothing but peace and happiness.

My brother Johnny tells me he was concerned at first that people would gossip or ask him hurtful questions after the release of *Under the Banner of Heaven*, but he's found that most people have been understanding and respectful, largely because of the way he respects himself and others. Johnny is a medical professional and is happily married with six kids. He speaks to my father occasionally.

My younger sister, Rachel, received great support from her congregation after having the courage to open up after the television series aired. She was embraced by the women who surrounded her and was able to

---

* My mom has given me permission to talk about her in this book, but she has made it clear that this is my story, not hers. I have changed her name to protect her privacy.

heal some of the pain and shame she had been carrying for so long. I am so proud of her and her faith and fortitude. Rachel says that she forgives Dan (she does not call him Dad) and has found great freedom in doing so. Although she can forgive him, she has no desire to talk to him or let him into her life. She told me, "I can forgive him from afar. He doesn't hold those chains around me [anymore]. I forgive him and take accountability for that, and I get my strength from the Lord." Rachel is a mother of two boys. Her family is everything to her.

My two younger brothers, Christopher and Brian, have very little to say about my father. Christopher accepts who our dad is and communicates with him from time to time, but he is busy with his own life. He has a very successful business and is married with two little girls.

Brian has no memories of our father and no desire to speak to or about him. He is a skilled tradesman who has also earned great acclaim in his community and works on many high-profile jobs. He is currently enjoying bachelor life.

All of us have experienced and handled grief in our own ways. Some of us have healed by opening up and sharing, and some of us don't feel the need to talk about it. Regardless, we can find comfort in the fact that we all survived and have each other, and I know our love will always prevail.

I reached out to my uncle Allen while I was finishing the book. He told me he's in the best place he's ever been. He spends his time mentoring others who have gone through difficult experiences. "Hard things bring out the good in you if you allow it," he told me. "There is always a fork in the road where you can choose victimhood, or you can stop and be willing to look and learn and listen to our Heavenly Father as He will lead you through."

I asked him what he would like people to know about him and his story. He told me, "We are all on the same path. Some of us are doing better [than others]. I trust my Savior." His advice to me and anyone reading this was: "Learn to forgive. We are here to help each other out. We should be lifting each other up."

Thank you for reading my story. No matter where you are on your journey, I have so much love for you. We are all in this life together. It is so much easier to love, and to feel loved, when we seek to understand each other's hearts. As Gabor Maté writes, "If we are to dream of a healthier, less fractured world, we will have to harness and amplify compassion's healing power." It is so worth taking steps toward becoming whole and empowered. Only once we've addressed our inner wounds can we experience real love, which ultimately comes from within. This is the source of true freedom. It is my deepest desire that everyone experience this freedom and live to their fullest potential. We are eternal beings, so we will always be growing and expanding, but we can experience so much joy in the process.

Now that I have finished this book, I finally feel at peace. I have processed and released the burdens that I have carried for so long. I have forgiven those who have wronged me and paid my debt to family members who have craved reconciliation and understanding. I have written my story, with tears and with love, in the hope that my family, my children, and anyone who searches for inner peace, can awaken from the darkness of life's challenges to a bright new day and this message of hope:

Love *is* there, for all of us.

ACKNOWLEDGMENTS

It takes a village to raise a child—and an even bigger village to publish a book. I'm so grateful to all of the people who helped me on this journey. I wouldn't be here without you.

I first want to thank my amazing mother for always supporting me and for allowing me to write publicly about her pain as well as her resilience. Our beautiful family is a testament to your strength. I love you so much.

I also want to thank my siblings for giving me permission to share details from our childhood and for supporting me in this endeavor. I'm so grateful for your love and example.

Thank you to my Lafferty family for holding space for my experience and for loving me without judgment. Immeasurable thanks to my uncle Allen for speaking with me openly about the suffering he endured and for being a tremendous example of love and forgiveness, to my uncle Watson for sharing Grandma's letter, and to my uncle Mark for the compilation of home videos. Your support means the world.

I'm so grateful to my daughter, Erin, who has helped me embrace my inner strength by seeing that strength within me first, and to my sons, Nathan and Max, who along with their sister have brought meaning, purpose, and joy to my life. You motivate me every day to be a better person. I love you more than words can say.

To my partner, Josh, thank you for supporting me at every step of this process and for seeing and loving the real me.

Thank you so much to my cowriter, Katie McNey, for believing in my story and helping me shape it into a readable form. And thank you to Sharon King for connecting us. I'll forever be grateful to you for giving me the nudge I needed to finally make this book a reality.

Endless thanks to my mentor, Darla, for seeing me as more than my trauma and encouraging me to put my story into words. I owe so much of my healing to you.

All of my love and gratitude to Brenda's sister, Sharon, for opening her heart to me and sharing stories and insights about her sister.

Brenda and Erica, we love and miss you always. Thank you, Brenda, for being a light in our lives and for seeing me when so few did.

A huge thanks to my literary agent, Kurestin Armada; my film agent, Mary Pender; and everyone at Root Literary for working tirelessly on my behalf to bring this project to life. And thank you to my amazing editor, Barbara Berger, and the entire team at Union Square & Co. I'm so grateful for your vision and guidance.

I give thanks always to my angels and Heavenly Father for guiding me throughout my life, especially in my darkest moments, and to Jesus for his everlasting example of forgiveness and love.

Finally, I want to thank my own inner spirit. Little Rebecca has stood by my side through it all, holding my hand as I've stripped away the layers of pain to discover the truth of who I am. It is because of her that I can now stand proudly in the light and share my story in service of hope, healing, and love.

RESOURCES

I recommend the following resources to anyone dealing with trauma or wanting to reprogram their limiting beliefs and change the trajectory of their life.

Dispenza, Joe. *Becoming Supernatural: How Common People Are Doing the Uncommon*. Carlsbad, CA: Hay House, 2017.

———. *Breaking the Habit of Being Yourself: How to Lose Your Mind and Create a New One*. Carlsbad, CA: Hay House, 2012.

———. *Evolve Your Brain: The Science of Changing Your Mind*. Deerfield Beach, FL: Health Communications, 2007.

Estee. "How to Reparent Yourself: A Step-By-Step Guide," *Hopeful Panda: Hope After Childhood Abuse*, June 29, 2022, https://hopefulpanda.com/how-to-reparent-yourself.

Hay, Louise. *You Can Heal Your Life*. Carlsbad, CA: Hay House, 1984.

Hicks, Esther and Jerry. *The Astonishing Power of Emotions: Let Your Feelings Be Your Guide*. Carlsbad, CA: Hay House, 2007.

Lainus, Ruth A., Eric Vermetten, and Claire Pain, eds. *The Impact of Early Life Trauma on Health and Disease: The Hidden Epidemic*. Cambridge, UK: Cambridge University Press, 2010.

Maté, Gabor. *The Myth of Normal: Trauma, Illness & Healing in a Toxic Culture*. New York: Avery, 2022.

Meurisse, Thibaut. *Master Your Emotions: A Practical Guide to Overcome Negativity and Better Manage Your Feelings*. Self-published, 2018.

Miller, Alice. *The Body Never Lies: The Lingering Effects of Hurtful Parenting*. Andrew Jenkins, trans. New York: W. W. Norton, 2006.

Scaer, Robert. *The Body Bears the Burden: Trauma, Dissociation, and Disease*, 3rd ed. New York: Routledge, 2014.

Truman, Karol K. *Feelings Buried Alive Never Die*. St. George, UT: Olympus Distributing, 1991.

van der Kolk, Bessel A. *The Body Keeps the Score: Brain, Mind, and Body in the Healing of Trauma*. New York: Viking Penguin, 2014.

Wolynn, Mark. *It Didn't Start With You: How Inherited Family Trauma Shapes Who We Are and How to End the Cycle*. New York: Viking, 2016.

If you or someone you know has been abused or is experiencing suicidal ideation, you can find support on this resource page created by Netflix: wannatalkaboutit.com. If you're in the United States, you can also call the Suicide and Crisis Hotline at 988. The National Domestic Violence Hotline is 1-800-799-7233.

Wherever you are in your healing journey, I highly recommend finding a group of people who share the same intention to heal without giving advice or trying to fix each other. I cannot express enough the therapeutic value of having someone else simply listen to you and witness your story in a state of compassion.

Finally, if you are interested in regression therapy, please feel free to contact me at rebecca.thecenterwithin@gmail.com. I am a CHt (Certified Hypnotherapist) and have been specializing in inner child work since 2013. I offer regression sessions via Zoom or Skype. You can learn more on my website: rebeccalafferty.com.

NOTES

17 **"Studies have shown that children can be severely mistreated":** Susan Radcliffe, "Why Some Children Want to Stay with Their Abusive Parents," *New Jersey Law Journal*, July 5, 2021, https://bit.ly/4hsoqO8.

49 **"Joseph Smith founded the Church of Jesus Christ of Latter-day Saints":** Beginning in the mid-1900s, the Church of Jesus Christ of Latter-day Saints (LDS Church) began refuting that Smith used a seer stone to translate the Book of Mormon. The church changed its position in August 2015, when it released a picture of the brown stone Smith was said to have used; an October 2015 article from the church's *Ensign* magazine describes Smith receiving the stones, which the Book of Mormon calls "interpreters." (See: Eric Johnson, "Did Joseph Smith Use the Seer Stone . . . or Didn't He?," Mormonism Research Ministry, mrm.org/bom-seer-stone; and Richard E. Turley Jr., Robin S. Jensen, and Mark Ashurst-McGee, LDS Church, "Joseph the Seer," bit.ly/4gyql19.) And in a later post, the church acknowledged Smith's early use of a seer stone to look for lost objects and buried treasure. (See: "Book of Mormon Translation," LDS Church, bit.ly/4gObWQs.)

In *No Man Knows My History: The Life of Joseph Smith*—one of the first non-hagiographic biographies of the Mormon founder—Fawn Brodie explains that Smith was sued for defrauding clients with his treasure-hunting scheme, and that his father-in-law Isaac Hale was relieved to hear that Joseph had "given up what he called 'glass-looking.'" (See: Fawn Brodie, *No Man Knows My History: The Life of Joseph Smith, the Mormon Prophet* [New York: Alfred A. Knopf, 1945], 29, 42.)

Richard Bushman, a practicing member of the LDS Church and a professor emeritus at Columbia University, acknowledges that Smith was taken to court for treasure hunting. However, Bushman contends that the charges were intended to discredit Smith, who used the stone to "help people find lost property and other hidden things." (See: Richard Lyman Bushman, *Joseph Smith: Rough Stone Rolling* [New York: Vintage, 2007], 49.)

The LDS church has published an article addressing Smith's glass-looking and court trial here: "Joseph Smith's 1826 Trial," LDS Church, bit.ly/3PjADs8.

49 **"Smith adopted increasingly radical ideas . . . introducing them as revelations":** Smith was a religious innovator with a vivid imagination. He freely borrowed ideas from organizations and religions that intrigued him and then presented these ideas as doctrines in the form of revelations or translated Scripture. By November 1831, Smith had recorded at least seventy revelations that he claimed to have received from God. That month, a conference of elders held in Hiram, Ohio, decided to compile a selection of these into a "Book of Commandments." (See: "Introduction to the Doctrine and Covenants of Church History," LDS Church, Lesson 1, Study Guide, bit.ly/40dLg66.)

The Book of Commandments (1833) was eventually republished as the Doctrine and Covenants (1835). Many of the original revelations were revised for the new publication. Mervin J. Petersen found that 703 words were changed, 1,656

words added, and 453 words deleted. (See: "A Study of the Nature of and Signif-
icance of the Changes in the Revelations as Found in a Comparison of the Book
of Commandments and Subsequent Editions of the Doctrine and Covenants,"
master's thesis, Brigham Young University, 1955, 147, scholarsarchive.byu.edu
/etd/5034.) While some of Smith's supporters were troubled by these revisions,
believing the original revelations were correct as received, the revised Doctrine and
Covenants (D&C) and the concept of ongoing revelation allowed Smith to shape
church governance and doctrine as he saw fit.

    While devout Latter-day Saints today consider the D&C to be one of the stan-
dard works of Scripture, some scholars have questioned the divine provenance of
Smith's revelations—not only because of the revisions made to the D&C but also
because of the contents of the revelations. For example, several of the revelations
offer Smith leverage in managing conflicts with his associates like Oliver Cowdery
and his wife, Emma. (See section 132, verses 54–65, bit.ly/3Dwcf3J, a revelation
given after Emma discovered that Smith was practicing polygamy. The headnote
of the section acknowledges that, although the revelation was recorded in 1843,
the principles of plural marriage were known by Smith as early as 1831, over a
decade before he disclosed them to Emma. She is commanded to obey the new
laws of polygamy or else "be destroyed" (verse 54). See also: Brodie, *No Man
Knows My History*, and Dan Vogel, *Joseph Smith: The Making of a Prophet* [Salt
Lake City: Signature Books, 2004].)

49   **"One of these was polygamy":** Joseph Smith claimed that he was commanded by
God to practice polygamy and that an angel with a flaming sword had threatened
to destroy him if he did not obey, as noted in an article released on October 22,
2014: "Plural Marriage in Kirtland and Nauvoo," LDS Church, bit.ly/40fANXC.
This same article acknowledges that there is some evidence that Smith took Fanny
Alger as his first plural wife in the mid-1830s. Smith had legally married Emma
Hale on January 18, 1827. Fanny Alger was a teenager who lived in the Smith
home and was considered their adopted daughter. Ann Eliza Webb recalled, "Mrs.
Smith had an adopted daughter, a very pretty, pleasing young girl, about seventeen
years old. . . . Their affection for each other was a constant object of remark, so
absorbing and genuine did it seem." (See: Ann Eliza Webb, *Wife Number 19 . . .
Revealing the Sorrows, Sacrifices, and Sufferings of Women in Polygamy* [Hartford,
CT: Dustin, Gilman, and Co., 1875], 66–67, bit.ly/400bveH. See also: Todd M.
Compton, *In Sacred Loneliness: The Plural Wives of Joseph Smith* [Salt Lake City:
Signature Books, 1997], 25–28, 34–39, 41.)

    Smith began a relationship with Fanny without Emma's knowledge. Several ac-
counts assert that Emma discovered the pair consummating the union in the barn.
(See: Linda King Newell and Valeen Tippetts Avery, *Mormon Enigma: Emma Hale
Smith* [Champaign: University of Illinois Press, 1994], 66; and Richard S. Van
Wagoner, *Mormon Polygamy: A History* [Salt Lake City: Signature Books, 1989],
5–10, 85.) Webb wrote, "It became whispered about that Joseph's love for his adopted daughter was by no means a paternal affection, and his wife, discovering the
fact, at once took measures to place the girl beyond his reach. . . . Since Emma

refused decidedly to allow her to remain in her house . . . my mother offered to take her until she could be sent to her relatives" (Webb, *Wife Number 19*, 66–67).

Smith's next wife was Louisa Beaman, whom he married on April 5, 1841. Smith swore the attendants to secrecy, and Louisa wore a man's hat and coat as disguise. After Smith's death, Louisa married Brigham Young. (See: Compton, *In Sacred Loneliness*, 57–60; Van Wagoner, *Mormon Polygamy*, 6, 23, 27; Newell and Avery, *Mormon Enigma*, 95; and "Remembering the Wives of Joseph Smith," wivesofjosephsmith.org/PDFBooklet/PDFBooklet.pdf.)

Smith would go on to marry at least thirty-four women. All the sealings were conducted in secret. Eleven of the women were already married (with living husbands). Seven were teenagers. (Smith was thirty-seven when he married fourteen-year-old Helen Mar Kimball; see "Plural Marriage in Kirtland and Nauvoo.") Among the wives was a mother-daughter set and three sister sets. Several of the wives were Smith's foster daughters who lived in his home. Smith had been sealed to at least twenty-two other women before he was sealed to his first (legal) wife, Emma, of which she was largely unaware.

As the church did not openly acknowledge or discuss Smith's polygamy until the 2014 article, many church members were unaware that Smith had plural wives; polygamy was commonly understood to have started with Brigham Young. (See: "Response . . . About Joseph Smith's Polygamy," MormonThink, bit.ly/4fWqM6B.)

49 **"special temple rituals Smith adopted from the Freemasons":** Smith was initiated into the Freemasons in March 1842. Two months later, he introduced the LDS endowment ceremony, which was modeled almost entirely on the rituals he had learned from the Masons. The ceremony included secret handshakes and Masonic signs and symbols like the all-seeing eye, the compass and square, and the sun, moon, and stars. (Some of these symbols can be seen on the exterior of the LDS temple in Salt Lake City.) Many Mormon leaders, including Brigham Young and Heber C. Kimball, became Masons and organized a lodge in Nauvoo. Soon, nearly every male member of the church had joined the Masons. Fawn Brodie wrote, "The Mormon Temple endowment ceremony is without a doubt taken from the Masonic ceremonies Joseph Smith participated in just weeks before he introduced the temple endowment. The grips, tokens, covenants, secret words, keys, etc. were word for word the same when first introduced" (*No Man Knows My History*, 279–83). Mervin B. Hogan concurs: "The Mormon Temple Endowment and the rituals of ancient Craft Masonry are seemingly intimately and definitely involved." (*Freemasonry and Mormon Ritual* [Salt Lake City: Self-published, 1991], 22.)

Given the timing, it's extremely likely that Smith introduced the temple ceremony as a way of keeping polygamy a secret—not just from the general public but from his own followers—while introducing select members to the practice of plural marriage. (The "new and everlasting covenant" revealed in the temple ceremony referred to the practice of polygamy.)

50 **"Brigham Young, had fifty-six wives":** "Brigham Young," LDS Church, bit.ly/4gysRGX; "The Wives of Brigham Young," UTAH.gov, historytogo.utah.gov /wives-brigham-young.

50 **"by 1870, about a quarter of all Mormons practiced polygamy":** "Plural Marriage in Utah," LDS Church, bit.ly/41UHgIQ.

50 **"Wilford Woodruff, issued a manifesto ending plural marriage":** "Plural Marriage after the Manifesto," LDS Church, bit.ly/402fUOv.

51 ***The Peace Maker* was a small pamphlet":** Udney Hay Jacob, *An Extract, from a Manuscript Entitled The Peace Maker . . .* (Nauvoo, IL: J. Smith, 1842), contentdm .lib.byu.edu/digital/collection/NCMP1820-1846/id/4067; and Lauren Thatcher Ulrich, *A House Full of Females: Plural Marriage and Women's Rights in Early Mormonism, 1835–1870* (New York: Alfred A. Knopf, 2017), 102, 107.

51 **"Joseph Smith later disavowed the pamphlet":** Joseph Smith, Notice, *Times and Seasons*, December 1, 1842, centerplace.org/history/ts/v4n02.htm.

51 **"women can only be sealed to one man":** Jana Riess, "Eternal Polygamy? How LDS Temple Sealings and Cancellations Became a Raw Deal for Women," *Salt Lake Tribune*, May 18, 2024, bit.ly/40eUxdU.

52 **"In Mormonism, only men can hold the priesthood":** Women who have advocated for the right to hold the priesthood have been excommunicated. (See: Laurie Goodstein, "Mormons Expel Founder of Group Seeking Priesthood for Women," *New York Times*, June 23, 2014, bit.ly/4gywEnx; and Holly Welker, "The Mormon Church Just Excommunicated Another Feminist," Slate, June 23, 2014, bit.ly/3PjGk9t.)

52 **"blood atonement":** Brigham Young, *Journal of Discourses*, 4 (Liverpool, UK: S. W. Richards, 1857), 53–54, bit.ly/3BP0gOq.

53 **"My father was neither the first nor the last to hold these beliefs":** Historian and author Benjamin Park estimates that there are over four hundred denominations that have followed Smith's original movement. (See: Benjamin E. Park, *American Zion: A New History of Mormonism* [New York: Liveright, 2024], 17. Wikipedia lists several of these: en.wikipedia.org/wiki/List_of_denominations _in_the_Latter_Day_Saint_movement.)

53 **"Joseph Smith also preached that the laws of God took precedence over the laws of men":** Book of Mormon, Mosiah 29:12, bit.ly/3PhbIWf.

54 **"a government that fails in these duties should be removed":** Book of Mormon, Mosiah 29:16–17, 26, 28–29, bit.ly/3PhbIWf.

54 **"Smith himself decided to run for president in 1843":** Joseph Smith wielded a great deal of political influence. He was the governor of Nauvoo, a city the Mormons founded in Illinois in 1840, as well as the commander of the Nauvoo Legion, a force of 2,500 men that was nearly one-third the size of the US Army. By 1844, Nauvoo had reached a population of 12,000 people, making it the second-most populous city in the state, just behind Chicago. Smith asked his followers to vote in a bloc for candidates endorsed by the church. Consequently, Mormons held considerable sway in state elections.

In 1844, Joseph Smith announced his run for US president (with his first counselor, Sidney Rigdon, for vice president). Smith's platform called for the abolishment of slavery and for the reduction in the size of the US House of Representatives, believing that a smaller body would "do more business than the army that now occupy the halls of the national legislature." (See: B. H. Roberts, *The Rise and Fall of Nauvoo* [Salt Lake City: Deseret News, 1900], bit.ly/3BPF3nw.) He wanted to limit the number of government officials as well as their pay and power, while desiring protection for the Latter-day Saints from the federal government. (See also: Martin B. Hickman, "Joseph Smith's Presidential Platform: The Political Legacy of Joseph Smith," *Dialogue: A Journal of Mormon Thought*, Fall 1968, 3(3): 23, bit.ly/3DEFYYo; Richard E. Bennett, Susan Easton Black, and Donald Q. Cannon, *Nauvoo Legion in Illinois: A History of the Mormon Militia, 1841–1846* [Norman, OK: Arthur H. Clark, 2010]; and Christopher Cronin and Luke Perry, *Mormons in American Politics: From Persecution to Power* [Santa Barbara, CA: Praeger, 2012].)

82 **"the Mountain Meadows Massacre of 1857":** "Mountain Meadows Massacre," Wikipedia, en.wikipedia.org/wiki/Mountain_Meadows_Massacre; Gilbert King, "The Aftermath of Mountain Meadows," *Smithsonian* magazine, February 29, 2012, bit.ly/4gLCVwf; and Ronald W. Walker, Richard E. Turley, and Glen M. Leonard, *Massacre at Mountain Meadows* (New York: Oxford University Press, 2008).

173 **"The cycle of violence, or abuse, is a social theory":** Lenore E. Walker, *The Battered Woman* (New York: Harper & Row, 1979); Lundy Bancroft, *Why Does He Do That?: Inside the Minds of Angry and Controlling Men* (New York: Berkeley, 2002), 147–50.

173 **"Attachment theory is an area of psychology":** John Bowlby, *Attachment: Attachment and Loss*, vol. 1 (New York: Basic Books, 1969; H. R. Schaffer and P. E. Emerson, "The Development of Social Attachments in Infancy," *Monographs of the Society for Research in Child Development*, 1964, 29(3): 1–77, pubmed.ncbi .nlm.nih.gov/14151332.

234 **"When trauma and feelings are repressed instead of expressed":** See Bessel A. van der Kolk, *The Body Keeps the Score: Brain, Mind, and Body in the Healing of Trauma* (New York: Viking Penguin, 2014).

240 **"Almost everyone in Utah County has heard of the Lafferty boys":** Jon Krakauer, *Under the Banner of Heaven: A Story of Violent Faith* (New York: Doubleday, 2003), xi.

240 **"Baby Erica":** Ibid., xii.

244 **"Carnes asked Ron why they needed to kill Erica":** Ibid., 181.

245 **"Afterward, the four men drove to a gravel quarry":** Ibid.

246 **"According to Krakauer, Dad asked if Allen was home":** Ibid., 183.

247 **"At this point, Ron entered the house":** Ibid., 184.

248 **"Dad closed the door behind him":** Ibid., 186.

248 **"After taking the baby's life":** Ibid., 186–87.

249 **"Dad replied, 'It was no problem.'":** See *State v. Lafferty* (2001), caselaw.findlaw .com/court/ut-supreme-court/1270132.html#footnote_8.

249 **"The four men reached Chloe's house":** Krakauer, *Under the Banner of Heaven*, 278.

251 **"they were pulled over by a Nevada highway patrol officer"**: Ibid., 282.

251 **"While Ron and Dad got some rest"**: Ibid., 282–83.

252 **"However, he died of natural causes in November of 2019"**: *Utah v. Lafferty*, Wikipedia, en.wikipedia.org/wiki/Utah_v._Lafferty.

253 **"Mark Wolynn writes in *It Didn't Start with You*"**: Mark Wolynn, *It Didn't Start with You: How Inherited Family Trauma Shapes Who We Are and How to End the Cycle* (New York: Viking, 2016).

264 **"I had been reading stories from the book *Spiritual Midwifery*"**: Ina May Gaskin, *Spiritual Midwifery*, 4th ed. (Summertown, TN: Book Publishing, 2002).

267 **"Mark Wolynn explains that trauma is frequently inherited"**: Wolynn, *It Didn't Start with You*.

267 **"The first step is to face and repair our relationship with our parents"**: Ibid.

281 **"Paul said, 'Suffer not a woman to teach or usurp authority over the man"**: Jacob, *The Peace Maker*.

281 **"Who can find a virtuous woman? For her price is far above rubies"**: Proverbs 13:10, King James Version, bit.ly/40hWSVN.

284 **"My insanity messes with people's lives"**: Tara Fowler, "Convicted Murderer Says He Influenced Utah Couple to Kill Themselves and Their Children," *People*, January 30, 2015, bit.ly/41TkOzX.

289 **"I think back to the earaches I had suffered as a child"**: Jay P. Willging, Charles M. Bower, and Robin T. Cotton, "Physical Abuse of Children: A Retrospective Review and an Otolaryngology Perspective," *Archives of Otolaryngology Head and Neck Surgery*, 1992; 118(6): 584–90. doi:10.1001/archotol.1992.01880060032010.

306 **"In *The Urantia Book*, there is a passage that reads"**: Anonymous, *The Urantia Book* (Chicago: Urantia Foundation, 1955), en.wikisource.org/wiki/The_Urantia_Book.

308 **"*The Urantia Book* states"**: Ibid.

309 **"Mark Wolynn writes"**: Wolynn, *It Didn't Start with You*.

317 **"As Gabor Maté writes"**: Gabor Maté, *The Myth of Normal: Trauma, Illness & Healing in a Toxic Culture* (New York: Avery, 2022).